Say Goodbye to the Cuckoo

Say Goodbye to the Cuckoo

Michael McCarthy

JOHN MURRAY

First published in Great Britain in 2009 by John Murray (Publishers)
An Hachette UK Company

2

© Michael McCarthy 2009

The right of Michael McCarthy to be identified as the Author of the Work has been asserted
by him in accordance with the Copyright, Designs and Patents Act 1988.

A CIP catalogue record for this title is available from the British Library

ISBN 978-1-84854-063-7

Typeset in Adobe Caslon
by Servis Filmsetting Ltd, Stockport, Cheshire

Printed and bound by Clays Ltd, St Ives plc

John Murray policy is to use papers that are natural, renewable and recyclable products and
made from wood grown in sustainable forests. The logging and manufacturing processes are
expected to conform to the environmental regulations of the country of origin.

John Murray (Publishers)
338 Euston Road
London NW1 3BH

www.johnmurray.co.uk

For Jo

They've made it again,
Which means the globe's still working, the Creation's
Still waking refreshed, our summer's
Still all to come –

Ted Hughes, 'Swifts'

Contents

ONE

Spring-Bringers

Willow Warbler

I f we could see it as a whole, if they all arrived in a single flock, say, and they came in the day instead of at night, we would be truly amazed: 16 million birds. How other than with wonder could we view the sight of 16 million swallows, martins, swifts, warblers, wagtails, wheatears, cuckoos, chats, nightingales, nightjars, thrushes, pipits and flycatchers pouring into Britain from sub-Saharan Africa? They would cover the sky from horizon to horizon: it would be the greatest of all natural spectacles. Work would stop; people would gather to watch it. That night it would lead the television news; next morning it would dominate the papers, and the nation would celebrate, not only for the giant, scarcely credible journeys that these huge numbers of diminutive creatures have just completed, but for a reason which moves us even more: that in coming, they have brought the spring.

We do not see it, most of us, the Great Arrival: the advent of the migrant birds that every year leave Africa, where they have wintered, and come to Britain, and to all of Europe, to spend the summer breeding. Or rather we do not perceive it as the single, phenomenal event that it is. It is spread out geographically and temporally: different species of birds arrive over a period of about ten weeks, from mid-March to the end of May, and much of their journeying is done at night, when cooler air means less energy expended in flying and less danger from predators, so the arrival is often in darkness. Indeed, urbanized as most of us are now, living in a motorized and electronic society that hears birdsong only at weekends – and mostly not even then – we may not perceive it at all.

But it is one of the enduring wonders of the natural world, its sheer scale hard to grasp. Sixteen million is the estimate of the birds that fly to Britain from Africa every year, but that is a drop in the ocean compared to the total that set off every spring from their African wintering grounds not just for Europe, but for Eurasia as a whole, the land mass that stretches from Spain to Siberia and across to China: their numbers are estimated at 5 *billion*.

Every one of them faces the most daunting of journeys: in each case, a personal struggle to cross enormous obstacles, such as the Sahara Desert or the Mediterranean, the outcome being dependent on bodily fuel reserves, ability to navigate, and the maintenance of great effort over long periods. And these are small, often tiny, creatures to undertake flights of such epic proportions: a swallow that covers the 6,000 miles from South Africa to Britain is smaller than a TV remote control. Yet none can refuse; none can say, as we well might, *Er, I think this year I'll give it a miss.* If you are a swallow, or a willow warbler, or a spotted flycatcher, you are born to these twice-yearly odysseys: they are your fate; you have no choice.

Many die en route. A sudden and violent end is threatened by human hunters, birds of prey, even bats (scientists have discovered in the last decade that Europe's largest bat, the greater noctule, hunts migrant songbirds passing in the night over Spain). A more likely end is from adverse weather conditions, in particular the failure of rain in the Sahel, the arid zone south of the Sahara which countless numbers of birds use as a refuelling stop, to fatten up before attempting to cross the empty vastness of the desert. If there is drought, the

2

food supplies disappear. So sometimes, millions fail. But billions of individuals, of nearly 200 species, still get through.

This fantastic traffic is not confined to the Old World. It is replicated across the Atlantic, where every spring another awesome assemblage of birds – perhaps 3 billion this time – leaves wintering grounds in the Caribbean and Central and South America for North American breeding territories. Once again there are countless minuscule creatures tackling marathon trips, from the thirty or so species of brilliantly coloured American warblers to the ruby-throated hummingbird, heading out across the Gulf of Mexico for the North-Eastern US running only on nectar.

There is a third migration system, the least known one, which involves birds from the eastern end of Eurasia and even Alaska heading down into southern Asia and Australasia. And this features the most spectacular migration by any land bird, and perhaps the longest single point-to-point journey by any living creature: the flight of the bar-tailed godwit, a handsome, streamlined wader half the size of a curlew, from its breeding grounds in Alaska to winter quarters in New Zealand.

It does it in a single hop. It covers 8,000 miles across the Pacific in a continuous flight lasting eight days. This was long suspected, but proved conclusively only in 2007, when a female bird given the number E7 was fitted with a satellite transmitter and tracked all the way. When the godwits get to New Zealand, and land on the coast near Christchurch, there is a celebration: the Christchurch cathedral bells are rung – as well they might be.

Nothing tops the godwits' flight, but all around the world, birds are making incredible journeys. The present routes are thought to date from the ending of the last Ice Age, being dictated by the ways in which the vast ice sheets of the northern hemisphere melted and retreated and opened up new swaths of feeding and breeding territory, which birds living south of the ice, as in Africa and South America, could move northward to exploit in the summer, before moving back south again as the northern winter closed in.

But migration is far, far older than that. It goes back way beyond the 18,000 years since the most recent great freeze began to thaw, for millions, many millions, of years – almost certainly to birds' reptilian ancestors, those medium-sized dinosaurs which eventually grew flight feathers and took off. Close your eyes and imagine the V-shaped skein of wild geese, heading for Greenland, replaced by pterodactyls. It might seem strange, but it shouldn't: modern-day reptiles undertake long-distance migrations – the leatherback turtle, for example, swims across the Atlantic in summer in search of its jellyfish diet – and so do mammals, fish and even insects.

For migration occurs whenever a species can move fast enough to take advantage of the premier consequence of the earth's orbit around the sun: seasonality. There are great differences in living conditions and food resources at different seasons, in different parts of the world, and it may pay you to make the effort to move between them. For two-thirds of the year the tundra of the High Arctic is a frozen, forbidding penal colony, but during a balmy window of opportunity in the summer it is a holiday resort, from a bird's point of view, with gorgeable masses of insect food, exceptionally long daylight hours to feed in, few predators, and not an enormous amount of competition: an ideal place to bring up the chicks – as long, that is, as you accept the trade-off, which is that as soon as autumn arrives you have to scarper, as you will not survive the winter.

A whole suite of bird species has found this trade-off acceptable. In fact the great majority of the Arctic's breeding birds migrate up in the spring and fly back south to Europe or Africa with the onset of autumn.

On the equator, however, the position is reversed. In equatorial Africa's rainforests, conditions are largely unchanging from one season to the next, food is available continuously, and living conditions do not deteriorate, so migration is pointless, and as a result virtually all the breeding birds are year-round residents. There is actually an observable statistical relationship, in both Europe and **4** North America, between distance north from the equator and the proportion of breeding birds that will be migratory. The bigger the difference between summer and winter, the more migrants you find, and the further north you go, the bigger that difference is. By the time you get to the Arctic island of Svalbard, at 80 degrees north, the proportion is nearly 85 per cent.

Britain is about a quarter of the way up this ladder: about fifty British breeding bird species, roughly 25 per cent of the total, are summer visitors which arrive from Africa in the spring. Among the first, in mid or even early March, is the wheatear, a striking, very energetic relation of the thrushes with a grey back and a buff breast, and the stone curlew, one of the weirdest-looking British birds, with bulging eyes (used for hunting insects at night) and knobbly knees on its long legs. Later in March they are followed by three warbler species the size of a hen's egg: first the chiffchaff, then the blackcap and the willow warbler, this last perhaps the most numerous of all the migrants, its numbers possibly exceeding 4 million.

Arrivals at the same time include the ring ouzel, which is the blackbird of the mountains, and the sand martin, the first of the swallow family. The swallow itself arrives in early April from the far end of Africa, and is soon followed by several migrant close relatives of year-round-resident British birds, including the tree pipit, the yellow wagtail and the redstart. Mid-April sees the grasshopper and sedge warblers and the whitethroat (another warbler); the last of the swallow family, the house martin; our migratory falcon, the hobby; and the cuckoo, and then the nightingale. In late April three more warblers drop in – the reed and garden warblers and the lesser whitethroat – followed by our migratory hawk, the honey buzzard; and then at the end of the month the swifts are here, dark scimitars in the sky, similar in design and behaviour to swallows but not actually related, though anticipated and enjoyed by many people in cities, where swallows nowadays cannot exist.

The last migrants, the ones that arrive in May, include the corncrake, the hen-like bird of the hayfields, which has now retreated to the Hebrides; the last and prettiest of the warblers, the green-and-yellow wood warbler; the nightjar, the hawkish patroller of the gloaming on lowland heaths; the turtle dove, our only migratory pigeon; and the spotted flycatcher, a small songbird which is understated and unspectacular but nevertheless of great charm and elegance and much loved by people lucky enough to have it nesting on their property (it is fond of gardens).

This is not the whole story, but it is the general picture of the Great Arrival, this exceptional natural event which we do not see – or rather which we did not see until recently. Seven years ago, Britain's principal bird research organization, the British Trust for Ornithology, worked out a way of making it visible, at least in virtual terms, by harnessing a cross-country network of several thousand amateur observers to the internet. Their daily sightings appear as red dots on constantly updating maps, and so give an unfolding picture of the return of each species, from the first trickle of early individuals to the final tide weeks later. The scheme is called BirdTrack. Watching the dots multiply on the animated map sequences, until the country is covered in red – rather like watching Britain contract chickenpox – for the first time gives a real sense of the remarkable dimensions of the migratory influx into Britain from Africa, with astounding numbers of journeys, each astounding in itself.

Yet that is not why for millennia the Great Arrival has been celebrated. Hear it from a poet writing nearly three thousand years ago: 'For, lo, the winter is past, the rain is over and gone; the flowers appear on the earth; the time of the singing of birds is come, and the voice of the turtle is heard in our land.' The author of the Song of Solomon had no way of knowing that turtle doves left ancient Israel and flew to sub-Saharan Africa for the winter, but he (or she) did rejoice when their purring was suddenly heard again on their

return the following year, just as it can still be heard today in modern

Israel and Palestine, or across the whole of Eurasia from to Britain to China. For, as much as the flowering of plants or the emergence of butterflies, it signals the coming of spring: the migratory birds from Africa are the spring-bringers.

Every one of them is a stirring symbol of the new season for somebody, from the hillwalkers who catch sight of the first wheatears bouncing around the crags of the uplands in March, to the retired couple in the Cotswolds who quietly rejoice in May that a pair of spotted flycatchers has come back, and once more chosen their manicured garden to nest in.

Yet there are a number of the spring-bringers which, over the centuries, have taken on something more like a universal significance. Swallows go back (like the turtle dove) to the Bible, and flit through Greek and Latin literature as streamlined spring and summer emblems, giving rise to one of the most haunting lines in poetry (from the late-Latin *Pervigilium Veneris, The Festival of Venus*): 'When will my spring come, when I may be like the swallow?' They swoop through Shakespeare and dip in and out of much of our other literature and folklore, to end up firmly perched on a proverb: one swallow doesn't make a summer. You know what it means. But it's wrong, really, because for many people one swallow definitely *does* make a summer, in that as soon as they catch sight of their first one, all tail streamers and acrobatics, just back from Cape Town, they know with a rush of elation that the warm times, beyond all doubt, are just around the corner.

Nightingales are not visually thrilling like swallows, not much to look at at all really – small brown thrushes skulking inside scrub – but the sound they make, for the short six weeks after they arrive from Nigeria or Ghana, has been held up as the quintessence of birdsong by all of civilized Europe for 3,000 years, and has given the bird an unparalleled position in our culture. It has formed the basis of a Greek and Roman myth (of Philomel and Tereus) and of one of Aesop's fables (the peacock and the nightingale); it has been used in simile by Chaucer, in metaphor by Shakespeare, and as the 7 subject of a wonderful ode by Keats. But the real thing far surpasses the literary references, and to hear a nightingale singing, its clear-cut, liquid voice piercing the darkness on a warm May night, is one of the most intense experiences the natural world can provide. This uniquely powerful song would almost certainly be spring's anthem – were it not for one other.

It is curious that the bird we regard as the spring-bringer supreme should be famous also for its deviant habits. The cuckoo is our only brood parasite – it lays its eggs in other birds' nests – and has long been a symbol of sexual deception. Yet it has a double identity for us, and the other side of its image is inspiring. No sound in nature is more familiar, more instantly recognizable or more celebrated than the male cuckoo's call, the two descending notes which from the middle of April echo, bell-like, through the countryside when the bird comes back from Kenya or Ethiopia.

It may be its similarity to the human voice, often remarked upon; it may be its striking, metronomic simplicity; it may be its sheer musicality (for the interval is an exact minor third). Whatever the reason, the cuckoo's call has such a deep resonance for us, as the great marker of the arrival of spring and the advent of summer, that it too has caught imaginations for centuries: it forms the chorus of the oldest extant song in English, 'Sumer is icumen in', written 750 years ago (probably by a monk in Reading Abbey).

It is universally known: even people who have never heard a real cuckoo could imitate it. In Europe, it is one of the fundamental sounds of our world, the supreme signal of the soft days coming again, with the trees in full leaf and the high blue skies, and to have it drift to your ears for the first time in any spring is to know true exhilaration.

Exhilaration with all of them. Yet underlying the exhilaration there is something more. The spring-bringers stir in us something deeper than mere delight when we encounter them (though that is certainly part of it). What it is is hard to tease out at first. Eventually, though, you realize that it is not simply the fact of their arrival, and its marking of the seasonal change, tremendous though that is, that so affects us: it is the recurring nature of it. In coming back year after year after year, against all the odds that they face, the spring migrants are testaments to the earth's great cycle. They remind us that, although death is certain, renewal is eternal, that although all life ends, new life comes as well.

Perhaps what they mean to us, really, is hope. Hope is there in the annual arrival of all of them, small creatures, tiny creatures even, making their giant, incredible journeys and then pouring into our countryside in a multicoloured, singing cascade – wheatears and willow warblers, stone curlews and sand martins, redstarts and ring ouzels, whinchats and whitethroats, hobbies and honey buzzards, tree pipits and turtle doves and nightjars, as well as the nightingales, swallows and cuckoos – every single one of the whole 16 million a feathered piece of hope, fresh from Africa.

What would it mean to us if the spring-bringers stopped arriving? If the great eternal migration machine started to go wrong; if trouble, serious trouble, got into the works, and the birds that for all our time as humans have come on their great journeys and announced that the winter is past, and the rain is over and gone, came no longer?

How much would it matter to us? How would we measure it, as a loss? It would not be immediately catastrophic, as the loss of bees would be catastrophic (for then much pollination would stop and swathes of agriculture would collapse). Life would go on. But what would it mean to our souls? What – a strange exercise – could we compare it to?

Would it be like the loss of rainbows?

Would it be like the loss of roses?

Would it be like the loss of rivers, of running water?

Would it be greater than that? Would it be like the loss of music?

Would it be greater still, knowing everything the arrival of the spring-bringers stands for?

Would it be like the loss of hope?

We ought to start working it out pretty soon, for the process has already begun.

TWO

Out of Africa

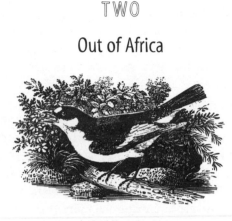

Pied Flycatcher

Is it a foolish enterprise, to seek to get to the heart of things? There are always limits to how we can know and apprehend the world, and my knowing and my apprehension will not be yours, and who is to say whose is closer, closer to the heart? If we seek to define, we may end up merely mistaken. Yet perhaps any attempt has value, for in the particular the essence may be glimpsed, and a glimpse is often the start of something. That there was a need, a need to seek out and proclaim the worth and essence of the spring-bringers, at least seemed clear; and in the end that was justification enough.

It was partly that no one ever appeared to have quite grasped what they gave us as a group, Europe's summer migrant birds. They had excited people and been admired since the beginning of literature, and doubtless earlier, individually, but the wonder of the whole phenomenon which brought them out of central Africa every spring, this stupendous natural marvel on the scale of the Gulf Stream, or the Indian monsoon, had passed people by. No great surprise in that: it was not even described in full, scientifically, until 1972. But it did mean that people were largely unaware of the remarkable dimension **11** of the heritage, of just how great was the resonance of the spring-bringers, taken together, in European literature, legend and folklore, from Greece and Rome onward. Nightingales, swallows, cuckoos and the rest, with their annual arrivals and performances to which people responded down the centuries with such animation, seemed to transcend national boundaries to become part of Europe's very essence, to be part of the continent's distinctive cultural furniture, as much as cathedrals, Latin, olive oil or wine.

Secondly, people seemed to be hardly aware of how, despite the heritage, they had themselves lost touch with them, lost the live links to these creatures, lost the very responses which had propelled the spring-bringers to such prominence in our culture. Once everybody knew them, for once everyone lived in intimate contact with the natural world: Shakespeare mentions more than fifty bird species, and his knowledge came from the countryside. But in the last two or three generations this generalized intimacy had faded, until more recently it had vanished altogether, as increasingly urbanized men, women and children shifted their gaze from the living world around them to electronic screens, and listened to electronic sounds. You could still find real interest in the spring-bringers, but it had largely become the interest not of people, as it were, but of specialists: of scientists, of birdwatchers (or birders, as we tend to say nowadays). Once it was *people* who listened to warblers and turtle doves, citizens going about their everyday business; more often now it was only experts, or special-interest groups, who made expeditions, who went out looking for them. If people in general did not register these creatures any more, how would our society understand the scale of the loss if a bleak and still scarcely conceivable April were ever to come when the spring-bringers did not return?

It was time that they were celebrated; that seemed to be not only right, but overdue. It was time to seek them out and restore them to their rightful place in the scale of what mattered in life, to hoist them up once more into our consciousness alongside the other pressing concerns of living in the twenty-first century. To do this was a quest of sorts, and like all quests it involved a challenge, as it was obvious that simply to seek out the birds themselves and write about them, however pithily, eloquently or quirkily, would be insufficient. Something more was needed, something to do with human responses, and it gradually became apparent that the challenge was not only to find the birds – itself not always a straightforward task – but, beyond that, to get to the heart of what they had meant and still may mean to people.

In attempting it I felt I had an advantage, if a perverse one: I was not an authority. I had been a boyhood birdwatcher, many years before, but I had not progressed into that much more single-minded, optics-laden and pager-alerted figure of later decades, the birder. Although I had friends who were birders and friends who were ornithological scientists, I did not have the real expertise of either (and the expertise of birders is terrifying); my knowledge of British and European birds amounted merely to a competence, albeit one I liked to think was animated by a love for them and by a love for the literature they had inspired. Yet that meant that if I were seeking to recapture the essence of the spring-bringers for people, rather than for specialists, it was as a mere person that I myself would be carrying out the exercise. I would be learning, more than I would be pronouncing (always a more trustworthy mode of being). It would be an exercise in discovery as much as one in dispensing knowledge from on high.

I spent a springtime doing it – the spring of 2008. It was a marvellous mission, for it took me into landscapes at the moment of their keenest beauty and showed me wildlife at the moment when it was most vibrantly alive. It felt like my spring, this one: instead of letting it pass me by as usual, with a hasty approving nod on the way to work, I watched it unfold in detail, from the first celandine in March to the first foxglove in June, and as it flowered around me I sought and found the spring-bringers, one after another, trying to get to the heart of them. Although the ones I pursued were birds that bred all over Europe, I mostly sought them in Britain, and, in Britain, mostly in England (with one journey into Wales). That **13** meant, unfortunately, that there was no place for the white storks, so venerated as bringers of luck and fertility as well as the spring on their annual return to nest on top of houses and churches and town halls right across mainland Europe; no place for the cranes and honey buzzards making the long haul back to Scandinavia; no place for that rainbow trio the hoopoe, the roller and the bee-eater, which add such eye-popping colours to summers in Italy and Greece (cinnamon, cyan, chestnut, primrose); no place for the lesser kestrel, the most charming of small falcons, returning from Africa to flutter in flocks around the heights of the cathedral in Seville.

As for France, the land I would adopt if I had to choose another, I discuss often with a French friend how his countrymen seem more and more uninterested in the natural world, or indeed even in the real world, saving all their enthusiasm for the abstract world of ideas, and I despair of them – and then I find a website put together by a young French scientist detailing all the colonies in central Paris of one of the loveliest of the spring-bringers, the house martin (the *hirondelle de fenêtre*, the 'window swallow') and my faith is restored.

But Britain was where my own spring-bringers were, and Britain was where of necessity I looked for them across the landscapes, the wetlands and drylands, the lowlands and uplands, even in the city, as the days grew warmer and the trees burst into leaf and the evenings lengthened – except right at the beginning of it all, when in the sharp-edged early morning light a small bird caught in a mist net was silhouetted, motionless, against the sky.

'What d'you think it is?' said Ian Thompson.

We were about 30 feet away. I strained my eyes. I shook my head.

'Nightingale,' said Ian.

My heart skipped a beat. The bird-legend. The bird-fable. Never glimpsed before. Right here.

We moved forward and he reached up and began to untangle it gently from the nylon web (called a mist net because the threads are so fine they are virtually impossible for birds to see). He said, 'There's an art to identifying birds at awkward angles. I saw the russet on the tail.' And as it came out of the dark confusion of netting, as it took shape in his hands like a bird produced by a conjurer, I watched spellbound: here was the creature that poets had celebrated for millennia; here it was now, in Ian's hand, in the 'ringer's grip', the head gently held between the first and second fingers, the body in his folded palm. It was exquisite: plainly coloured, but in strong plain colours that a good designer might have chosen – a back the colour of milk chocolate, a tail the colour of an old terracotta flowerpot, a belly the colour of cream. And the eye, the black eye that was watching me warily, how bright it was; how big. 'That's for low-light vision,' said Ian – 'hopping around in the dark.'

We were in Gibraltar; we were on the Rock. I had come to the hulking lump of British limestone at Spain's southern tip to witness the start of the Great Arrival, the beginnings of the mass movement of African migrant birds into Europe, for Gibraltar is where many of them make their first landfall. But in going there I learned something more than the times and routes of their travelling: I began to understand something of their essence.

Gibraltar has a double identity. The familiar one is Little Bit of Britain Stuck on the End of Spain, the one that offers itself to the crowds who swarm ashore every day from the cruise ships: helmeted bobbies, double-decker buses, English road signs, shops and pubs. A British territory since 1704, Gibraltar has seen its long-time function as the UK's most important foreign naval base, guarding the entrance to the Mediterranean, much reduced over the last twenty-five years, and what has replaced it is hardly inspiring: the town is now a traffic-fume-filled, building-site-scarred, jam-packed, clattering tax-free shopping centre. It is almost a mini Hong Kong. Development is everywhere, much of it on land reclaimed from the harbour, and this has swamped the town's former outlines, with tower blocks hiding the old walls and bastions, so that what until relatively recently was a very obvious eighteenth-century fortified port now looks like Swindon.

Yet there is another Gibraltar, and its second, much less well known, identity is that of fantastic bird staging post. It's simple **15** geography. The Strait of Gibraltar provides the narrowest crossing of the Mediterranean from the vast African land mass to the south, and the Rock (with its Andalusian environs) is in the centre of a bottleneck through which millions of birds are funnelled twice a year. This is most notably the case with the migratory soaring birds such as storks, vultures, eagles and other large birds of prey. These are so heavy and long-winged that they have evolved to travel by soaring upward on thermals, the currents of air which rise from the land as it warms in the sun, and then gliding downward and forwards until the next thermal takes them back up again. But thermals do not form over the sea in the Mediterranean, so to cross it they need to rise on a thermal on one side and then glide over to the other all in one go.

Only the strait between Gibraltar and Morocco is narrow enough to allow this, being less than 10 miles wide at its narrowest point, a little way to the west in Spain. So the soarers, along with many other birds, congregate at the narrows and pass through in spring and autumn in awesome numbers, and at certain moments the sight can be unforgettable. John Cortes, secretary of the Gibraltar Ornithological and Natural History Society (known affectionately to its adherents as 'Gonze'), remembers a September day in the 1970s when he stood on the Rock and watched 11,000 honey buzzards fly south in an aerial pageant which took from morning till evening to pass.

But countless small migrants also choose the Gibraltar route in and out of Europe, making grateful landfall on the Upper Rock, which, surprisingly and happily, is entirely preserved as a nature reserve; it is a limestone landscape of maquis, a scrub of wild olive, lentisk and other aromatic and shrubby plants, and in effect an unspoiled Mediterranean island sitting on top of the raucous and polluted tourist trap below. Extraordinary: two completely different Gibraltars, separated vertically, layers in a cake. In so far as tourists get to the Upper Rock at all, they generally pop along in a taxi to see the 'apes', the tribe of semi-wild, tailless macaques maintained by **16** the Gibraltar government as a visitor attraction, which are the only monkeys in Europe. They're famous. And they hang around parts of the Upper Rock like aimless teenagers in a shopping mall, waiting to be fed. Go and gawp at them if you want. But they are sad creatures. And they'll bite you.

The real wildlife of the Upper Rock is infinitely less publicized and infinitely more engaging: sparkling butterflies like the Spanish festoon, the Cleopatra and the two-tailed pasha (Europe's showiest insect); arresting plants such as the giant Tangier fennel, the wild gladiolus and the Gibraltar candytuft; the barbary partridge, Gibraltar's special bird (found only here and in Sardinia); and when I visited, in mid-April, the migrant songbirds heading north into all of Europe, but resting first from their flight across the strait. High overhead the raptors were gliding, and not always comfortably – I watched a short-toed eagle, a snake-hunter perhaps heading for southern France, being hammered mercilessly by the local yellow-legged gulls – but down on the Rock the Europe-bound pied flycatchers and woodchat shrikes, the blackcaps and whitethroats, darted in and out of the lentisk bushes and the wild olive trees, and ended up in Ian Thompson's mist nets.

Ian was the Gibraltar Ornithological and Natural History Society's bird ringer. Tough-minded and intensely practical, at 56 he was a former British Telecom executive from Hatfield in Hertfordshire who had taken early retirement to devote himself full-time to ringing. That's the sort of commitment often inspired by the activity of catching birds, putting a small numbered metal ring on their legs, and letting them go. Closely controlled, and involving long training under strict supervision, ringing provides priceless knowledge, essential for conservation policy, of bird movements. (A ringed bird caught again somewhere else reveals its origin and its destination – possibly a previously unknown wintering ground – and enables a good guess about its journey between the two points.) To the ringer, it offers an intimacy of contact with wild birds which is unparalleled.

For the previous six years Ian had based himself, in the spring, at the Jews' Gate field station of GONHS, at the edge of the Upper **17**

Rock nature reserve, and he had caught and ringed thousands of migrant songbirds on their way from Africa to breed all over western Europe. As the dawn light filled the sky, he and his assistant, Yvonne Benting, opened up the nine long mist nets hidden in the maquis on the Rock's steep slopes, and soon they were picking up a few of Gibraltar's common resident birds: robins, blackbirds, blue tits and the species which is the Mediterranean bird par excellence, the Sardinian warbler, a songbird with a black head, a bright red eye-ring and a constant scratchy refrain which enlivens the scrub all round the littoral from Spain to Egypt – hire a holiday villa in Crete and there'll be a pair in your garden.

More interesting to me, though, were the migrants from Africa that were passing through on their way north. Many were warblers, small attractive cousins of the Sardinian such as blackcaps, whitethroats and subalpine warblers, and even-smaller leaf warblers such as willow warblers and chiffchaffs. These were among the spring-bringers I would be looking for back in Britain, and I found it mesmerizing to see at such exceptionally close quarters these creatures usually glimpsed only as a blur in a hedgerow or a silhouetted blob high in a tree. They were taken from the mist nets quickly – the nets were constantly visited – and placed into soft cloth bags which seemed to calm and settle them, like a hood calms a falcon. None I saw was harmed in any way, although watching the collection of them it struck me forcefully that on Mediterranean islands such as Malta or Cyprus this would be a harvest, and only one fate would await these birds: the pot. Here on the 'island' of Gibraltar they sacrificed twenty minutes of freedom in the cause of ornithology, and were sent on their way.

The bags were brought back from the nets to the ringing station by Ian and Yvonne, and watching the birds come out of them – I mean the ones I hadn't seen being put in – was like opening Christmas presents. What's this now? It's a whitethroat. Wow. I'd never realized just how pretty a whitethroat was, but looking at this one motionless a few inches away, as Yvonne examined its plumage to age it and sex it, checked its fat and muscle reserves, slipped the ring on to its leg and weighed it before letting it go, I could see how strikingly the grey head contrasted with the pure white throat and how all that was so handsomely set off by the rusty wings and the hint of a pinkish flush on the breast. What's this one? I was stumped for a second: a small browny-grey bird of clean lines, but distinguished by its very lack of any distinguishing features whatsoever. Then I realized. Of course. It was a garden warbler. Seen this close, even its simplicity was eyecatching. And then out of a bag came a jewel.

'What's this then?' said Ian, shifting it into the 'photographer's grip', where the bird is held gently by the legs so the whole body is visible.

'Well, it's a *Phylloscopus* warbler [a leaf warbler],' I said.

'Yeah,' he said slowly, with the ominous cadence of John Wayne. 'Go on.'

Being merely a person, rather than a birder, I struggled. It wasn't a chiffchaff, a willow warbler or a wood warbler, the three leaf warblers which breed in Britain, although it was clearly related to them. Yet it was as unfamiliar to me as it was intensely attractive: smaller than all the others and brighter, its olive-green back set off by a bright yellow-green rump, and white underparts giving it a sort of frosted appearance. I tried to remember the other leaf warblers. Yellow-browed? Arctic? Greenish? Ian shook his head.

I gave up.

'It's a Bonelli's warbler,' he said. 'You can find it in France. Birders would travel to see that in Britain. That would be a good bird.'

I gazed at it, and once more Christmas came into my mind: in its perfect prettiness it seemed for all the world like a Christmas-tree decoration, ready to be clipped to the branch of a silver fir amid the glossy hanging balls. It was great.

They were all great, the whitethroats and blackcaps, the pied fly-catchers, the subalpine warblers with their white moustaches above their orange breasts, terrific with their colours seen so intimately. Yet for me the nightingale, in its dun uniform, outshone everything. It was the first migrant caught that morning, and to see it for the **19** first time, and so closely, excited me beyond words, for it was almost more mystic creature than bird; I think I'd have been hardly more energized if we'd caught a unicorn. For anyone interested in poetry this was the bird supreme, and gazing on it, layer upon layer of legend came into my mind.

I thought of Keats, hearing it in the garden at Hampstead in the spring of 1819 when he was probably already ill with TB, and I thought that even for him, 200 years ago, it was a bird with a distant past, he felt the legend behind it:

The voice I hear this passing night was heard
In ancient days by emperor and clown.

And I thought of the unknown poet who wrote one of the most moving of Latin poems, the *Pervigilium Veneris*, the *Festival of Venus*, who spends nearly a hundred lines celebrating the coming of spring and then bursts out that the nightingale is singing but that *he* cannot sing, and we never find out why, only that his silence is destroying him – and for him too, 1,700 years ago, even then this was a legendary bird: it was *Terei puella*, the girl of Tereus in the gruesome legend of Tereus and Philomel, she who was turned into a nightingale by the gods after Tereus, her brother-in-law, ravished her and cut out her tongue. I thought too of how the celebration of the bird grew with poet after poet, through the late-Latin versifiers and then the troubadours in Provence and the minnesingers in Germany and the love poets of the Renaissance, all across Europe, then all the way through the romantics, through Keats and Coleridge and poor John Clare who went mad and everybody else, and then I looked up.

I looked up past the bird in Ian's hand, and out to where it had just come from, out across the shimmering blue strait to Jebel Musa, the mountain in Morocco 15 miles away – the other limestone peak which, with Gibraltar itself, was one of the twin Pillars of Hercules, guarding the Mediterranean's entrance for the ancient world. It was sharply visible now, its every indentation edged in shadow by the slanting rays of the rising sun, and the thought suddenly struck me forcefully, *that* was never part of it: Africa.

Africa was never part of the legend, of the stories clustering about the nightingale, of what today we would call the narrative of the nightingale. It was not part of the Greek or the Roman view of the bird, or the French or the German view of the bird, or the English view of the bird. Listening to it, ineffably moved, John Keats let his imagination take wing: he thought of Provence, he thought of Hippocrene, the fountain of the Muses on Mount Helicon, he thought of the biblical story of Ruth (somewhat modified), and he thought of faraway fairy lands, but it never occurred to him that the bird he was so raptly adoring might have been pouring forth its soul abroad in such an ecstasy a month earlier in a piece of savannah in what is now Gambia.

It did not dawn on him that the bird he was listening to in the garden at Wentworth Place in Hampstead, north London – the 'Dryad of the trees' – had come to him not from Greece, say, but from a hot, dry land of elephants and giraffes, of locusts and termites, of baobabs and acacia trees. How could it? There was simply no appreciation in Europe then that the nightingale had another life, that it had another existence outside its song season. Indeed, the very fact that its post-song season was a mystery was itself a fascinating element of its folklore, even part of its poetic appeal:

Ask me no more whither doth haste
The nightingale when May is past;
For in your sweet dividing throat
She winters and keeps warm her note

wrote the cavalier poet Thomas Carew sometime in the 1630s, charmingly but inaccurately (it is the male bird which sings, although all poets made this mistake before the twentieth century).

Here we have a striking paradox: that the continent of Africa, with all its divergence from Europe in terms of ecology, habitats, **21** landscape, weather patterns, human settlements and vastness, has featured not at all in the voluminous European literature and folklore of *Luscinia megarhynchos*, in our image of the nightingale – while in the bird's actual life it most assuredly plays a quite enormous role.

We know now; but it took a very long time to uncover just what a significant part Africa does play in the lives of all our spring-bringers, and in fact it was not worked out in full until less than forty years ago, after humans had taken to the air, split the atom, and landed on the moon.

People had always had a vague notion of migration: ever since civilization began in Eurasia it had been realized that some birds made seasonal journeys, towards the south in the autumn and back towards the north in the spring. When men and women still lived in intimacy with the natural world and there were few man-made distractions, the winter vanishing of certain species was perfectly obvious, and as for the bigger birds, they could hardly be missed even as they travelled: the storks and the cranes, forming into squadrons and setting off determinedly on course like bombers on a mission, the raptors which sometimes massed in enormous numbers at other Gibraltar-like choke points on their journeys, such as the Dardanelles. 'Yea,' says the Lord to the Old Testament prophet Jeremiah, 'the stork in the heaven knoweth her appointed times, and the turtle [turtle dove] and the crane and the swallow observe the time of their coming.' Earlier, pompously reminding poor old Job who is boss and who made the world, God says, 'Doth the hawk fly by *thy* wisdom, and stretch her wings toward the south?' Several times in the Bible we encounter migrating flocks of quail, such as the one that falls about the hungry Israelites as they wander in the desert, in the Book of Exodus. The winged comings and goings were part of many ancient cultures. Homer, with animal similes at the heart of his poetry,

opens Book 3 of the Iliad by describing the Trojans advancing on the Greeks: 'They filled the air with clamour, like the cranes that fly from the onset of winter and sudden rains.'

The first person to think scientifically about migration was Aristotle, the fourth-century-BC student of Plato and tutor of Alexander the Great, who was the first person to think systematically about so many subjects, from logic to literary criticism. Aristotle wrote extensively on biology, and a lot of what he wrote remains relevant today, but on the subject of bird migration he unfortunately left a confused intellectual legacy, and this confounded writers on the natural world, who bowed to him as their principal authority for more than 2,000 years. The problem was that much of what he set down about natural history, fish, flesh and fowl, was obviously based on stories passed to him by people such as fishermen and bird-catchers, and not only are some of these stories far-fetched – the fishy ones in particular have to be taken with a generous flick of the salt-shaker – but others are contradictory; yet Aristotle repeats them uncritically, and this is the case with migration.

His thoughts on it can be found in Book 8 of *The History of Animals*. In Part 12, Aristotle clearly recognizes that migration is a response to changing seasonality: 'For all animals have an instinctive perception of the changes of temperature, and, just as men seek shelter in houses in winter, or as men of great possessions spend their summer in cool places and their winter in sunny ones' – nothing's changed there – 'so also all animals that can do so shift their habitat at various seasons.' He instances cranes, pelicans, swans and quail as migratory species, saying that cranes migrate from Scythia – roughly the central-Asian republics of the former Soviet Union – to Egypt, which is more or less true, even today, and he adds cushats (wood pigeons) and turtle doves as other migrating species, saying that 'cushats and turtle doves flock together, both when they arrive, and when the season for migration comes round again.'

However, in Part 16, the sage introduces the idea of hibernation, which was to bedevil thinking about migratory birds for two millennia. He writes, 'A great number of birds . . . go into hiding; **23** they do not all migrate, as is generally supposed, to warmer countries ... Swallows, for instance, have been often found in holes, quite denuded of their feathers, and the kite on its first emergence from torpidity has been seen to fly out from some such hiding place ...' And he adds, 'The case of the turtle dove is the most accepted of all, for we would defy anyone to assert that he had anywhere seen a turtle dove in winter-time; at the beginning of the hiding time it is exceedingly plump ...' – and this of a species which he has described as migratory only a few pages earlier.

Modern ornithology has surprisingly shown that Aristotle was not entirely wrong to canvass the possibility that birds hibernated. In 1946 an American naturalist specializing in desert wildlife, Dr Edmund Jaeger, discovered a common poorwill, a species of small nightjar, in a state of extended torpor, which amounted to hibernation, in a rock crevice in the Chuckwalla Mountains of southern California. Further research showed that the species did effectively hibernate, and that the name given to it by Native Americans of the Hopi tribe meant 'the sleeping one'.

But that's it. Out of the 10,000 or so bird species in the world, there are no other known hibernators in the wild, and so Aristotle sent naturalists off on a wild goose chase which lasted until the early nineteenth century. Many subsequent authors, even the great Linnaeus, the father of modern scientific taxonomy, followed him in suggesting that disappearing birds hibernated in winter, though no evidence was ever produced for it, and evidence that they migrated began to mount steadily from the Renaissance onward. (A bizarre but particularly persistent version of the hibernation theory being that swallows and martins submerged themselves in lakes and ponds to pass the winter under water.)

The two conflicting theories met in the mind of Gilbert White, the eighteenth-century parson whose account of the wildlife of his native Hampshire village, *The Natural History of Selborne*, became a literary classic which has never been out of print since it was published in 1789. White is often thought of as the first birdwatcher, or

24

the first ecologist, in that, unusually for his time, he specialized in recording the behaviour of living creatures in the field rather than studying skins and specimens, and it is the scale and freshness of his observation of an English countryside much richer then than now in birds and animals, plants and insects, which gives his work its timeless appeal. Using only the naked eye – binoculars did not come along until 1894 – a finely tuned ear for birdsong, and endless patience, he made numerous fascinating discoveries about the natural world that surrounded him, from the identity of the wood warbler to the startling fact that swifts were capable of mating on the wing.

Every year, White was acutely responsive to the returning migrants – or summer birds of passage, as he termed them – noting down their arrival dates, and later their departure dates, and even working out for himself that some birds were migrants which had not hitherto been so regarded, such as the ring ouzel, the mountain relative of the blackbird. He accepted the idea of migration entirely – except for one curious blind spot. He thought it possible that hibernation was practised by swallows, martins and swifts, holding on to this belief to the end of his life; and the picture of the scrupulous parson/observer trying (in this one situation only) to convince himself of something which was not the case adds not a little to *The Natural History of Selborne*'s charm.

But the arguments for bird hibernation were getting steadily weaker, in the absence of any observation whatsoever of this, and by the second decade of the nineteenth century the idea had more or less been abandoned. From then on it was accepted that birds which vanished in winter from temperate regions such as Britain, from swallows to cuckoos, had migrated south to warmer climates. But to where, exactly? There were only the haziest notions. To Spain? To Italy? To the Mediterranean? To Africa? Where in Africa? What do we know of Africa?

The first piece of concrete evidence that European migrants actually penetrated deep into the African continent, and indeed went south of the Sahara Desert, came in May 1822, when a German **25** nobleman, Count Christian Ludwig von Bothmer, shot a weird-looking white stork on the thatched roof of a house near his castle in Mecklenburg, not far from the Baltic coast.

The bird's singular appearance had a singular cause: the stork turned out to be carrying an arrow in its neck, nearly 3 feet long – it had entered the neck obliquely and almost lay alongside it – and this was subsequently recognized as being of central-African provenance. (Imagine the creature's journey back to Mecklenburg . . .) This queer bird was the first proof that the spring-bringers really did come out of Africa's heart, and at the time it created a stir; but although subsequently much has been made of the '*Pfeilstorch*', or arrow stork, as it is known – the specimen is kept in the zoology department of Rostock University and is now seen as marking a paradigm shift in the study of migration – in truth it was a false start. The European bird with Africa drilled through its gullet was soon forgotten, and ignorance continued about the true extent of the exchange between the two continents until the end of the century and beyond.

This might seem surprising, because these were the decades in which European colonizers were 'opening up' Africa, delineating the mountain ranges, rivers and forests, founding countries and settlements, and starting to exploit the raw materials and the people; and in the wake of the explorers, soldiers and administrators came a wave of gun-toting European naturalists who began methodically to document Africa's stunning avifauna. They did this not so much with pen and paper as by making extensive collections of skins and specimens, shot on a grand scale, and they specialized in what became known as 'faunistics' – the compiling of exhaustive lists of the species to be found in a given area, as in *List of a Collection of Birds From the Colony of Natal in South-eastern Africa* by J. H. Gurney, 1859. During the nineteenth century's course they covered most of the continent, yet, although they encountered wintering European birds and noted them down, they never seem to have paid them much attention or addressed them as a group.

It's not hard to understand why: here were 2,300 new species to gaze upon, more than four times the number that Europe held, and many of them exotic beyond anything found north of the Mediterranean. Why bother with a boring old willow warbler when there was a paradise flycatcher to be amazed by? Why get excited by a European cuckoo when there were ten native species of cuckoo to distinguish and feast your eyes on in South Africa alone (before knocking them off and setting them up in the cabinet, naturally)? All through the century, the professional ornithologists whose age it was – museum men and academics, with their collections of skins and eggs – paid no heed to the African presence of European birds as a question in itself, and when it was eventually considered for the first time, it was done by a quite new type of ornithological being: the amateur. A bird watcher. (The term was coined in 1901. Not yet a birdwatcher; far less a birder).

Eliot Howard was a prosperous businessman (director of a Birmingham steel company) who watched birds every morning before breakfast, near his home in the Severn valley in Worcestershire. Uninterested in collecting specimens, Howard followed Gilbert White a century earlier in being absorbed by the behaviour of living species, and as the twentieth century began he decided to focus his interest on a group of songbirds prominent among the spring-bringers, several of which he could observe locally: the warblers.

Easy enough to watch them come out of the ringing bags in Gibraltar; much harder to keep track of them zipping in and out of the Worcestershire hedgerows. Yet such were Howard's powers of patient observation and intelligence that this study led him to one of the great biological breakthroughs of the twentieth century: the discovery of territory. Howard worked out that, for male birds in the breeding season, holding an area and defending it against other males was the activity that was key to everything else. It was over territories, not females, that competing males actually fought, but the winner of the fight and consequent occupier of the territory was the bird that will attract a mate, for territory ensured a nesting **27** area, a guaranteed food supply, and a potential refuge from predators. Howard's discovery also began to explain the true function of bird-song, which, almost always performed by the male, was an aggressive warning to other males to keep right out, and a seductive invitation to females to come on in. (Before this, the general assumption was that female birds did the singing.) Howard's book *Territory in Bird Life*, published in 1920, is one of the landmarks of twentieth-century ecology. Belittled at first by the ornithological establishment because their author was an amateur, the book's ideas gradually became accepted into the mainstream and gave Eliot Howard a permanent place in biological history.

However, his study of warblers had already borne independent fruit. In 1907 he began the publication of a nine-part work entitled *The British Warblers: A History, with Problems of their Lives*, which in its own way was just as exceptional as his later territory volume. It was an astoundingly opulent production, with exquisite illus-trations – both coloured plates and photogravures – by the Danish artist Henrik Grönvold, and retailed at 21 shillings per part. A guinea a time! Nine gold guineas for the set! Converting this to present prices depends on which method you use, but if we base it on a comparison of average earnings then and now, it works out at something like £400 per volume, and so £3,600 for the set. Who was to buy this? What market did Howard have in mind? One suspects he had none; he was independently wealthy, and simply wished his work to be produced in a way that was as close to per-fection as possible. You would have to say that he succeeded: today it is a much-sought-after treasure of ornithological literature, and just holding it and leafing through it in a library (when it had been brought out of the locked rare-books cabinet) left me lightheaded with covetousness.

Yet *British Warblers* was far more than just a book for the Edwardian equivalent of the coffee table. It was a startlingly original account of the life cycles and breeding biology of a whole group of

birds which are far from easy to observe, detailing from first-hand knowledge not only their descriptions and their distributions, but also their songs, their displays and their breeding behaviour – including their copulations, to the embarrassment of some of his contemporaries – in a way that had never been done before.

Most original of all, we can see now, were the maps. Of the fourteen species of warbler which breed in Britain, twelve are African migrants, and for ten of them Howard, the amateur indefatigable, drew up double maps of their distribution: one for the British summer or breeding range, which was enterprising enough, and the other for the winter or non-breeding range – *this one in Africa*. For the record, the species he featured were the willow warbler, chiffchaff, wood warbler, blackcap, garden warbler, reed warbler, marsh warbler, sedge warbler, grasshopper warbler and Savi's warbler. There were also similar maps for two further species which occur in Britain on passage but do not breed here: the great reed warbler and the aquatic warbler.

Professor Tim Birkhead of the University of Sheffield, an authority on early ornithology (and the fortunate owner of a copy of the book), drew my attention to these quite remarkable pages, which as far as I am aware have never been commented upon but appear to constitute the first graphical representation of the presence of European breeding birds on their wintering grounds in Africa. If you consider the absence of anything remotely similar in the literature previously, it is astonishing to gaze on the pale-blue map of the African continent and look at Howard's estimate of the winter distribution of the willow warbler, marked over it as a stippling of red dots – all the more so when one remembers that this and the other eleven maps like it were produced from a house in Stourport-on-Severn a hundred years ago, in the spare time of a man running a steel firm.

How had he done it? From the text, it is clear that in between managing his business and stalking his warblers he had also mastered all the extant ornithological literature and had combed it exhaustively for African references. For the field naturalist Eliot Howard, the practitioners of faunistics, the collectors of skins and eggs, could have their uses. Of the willow warbler he writes: **29**

Its winter quarters in Europe may be said to begin in the south of France and extend through Spain, parts of Italy, Sicily, Greece and Asia Minor. The majority, however, pass on to Africa, where they have been traced to Morocco, Algeria, Tripoli, the Oases of the Sahara, Egypt and the vicinity of the White Nile, Abyssinia, Somaliland, East Africa, Uganda, the Congo Free State, Rhodesia, the Transvaal, Orange River Colony, Cape Colony and up the West Coast through Namaqualand, Darmaraland, Fernando Po, and Sierra Leone.

There's a lost geography for you. But consider the word 'traced': it is clearly referring in every case to a monograph, or to somebody's note on a specimen collection, or to a paper in *Ibis* (the journal of the British Ornithologists' Union). Howard's achievement was once again amazing for an amateur, and almost on a par with his discovery of territory (though this one has had no recognition): it was not only to assemble all this information, but, more than that, it was to see that the information was there for the assembling. For *British Warblers* represents not just the first attempt at mapping the spring-bringers in their African distribution: it is the first attempt to show they had another life, outside Europe.

Yet, like the arrow stork, it was not remarked upon by the world at large. Howard's luxury volumes, his guinea-a-time tomes, drew a leisured as much as a scientific readership, and the ground-breaking maps were included virtually without comment on his own part. For all their originality, they passed unnoticed (at the time). It was another, concurrent, development which made the world sit up and take notice of the reality of Africa in the lives of the spring-bringers, and that was the advent of ringing.

The idea of marking birds and then recovering them as a means of communication goes back to antiquity, and there are various accounts of swallows and other species being sent as messengers with toes cut off or cotton tied to their legs; but the formal practice of **30** fitting a numbered or address-bearing ring to the leg of a bird, as

Ian Thompson was doing with his songbirds on Gibraltar's Upper Rock, in the expectation that it may be recovered elsewhere and thus enable the bird's journey to be reconstructed, is just over a century old.

It was begun in Denmark by a teacher, Hans Christian Mortensen, who in 1890 attempted it with rings made out of zinc. The metal proved too cumbersome for the birds to cope with. By 1899, however, aluminium had become available, and Mortensen tried again, ringing 162 starlings in that year and hoping for recoveries. There were none; but as the century changed, so did his luck, and two of the birds he ringed in Denmark in 1900 were found again, one in Holland and one in Norway.

Europe's ornithological establishment noted this; they saw the point, and the Germans, who were then the establishment's leaders, acted at once. Ringing became the focus of a new bird observatory opened by the German Ornithological Society in 1901 in East Prussia, the ancient German province anchoring the south-east corner of the Baltic Sea (and destined to vanish from the map completely as Europe was chopped up and reconfigured in 1945).

The new ringing station was at Rossiten – it's now Rybachy in Russia – a small fishing village on the Courland Spit, a long, narrow, sand-covered shingle bank which separates the sea from the Courland Lagoon behind it, in an arrangement similar to Chesil Beach and the Fleet Lagoon in Dorset, except on a much grander scale, as the Courland Spit is 60 miles long (although barely half a mile wide in places). The Vogelwarte Rossiten, or Rossiten Bird Observatory, was established in the dunes of the spit by its first director, Johannes Thienemann, as the area lay on one of the Baltic's major migration routes, and at the height of the autumn passage might easily see a quarter of a million birds stream past in a day.

The energetic Dr Thienemann, who later was responsible for resurrecting the Rostock arrow stork from obscurity and underlining its significance, began his ringing programme in 1903 with migrants **31** passing from one part of Europe to another, especially hooded crows and gulls – they were caught for him by local bird-trappers – and began to obtain recoveries from a broad band of the continent from Finland to France. But then he spread his wings, as it were, and started ringing birds nesting all over East Prussia; and inevitably, given the bird's rooftop visibility and iconic status, he turned his attention to the white stork.

The results were historic. On 21 June 1906 Dr Thienemann ringed a brood of three white stork chicks near Königsberg, the East Prussian capital (now the Russian city of Kaliningrad), and in the following October a foot of the first of these, still bearing its ring, was brought by a local man who had shot the bird to a French officer near Lake Chad, which was then part of French Equatorial Africa, and 3,000 miles from Königsberg. The next year an even more striking result was obtained. In July 1907 a colleague of Dr Thienemann's, Franz Bahr, ringed another white stork brood of three chicks, this time near Köslin in Pomerania – now the Polish town of Koszalin – and in the December one of these birds was shot near Fort Jameson in north-eastern Rhodesia, which is now Chipata, Zambia, and 5,000 miles from Poland.

The shooting and the finding of this ring were reported to the hunting journal *The Field*, in London, by the local colonial administrator, Harry Scott Thornicroft, one of the more noteworthy of the servants of British Empire – he married a local African woman, fathered eleven children, and had a subspecies of giraffe named after him (Thornicroft's giraffe, sometimes spelled Thorneycroft's giraffe, which is found in Zambia's Luangwa valley).

In his letter to *The Field* dated 16 December 1907, from the Native Commissioner's Office, Petauke, Fort Jameson, North-Eastern Rhodesia, Thornicroft wrote:

A curious thing happened here last week. A stork (Ciconia alba) was shot in the gardens of the native village near by. It had a metal ring on one of its legs marked Vogelwarte, Rossiten

163, Germania. It was flying wild with others when shot. It would be interesting to know whether this bird had escaped from some owner and flown here from Europe, and if the date and other details of its escape are known. I have preserved the skin complete with legs attached bearing the metal ring, and should be glad to forward it to the orginal owner of the bird if possible.

Thornicroft's puzzlement about the nature and purpose of the ring serves to underline what a dramatic step forward the whole process was: a curtain was at last opening on the true nature of the odysseys the spring-bringers made, which may have been suspected before in general terms, but was now being pinpointed and laid out, before the world, and beyond peradventure, in all its wonder and scale: Russia to Chad; Poland to Zambia. Yet an even greater feat of voyaging was about to be illustrated, this time from England.

The story of John Masefield's swallow represents the most dramatic milestone of all in the understanding of bird migration. Masefield was a prosperous small-town solicitor from Staffordshire – not to be confused with his near-contemporary John Masefield the poet, who was England's Poet Laureate from 1930 until his death in 1967 (and appears to have been no relation, despite occasional claims to the contrary). Solicitor-Masefield could stand as the examplar of Victorian middle-class uprightness and responsibility. Born in the town of Stone in 1850, son of a doctor, after Cambridge he was articled to a solicitor's firm in nearby Cheadle, married the senior partner's daughter, and then led a blameless life of religious observance and civic activity, reading the lessons in Cheadle parish church every Sunday, sitting as a magistrate, and serving on everything from the Staffordshire County Pensions Committee to the management committee of the William Salt Library in Stafford. He could be a character from *Middlemarch*. He also underwent the agony that befell many a late-Victorian paterfamilias: his only son, Charles, who had joined the firm, but in his leisure time was a published **33** poet, was swallowed up by the Great War, having answered the call of Kitchener at the age of 35 and being killed in France in July 1917, a month after being awarded the Military Cross.

That was towards the close of Masefield senior's life; his earlier decades were uneventful, but filled with a passion: natural history. A leading member of the North Staffordshire Field Club from 1884 until his death in 1932, he was the archetypal amateur naturalist in the acquisitive Victorian manner, making substantial collections of moths, butterflies, dried wild flowers and birds' eggs, and, his pride and joy, 'a complete collection of the land and freshwater shells of the county', which was eventually purchased by the City of Stoke-on-Trent for its museum. The collections filled his large house, Rosehill; its gardens were filled with nesting boxes for birds. And, although entering his seventh decade, Masefield took enthusiastically to bird ringing when it was brought to Britain by Harry Witherby, a publisher who in 1907 founded the journal *British Birds*, aimed at the new generation of amateur ornithologists – the bird watchers – who were not catered for by scientific publications such as *Ibis*. The magazine was an immediate success, and in 1909 Witherby went on to organize the first British ringing scheme, and used *British Birds* to publicize it.

Up in Cheadle, Masefield began ringing the chicks in his nest boxes, and among those he ringed were the swallows which nested in the porch of Rosehill. On 6 May 1911 he fitted one of these birds with one of Witherby's rings, numbered B830. What happened to this swallow was recorded in *British Birds* just over eighteen months later in a letter dated 27 December 1912 from Mr C. H. Ruddock, proprietor of the Grand Hotel, Utrecht, Natal, South Africa. Mr Ruddock wrote:

Dear Sir,
On December 23, a Swallow was caught in the farmhouse of the farm 'Roodeyand', 18 miles from this town, with a metal label round its leg, with the words Witherby, High Holborn,

London, and on the other side B830. The farmer, Mr J. Mayer, took the label off and has it in his possession. As I am interested in birds of any sort and the migration of same, I shall be glad to know if you received this letter safely.

In the *Transactions of the North Staffordshire Field Club* for 1931–2, John Masefield's obituarist records, 'The garden at Rosehill was a veritable bird sanctuary. Almost every tree had its nesting box or boxes. Soon after hatching, the young birds were ringed, and great was the joy of Masefield's heart when the following year some of his ringed birds returned, or were heard of in Scotland, or Wales, or even as far away as S. Africa.'

That hardly does justice to the singular nature of the recovery of swallow B830. Perhaps in his last years Masefield was more preoccupied with what had happened in Flanders rather than what had happened in Natal, and who could blame him? But in *British Birds* Witherby described it as 'extraordinary', and he did not exaggerate. It established for the first time that swallows breeding in the British Isles migrated in winter to South Africa, something which even today we find hard to credit: a bird not much bigger than a box of matches flying 6,000 miles down the whole length of the African continent.

The fact that the swallow was found so far to the south-*east* of Africa Witherby also found remarkable, thinking it unlikely that the bird could have flown down the continent's eastern side. But what was the alternative? Crossing the Sahara Desert? Surely not. However, just over a year later another British swallow was recovered in South Africa, this time a bird ringed by Mr R. O. Blyth at Skelmorlie, Ayrshire, on 27 July 1912, which was found at Riet Vallei in the Orange Free State on 16 March 1913 (about 150 miles away from the first recovery).

Commenting on this bird, and on the earlier Masefield recovery, Harry Witherby pointed out that in the meantime the Anglo-German ornithologist Dr Ernest Hartert had 'shown by his observations in the middle of the Sahara, that deserts are not necessarily a bar to the **35** passage of migrating birds, as was formerly supposed', and so 'it may perhaps be presumed that these Swallows take a more direct line than one would previously have thought possible.' And so it proved. As the African ringing records began to mount up – there were half a dozen swallow recoveries by 1920 – they showed that Europe's summer migrants clearly do cross the Sahara and penetrate deep into Africa, and wander all over the continent.

Yet they were but glimpses, only pointers to an enormous truth, these recovered rings, like a few scattered arrowheads found in a field that barely hint at the titanic clash of armies that had once taken place there. For the whole phenomenon of the birds leaving Africa and going north to Europe in the spring and then returning in the autumn, this vast aerial river of life annually switching direction of flow, is one of the earth's great natural marvels, like the trade winds or the leafing of trees. But not only is it enormous: it is invisible, as a discrete event. It is so huge that it is scattered in time and distance and almost impossible to conceive of in its entirety.

It took one special individual to grasp it and set it all down in its true scale and significance. He was a man who was supremely well qualified to do it, who came along just at the right time, but it still took great experience, effort, intelligence and most of all a considerable leap of the imagination to see the phenomenon in the round. His achievement is truly significant, and is recognized in the world of scientific ornithology: but, because the book in which he set out his thinking is specialized and fairly technical, his name is scarcely known to the general public, nor even to the nature-loving, birdwatching public.

It was Reg Moreau. He was an ornithologist who had learned his discipline over twenty-five years in the service of the British Empire in Africa, and came back to practise it as an academic in Oxford over a similar period, despite having left school at 17 and possessing no formal scientific qualifications whatsoever. He was a spectacularly late developer. But by the end of his career, when he turned his attention to the spring-bringers – in the years of his final illness, in fact – he had achieved a perspective on them so singular as to be in effect unique, which was that he could see the migrants from an African viewpoint every bit as much as from a European one.

Moreau's great book, where, in 1972, for the first time he made the immense aerial river of birds conceivable in its full scale, is called *The Palaearctic–African Bird Migration Systems*. The title requires a word of explanation. The Palaearctic is one of the eight faunal or biogeographical regions into which the world is divided by zoologists for the purpose of locating wildlife, and it corresponds roughly to Eurasia – that is Europe, plus Asia north of the Himalayas – and also part of North Africa. (The other faunal regions are the Nearctic – North America; the Neotropical – Central and South America; the Afrotropical – Africa south of the Sahara; the Indomalayan – Asia south of the Himalayas; the Australasian, which is self-explanatory; the Antarctic, ditto; and the Oceanic, which covers the Pacific.)

The point is that the great winged river flowing in springtime out of Africa does not only flow due north or north-west to Europe: its streams branch out across the whole of Eurasia, from Ireland at one end to Kamchatka 5,000 miles away at the other. Moreau's vision encompassed all of it, and all the bird species involved: not just the 50 or so that come to Britain, or the 120 or so that come to what we think of as Europe, but the 180-plus which throng from the end of one continent to the end of the other in their teeming billions. He put the whole picture together, and in doing so he made a major leap forward in our understanding of the natural world. But it was a long journey to get there.

Reginald Moreau, known universally as Reg, was born in 1897 in genteel suburbia, at Kingston upon Thames just outside London, the son of a stockbroker. He had neither a youthful interest in birds nor an auspicious start in life. Although his early years were comfortable in a lower-middle-class way – he was sent as a boarder to Kingston Grammar School – calamity arrived in the morning rush hour. In his own words, 'My father was hit when an express train **37** came through Surbiton station with the door open.' Mr Moreau senior never recovered, became a manic depressive, and ceased to be the family provider; Mrs Moreau took in paying guests. At 17, young Reg left school to start contributing to the household budget. He was not healthy; he had worn a sling for two years for what was diagnosed as a 'tubercular wrist'. He applied to join the Home Civil Service, scraping in at 99th in the list of the 100 places on offer, but by the time his appointment came through it was September 1914 and Britain was at war; he was classified as C3, the lowest class of fitness in the British Army, and sent to join the Army Audit Office, to spend his days counting blankets and pounds of cheese.

The following years were friendless and unhappy until in 1920 his health deteriorated even further and he developed rheumatoid arthritis in his hands and feet; his doctor said he needed a 'complete change', and Moreau applied for, and obtained, a posting in the Army Audit Office station in Cairo. That changed his life. He had just begun an interest in birds, and over the next eight years, in the unstable British protectorate which Egypt then was, the interest became a passion; guided by some of the colonial scientists who befriended him, he began to write up his observations of African bird species for various journals. He also met his wife, Winifred, on the coastal plain near Alexandria – 'Here one March afternoon, where the steppe was bright with flowers and twinkling with short-toed larks and wheatears, I met a small person picking scarlet ranunculuses . . .'

In 1928 he was given the opportunity to make his interest pro-fessional when another British Empire posting arose – this time at the nascent Agricultural and Forestry Research Station at Amani in what was then Tanganyika and is now Tanzania. Joining the Colonial Service, Moreau became secretary-librarian to the sta-tion, and remained there with his wife until 1946. In the course of eighteen years of research and fieldwork in the rainforest of the Usambara Mountains, overflowing with wildlife, he became one of the leading experts on the birds of Africa – although he had no formal scientific qualifications or training – building up an Africa-wide network of correspondents and observers, and hosting at Amani most of the principal researchers on the subject in the English-speaking world (and commemorating the devotion of his wife in the naming of a small local songbird, Mrs Moreau's warbler, *Bathmocercus winifredae*).

When ill health brought both of them back to Britain after the end of the Second World War, Moreau had accumulated not only expertise but also a formidable range of contacts, and among them was the young prodigy of British ornithology David Lack, who had visited him in Amani. A well-bred former schoolmaster, Lack was a population ecologist who specialized in the natural regulation of animal numbers, but he was also an accomplished writer for a wider audience and had gained the beginnings of a public reputation with a remarkable book, *The Life of the Robin* (published in 1943), the first full-length behavioural study of a British bird.

At the age of 35, Lack had now been made director of Oxford's Edward Grey Institute of Field Ornithology (known to generations of DPhil students as the EGI), which was virtually the university ornithology department. Recognizing Moreau's abilities, Lack offered him a place at the EGI, making the unqualified researcher in effect an instant Oxford don (an honorary degree soon followed); and shortly afterwards Moreau's abilities were further recognized when he was offered, and accepted, the editorship of *Ibis*.

With an instantly memorable face – a king-size grin under a shining bald dome of a head – and a penchant for elaborately phrased English, for the next twenty years Moreau was one of the most popular as well as one of the key figures in British academic ornithology, producing a long string of scientific papers and several books, until in 1966 his rheumatoid arthritis returned and his health broke down completely, and he retired to Herefordshire to live near his daughter. It was then, in the four years of life remaining to him, when he was increasingly punished by his illness, that he produced his masterly synthesis of migration.

It began with a chance remark from David Lack, who asked him how the breeding habitats of some of the European migrant songbirds compared with the habitats of their winter quarters, and it spread out from there into a colossal bringing-together of virtually everything that was known about the ecology of the migrants, in Africa as well as in Europe. Moreau assembled it, a generation before the advent of email, by way of a giant correspondence with the teeming number of experts on African birds whom Britain's colonial rule across the continent had produced, and all of whom he knew intimately – a lost generation now – and he put it all together from his paper-strewn sickbed, the more excited by the project the more his ill heath worsened, racing against his end like the crippled and dying scholar in Browning's poem 'A Grammarian's Funeral', and writing the preface to the book in Hereford General Hospital a short time before he died on 30 May 1970, the day after his seventy-third birthday. He hoped it would be, in his own inimitable expression, 'no bum swansong'.

Indeed it is not. He dealt in detail with 'every species that nested in the Palaearctic and wintered south of the Sahara'. There were 187 of them, from the great reed warbler to the glossy ibis, and for each he gave an account of breeding and wintering habitats and food, competition with closely related species, journeys to Europe and back, journeys within Africa, faithfulness to territories, fat accumulation, ringing recoveries, and a mass of other information. There were maps for 164 species, showing summer and winter ranges both, which was an immense achievement, unlocking at last some of the ages-old mystery of where birds went when they left us; browsing through them, you start to get a feel for the immensity of the phenomenon that Moreau was outlining for the first time. Look, for example, at the maps for the twenty-nine warbler species and you see at once in your mind's eye the rushing streams of small songbirds, millions strong, pouring between the two continents.

Libraries full of books had been written on the spring-bringers in **40** Europe, but this was the first to examine in detail their African lives, which are often two-thirds of the total or more. The work is probably not better known because it is structured largely as a technical handbook and Moreau died before he could draw his conclusions together in a separate chapter (the work was prepared for publication by his friend James Monk and was finally issued in 1972). But it is undoubtedly seminal, making truly comprehensible for the first time one of the planet's greatest life events.

Having looked at the phenomenon in the round, as nobody else had done, Moreau was able to establish two key aspects of its nature. The first was its astounding scale, for which he made an estimate of numbers: 5 billion birds were involved – five thousand million pairs of beating wings whirred out of Africa every year – a figure which today is generally accepted.

The second was a profound lesson for us in considering the spring-bringers in the past, in the present, and most of all in the future: *that these are African birds as much as European ones.*

We think of them as our own – as our cuckoos and swallows and nightingales, our warblers and our turtle doves – but they are only half ours; we share them with the mighty continent to the south, and it behoves us to remember that: to remember that in a sense they are merely lent to us, each year, before Africa takes them back. They breed with us, they are born with us, but many spend more of their lives among the acacias and the baobabs in the hot dry savannah, or in the African skies, than they do among the oaks and the beeches and the cool temperate woodlands of the north. The cuckoo that calls in April and May is at the heart of the English spring, but, Eurocentric as we are, it is worth thinking, if we can make the leap of the imagination, of what it has seen and heard and lived through in the weeks and months beforehand. It is a bird out of Africa which is calling us.

That was what struck me so forcefully as I watched Ian Thompson take the nightingale from the net on the heights of Gibraltar, with the dawn-lit Jebel Musa in the distant background behind him, and all of the African continent stretching away behind the Moroccan mountain. Even if it was the bird-legend supreme, I realized, the **41** most mythified bird in the world for its voice in the European spring, the real life of the nightingale was no less a marvel, and more than half of it was spent cruising the heart of Africa, though that had remained hidden from us for so long.

So it was with a doubled sense of fascination that I followed Ian into the ringing station and watched him start to record that life precisely in the cause of science. From the moult stage of the feathers he inferred that the bird he had caught had hatched the previous year, and from the wing length – 82 mm – that it was a male. 'This bird is relatively early, so it's more likely to be a male anyway,' he said. 'Males come through first, before the females, because they go and establish territories.'

A singer then, a young singer. I watched it, captivated – it was held with such tender deftness in Ian's hands that it seemed unafraid, bemused as much as anything – and thought how in a week or so, if it got through, it would be sending its voice out for the first time, clear on the air of a spring night in Spain or France or Germany, or maybe even in England, and I began to imagine the moment, moonlit or starlit, when it would begin. But Ian was being purely practical. He turned the bird upside down and blew softly on the feathers of its breast and belly, exposing the sternum, to check its fat and muscle reserves; they were fine. 'It's arrived here relatively fit and healthy, with good body mass and fat reserves and very good muscle,' he said. 'Sometimes you can get them and if they've crossed the Sahara they're really wasted. This one hasn't really struggled.'

Then he ringed it, fitting ring number V973155 to its leg with special pliers, and then he weighed it – it weighed 20.3 grams – and then he made me an offer which took me completely by surprise. He said, 'Would you like to release it?'

Like anyone who takes pleasure in watching birds, I had seen inspiring sights over the years, from a cornfield flashing with hoopoes and bee-eaters in Spain to a pair of sea-eagles touching talons in a mid-air greeting over Mull, from gannets divebombing a mackerel shoal to a barn owl floating past on its hunt, both within yards of me; but nothing in all that compared to the intensity of the moment that followed: I held a nightingale in the palm of my hand.

It was not just the overwhelming sense of privilege at the intimate contact with such a creature as I took it in the ringer's grip with all the gentleness at my command yet not knowing who was the more nervous, the bird or me. What impressed itself upon me most as I took it out on to the balcony at Jews' Gate, and looked across from Europe to Africa, was the marvel of its double identity.

One identity from each continent, I thought, looking from Spain to Morocco and back: the mythical one from Europe, which has engaged us for thousands of years, the ecological one from Africa, which we are only just really discovering. Both were equally remarkable: on the one hand, the small bird whose voice in the dark had moved people for as long as human feelings had been written down; and on the other, the creature with these wings a mere 82 millimetres long which had just overflown the empty vastness of the Sahara and was now to navigate north, through a myriad threats and maybe another 1,000 miles, to bring the spring in its incomparable way, perhaps to my own home country.

Both identities were astounding, and they met and they merged in the feathers and flesh I held for those few seconds, feeling the small heart beating. And then I knew I must prolong the moment no longer and I looked out over the Bay of Algeciras and I launched him back into his freedom, and followed him as he flew, northward at once, until he was lost from sight.

It was 8.15 on the morning of 14 April 2008. I stood on the balcony letting the sounds of wakening Gibraltar below wash up over me: the metallic clangings from the dockyard, the first shrill drillings from the building sites, the growl of the gathering traffic.

Eventually I went back in. I was too moved to say anything. But Ian Thompson, supremely matter-of-fact, had the right words. He looked up from the logbook he was filling in and nodded.

'Let's hope he makes it,' he said.

THREE

A Sense of Wonder

Nightingale

Gibraltar was the prelude; the quest began in England. It seemed an unusual task I had set myself, not only to seek out the spring-bringers, but to find and capture elements of the springtime more fleeting and ephemeral than its flowers: human responses. They were responses which were much rarer now, as we had turned inward to our cities and to our screens, but they were still, I firmly believed, findable and recordable, still there somewhere at the end of a lane, deep in a wood, out on a marsh, maybe even in the city itself, to show what the spring migrant birds might mean to us.

As I began to address it, I realized that something beyond the birds themselves would need to be engaged with. In every case there would also be a landscape. The background counted. It would be a setting, like a setting for a jewel, perhaps – and I found that one of the spring-bringers truly was that – or, to be more precise, like a venue for a musician. That makes a difference. The essence of a gravel-voiced singing reprobate like George Melly or a cool trumpeter like Chet Baker is much more discernible in the dark and fug of a jazz cellar like Ronnie Scott's Club, and some ageing rock fans might contend that it's only in an arena the size of Wembley Stadium that the showmanship of the Stones is fully displayed. The landscapes in which birds exist are sometimes a powerful part of their appeal, and to understand the setting can help comprehend the creature.

And there was yet another element to the enterprise: in every case there would also be a person. Some quests are solo; this one was not. I was a learner, not a dispenser of wisdom, and I sought out the people who could unlock the worth and essence of the birds, asking them to teach me. In every case they did, with boundless generosity; and sometimes what I took away was as much about them as it was about the birds they had shared with me. They were remarkable individuals, without exception. They often helped locate the species; they always helped locate the meaning.

Three elements to the quest then: a bird, a person, a landscape. The fourth was the choice. The species I was concerned with were the long-distance migrants, the ones that crossed or went south of the Sahara twice a year, these being roughly 50 out of the total of about 215 British breeding birds: a standard figure given was 48. This included the two birds which had become extinct in Britain since the Second World War, the wryneck, a small brown woodpecker named for its ability to turn its head right around like the possessed child in *The Exorcist*, and the red-backed shrike, an exquisite sort of miniaturized falcon. Of the remaining 46, 13 were water birds, like the arctic tern and its relatives, which left 33 land birds bringing the new season out of Africa into our countryside.

All of those would have their partisans, but a single spring would be too little to encompass every one, so a choice would have to be made. Yet which? In the end I was guided by ecological importance, and so I could not avoid the warblers, for example, the nearest thing we have in Britain to a springtime chorus; but I was led still more by cultural resonance, and so I sought out those which most had moved us down the centuries, and the bird I began with was the nightingale.

I had thought a lot about *Luscinia megarhynchos* after holding it in my hand on the heights of Gibraltar and feeling its heart beat, and something had dawned on me: the place it had now come to occupy in our culture was peculiar. It might be the most versified bird in history, but it was the one which most was lost to us; and, in a bizarre paradox, the first condition was the cause of the second. Thinking about the legend and the wild creature itself, I realized that while almost everyone was familiar with the one, almost no one now knew the other. The legend had grown and grown, but the living creature had vanished almost totally from our lives (I mean, of course, from the lives of people, rather than the lives of specialists).

As this was merely my impression rather than a piece of statistically based research, to provide some backing for it, however humble, I decided on a little rough-and-ready opinion polling. Not being able to afford MORI or YouGov, I bought a clipboard and myself posed the question *Have you ever knowingly heard a nightingale?* to 100 randomly selected people – 50 office colleagues, 25 family members and relatives, and 25 friends, neighbours and acquaintances. Out of the 100, 9 convinced me to my satisfaction that they had. Yet all were perfectly familiar with the bird. It wasn't as if I'd asked them if they'd ever knowingly heard a spoon-billed sandpiper. All knew what I was talking about, because they all knew the legend, the myth, just as they knew the myth of the unicorn. And that was the point. For the vast majority, myth was all that remained: the nightingale's corporeal being had vanished, leaving only an image behind it, like the Cheshire cat's grin. The bird had been eclipsed by its own cultural profile.

Two developments seem to have brought this about, the first being the intensification of the nightingale's identity as a literary icon that took place in the Romantic movement. Symbol it always was, down the centuries – the bird that sings in the dark could not but be – but after romanticism arrived, at the beginning of the nineteenth century, it was elevated to new emblematic heights, the prime agency being John Keats's terrific ode (although Coleridge and John **46** Clare, the peasant poet from Northamptonshire who lost his sanity and ended his life in an asylum, also wrote substantial nightingale poems).

Keats's nightingale is recognizably real, and the pressure of felt experience in the poem is obvious, but the experience is framed in an especially literary way. It is fascinating to compare it with Clare's poem, written a few years later. Clare knew the countryside and the natural world intimately – far better than Keats did – and 'The Nightingale's Nest' concerns a closely observed wild creature rather than a classical symbol of immortality: it contains an accurate account of a particularly hard-to-find bird's nest down near the ground under a thorn bush. But it is Keats's poem which is remembered, which is widely taught, and which, more importantly, has entered our consciousness as one of the principal archetypes of the Romantic lyric.

It helped ensure that as the nineteenth century progressed, and romanticism gradually tired and began to generate clichés, nightingales became 'poetic'. They were plonked into that toolbox of handy lyrical spare parts which also contained roses, kisses, dreams, moonlight and rainbows. The twentieth century made things worse, for when modernism came along, it reinforced the stereotype by the very act of rubbishing it. There is a perfect example of this in one of the key ancillary texts of modernist literature, *New Bearings in English Poetry*, written in 1932 by the combatively single-minded critic F. R. Leavis. The prime purpose of Leavis's book is to shore up the reputations of T. S. Eliot and Ezra Pound as bearers of the modernist poetic torch; and when he has done this he looks for who will carry the torch forward, and picks out two unknowns, William Empson and Ronald Bottrall.

Both proved failures, at least in terms of the future Leavis had predicted for them. William Empson did achieve fame as a critic – he wrote *Seven Types of Ambiguity* – but it would be fair to say that Ronald Bottrall sank virtually without trace, and in an unpleasant 1950 postscript to the book Leavis bid him good riddance, clearly infuriated that his failure to develop as a poet had made the critic **47** look foolish in choosing him. Yet eighteen years earlier Leavis was all over the boy, and took four of Bottrall's lines as embodying the essential spirit of modernism, and quoting them not only in his text, but also as the epigraph for the whole book:

> *Nightingales, Anangke, a sunset or the meanest flower*
> *Were formerly the potentialities of poetry,*
> *But now what have they to do with one another*
> *With Dionysus or with me?*

It seems unlikely, from this, that Ronald Bottrall ever heard or saw a nightingale in the flesh (although one would not want to do him an injustice). But these nightingales of his have long since ceased to be real: far from being migrant members of the thrush family, they are merely prime representative images of what is characterized as an outmoded way of feeling. It is clear that nightingales had come to stand for something which the avant-garde could achieve authenticity through dismissing.

But the twentieth century wasn't finished with typecasting nightingales yet. There was a further twist to the process, which put the species outside the realm of reality for good and all. It was performed by Eric Maschwitz, a song lyricist and a very successful writer of musicals and revues for the West End theatre between the wars. More precisely, Maschwitz flourished in that period from the mid-1920s to the mid-1950s when, under the influence of Noël Coward, the British musical theatre seemed to focus exclusively on the social habits of the English upper classes, especially in their Mayfair haunts; you might say Maschwitz was a colonel in Coward's army. He was perfectly at home there. Born into a family of Lithuanian immigrants in Birmingham, his education – Repton and Cambridge – made him undeniably a gentleman, while the outsider element of his background clearly did not hinder his theatrical streak. Of that generation of showbusiness figures who had their publicity shots taken in evening dress, fingering their cufflinks, he spent his career alternating

48

between executive posts at the BBC – he was variously Assistant Head of Outside Broadcasting, editor of *Radio Times* and Director of Variety – and writing songs and generally successful shows with titles like *Waltz without End*, *Flying Colours* and *Carissima*.

Maschwitz is forgotten for now, but he was a good lyricist and he left behind two songs which will guarantee him a modicum of immortality. The first, which he wrote in 1935, is said to have been inspired by his regrets after an affair with the Chinese-American actress Anna May Wong:

> *A cigarette that bears a lipstick's traces,*
> *An airline ticket to romantic places,*
> *And still my heart has wings . . .*

Yes, Eric Maschwitz wrote 'These Foolish Things (Remind Me of You)' to Jack Strachey's melody (although you will find him credited on the sheet music under his pen name of Holt Marvell). First sung by Judy Campbell, Noël Coward's muse, 'These Foolish Things' can justifiably be called a standard, having been performed and recorded subsequently by scores, perhaps even hundreds, of singers, from Billie Holiday to Brian Ferry.

Five years later Maschwitz produced his other winner, his other standard; this was a love song set specifically in Mayfair, written for the revue *New Faces*, and once again given its baptism by Judy Campbell:

> *That certain night, the night we met,*
> *There was magic abroad in the air,*
> *There were angels dining at the Ritz,*
> *And . . .*

you know what's coming

> *. . . a nightingale sang in Berkeley Square.*

With that line, etched indelibly into million of brains by Manning Sherwin's smoochy melody, Maschwitz not only found a place in musical history: he completed the process of nightingale mythification. At a stroke of his pen he removed the bird from nature and consigned it to an imaginary world, as a magic creature existing on the same plane as angels in restaurants. And he did more than that. Though the romanticized nightingale may have already emerged in formal literature, Maschwitz now took it further, and planted it firmly in popular culture, so that it was no longer mythified just for the literati or poetry-lovers: it was now mythified for everybody in the English-speaking world. Henceforth everyone had a cultural reference point for the nightingale – it was the bird that sang in Berkeley Square! In subsequent years, with the song being performed by Vera Lynn, Glenn Miller, Nat King Cole, Blossom Dearie, Mel Tormé, Bobby Darin, Manhattan Transfer, Twiggy, Rod Stewart, you name them, no rival version of nightingale identity has emerged to challenge this one. It has lasted for three generations. Seventy years ago, Eric Maschwitz shunted the bird firmly into fantasyland, and it's been there ever since.

It could not have remained so, however, but for the second development that led to the living nightingale's eclipse, and that was the loss of birdsong from our lives. It's perhaps instructive to consider for a moment the phenomenon of birdsong in general, and think about it at its most basic. It is a curious fact that for thousands of years human beings have paid particular attention to certain of the vocalizations of one other group of vertebrate animals. The nature of this attention is unusual. We do take notice of the sounds of other animal groups, but in a very simple way. We look to see what a dog is barking at, or why a cat is miaowing. In Hemingway's short story 'The Short Happy Life of Francis Macomber' the eponymous central character is greatly affected by the roaring of a lion outside his safari camp at night, because it makes him afraid. That is explicable. But humans have a specific way of responding to the sounds of some bird species which does not seem to admit of explanation, and this would seem to be because the emotion felt is that of being moved, which might be defined as the experience of a sense of wonder.

With most human feelings, the roots are palpable and found in the nature of our being. Hunger, thirst, desire are clearly responses to our physiological needs; aggression and fear are obvious consequences of us having to share the world with others; and all these are experienced by creatures other than humans. Love and hate are more challenging, but these too can be found in the non-human world, as Dian Fossey's studies of the mountain gorillas of Rwanda, for example, made clear, and it is not difficult to understand how both devotion and personal enmity can arise once intelligent creatures begin acting together in permanent social groups.

But a sense of wonder?

Where does that come from?

There is no doubt that down the centuries countless men and women have experienced it, hearing birdsong; they have been moved. Folklore and literature are testament enough. Birdsong was long one of the most celebrated elements of the natural world, and in the nineteenth and early twentieth centuries virtually every major English poet wrote of it: Shelley with his skylark, Browning with his chaffinch, Hardy with his darkling thrush, Edward Thomas with the spirit-lifting blackbird he heard when his train stopped briefly at the Cotswold hamlet of Adlestrop. When Sir Edward Grey, later Viscount Grey of Fallodon, the British Foreign Secretary who is supposed to have said 'the lights are going out all over Europe' at the opening of the First World War, wrote a well-received book called *The Charm of Birds*, in 1927, the first six chapters were entirely devoted to song.

Let's be precise about what we are referring to. Bird vocalizations can roughly be divided into two: calls and songs. Calls are usually single notes or sharp bursts of sound, often signifying alarm and used to warn other birds of danger. Some of these can themselves be found moving. As a teenage birdwatcher on the marshes of the Dee estuary, which separates Cheshire in north-west England from Wales, I was much taken with the calls of two wading birds, the redshank and the **51** greenshank. Both consisted of three musical, ringing notes, the red-shank's slurred downward and the greenshank's level. Writing this, I feel how impossible it is for mere words to do justice to their allure; maybe this is because birdsong that affects us is also bound up with a sense of place, and it is certainly true for me that whenever I hear those calls I am instantly filled with the wildness and loneliness of the wide marshes under the open sky.

But what generally moves people is the more complex phenomenon referred to as song, which tends to mean the extended and sometimes intricate vocalizations of most of the males of one order of birds, the Passeriformes: the passerines, or songbirds. This grouping contains more than 5,700 of the 10,000-or-so bird species in the world (the precise total shifts as species are constantly being reclassified) and includes such familiar families as the warblers, the finches, the swallows, the tits and the thrushes. The possession of a syrinx, a resonating voicebox at the bottom of the windpipe (as opposed to the mammalian larynx, which is at the top), enables passerines to produce a staggering variety of sound which ranges from single notes to the hundreds or even thousands that pour out of a skylark during its song flight.

If we ask why people have for so long been affected by birdsong, we have to ask why people can be affected at all by complex created sound, and then we start thinking of music and its origins. Music is very old. There is no known human culture without music, and it is possible that music is as much a key part of what it is to be human as is language. Why we respond so powerfully to it is the subject of active scientific debate, but some outlines are clear: we mostly respond to melody, a pattern created from a recognizable and regularly ordered grouping of sounds. Yet although (with one great exception) birdsong does not fall on our ears as melody does, it may be that it has something in it which is near enough to music to trigger a similar response.

When, with the coming of literature, that response went from the simple to the sophisticated, it doubtless added to birdsong's charm that people thought it *was* music – the music of these small feathered creatures, produced for their pleasure as we produce our own. How could it be otherwise, with them singing their hearts out all day long? After all, that's why the vocalization was called *song*. Now we know differently. Eliot Howard's discovery of the role of territory in birds' lives ninety years ago revealed the truth: that birdsong was anything but entertainment; rather it was a key tool in territorial defence, which itself was an essential step in the annual cycle of reproduction. Song said 'Get out of here' to other males; it said 'Hi, honey' to passing females. It was a device with a ruthlessly specific survival purpose, an essential demonstrator of reproductive fitness. What it didn't say at all was 'I whistle a happy tune'.

And yet in one way that discovery hasn't changed anything. One might think that our knowledge of its utilitarian purpose might lessen birdsong's ability to move us. It doesn't. With much of its mystery taken away, a mystery remains, and that mystery concerns our response. Perhaps it is something to do with birdsong's nature as one of the essences of the natural world, in the way that rivers are of the essence. 'Eventually,' wrote Norman Maclean, the American scholar and professor of English, in his account of his life as a fly-fisherman, 'all things merge into one, and a river runs through it.' You might say birdsong is heard in it, too.

And now we have lost it. Familiarity with the song of birds, once universal, has gone from most people's lives, largely, of course, because we inhabit an increasingly urbanized society, not just in Britain but across the world – 2008 was the year when, for the first time, a majority of the world's people lived in cities and towns rather than in the countryside. Urbanized, and electronic: we turn away entirely from the natural world and its phenomena to the world inside the screen. Yet it is not just that we have stopped hearing birdsong in the trees, in the hedges, in the air: we have stopped hearing it in literature too. It has ceased to have cultural significance. There is no place for birdsong in a literary world whose predominant tones are knowing and sardonic. And there is no place for birdsong in an urban world whose focus is ever more directed by electronics. **53**

No wonder, then, that the most celebrated singer of all has dwindled into mere reputation; no wonder that all that remains of it for most of us should be a caricature, a worn-out symbol of old-fashioned sentiment. No surprise that at least a dozen of the fifty office colleagues I polled about it should laugh and mention Berkeley Square. While the myth may sit comfortably in a corner of our culture, the real nightingale is lost from our lives.

Could it be recovered, I wondered? Not just the bird, not just *Luscinia megarhynchos*, but the original experience of it as well, uncluttered by reputation, legend, fable and cliché? Could it be unBerkeleySquared? Could it be found again, and freshly, the experience of what had made it so special in the first place? I slowly realized what would be the *sine qua non* for such a project: an innocent listener. It needed someone who was starting from scratch and devoid of sophistication or even familiarity with nightingale legends and lore; and so, after much thought, and a wonderfully kind offer from Britain's greatest nightingale expert and celebrant, I chose a child. I asked my son Sebastian, who was 11, if he would like to come and listen to nightingales, and he said he would.

We sought them out in Surrey. Hardly a byword for wildlife, Surrey; much better known as the most affluent county in Britain, sitting on London's doorstep and crammed full of London wealth, of mock-Tudor mansions with swimming pools, tennis courts and three-car, four-car, five-car garages. Like Yvelines in Paris, or Westchester County in New York, Surrey serves as the capital's opulent rural extension. Yet, curiously, it is just as rich ecologically: it has the most extensive flora and the most extensive woodland cover (nearly 23 per cent of its surface area) of any county in the land. And what excites naturalists even more is the fact that, alongside its privileged and manicured enclaves, Surrey still contains extensive stretches of the wild landscape which was typical of England before fields were enclosed with hedges at the end of the eighteenth century. There are areas of common land and of lowland heath which are not only unploughed, but also untouched by the bane of our generation, agricultural chemicals, and consequently form superlative wildlife reservoirs.

Great Bookham Common is one of these, an area of old oak woodland and scrub grassland near the market town of Leatherhead, which was anciently known as a settlement on the river Mole and is now more familiar as an exit on the M25, London's orbital motorway. For hundreds of years the common was run by the monks of Chertsey Abbey as woodland pasture, where pigs and cattle were turned out to snuffle and graze underneath the trees; for most of the last century its 400 acres have been cared for by the National Trust as a public amenity. Sitting on the last of the London clay before the chalk slope of the North Downs begins, it is noted for its profusion of insect, plant and bird life, and among its birds, I knew, were nightingales – some of the closest to London, if not the closest of all. I also knew the National Trust warden, Ian Swinney, albeit slightly, and when I asked him if he would take us – me and Seb – to listen to his nightingales in return for dinner beforehand in the pub, he readily agreed.

We were happy in our timing. April 2008 was chilly, with an east wind so forceful and persistent that on the 23rd of the month a very rare bird, a black lark, was found in Norfolk, having been blown 3,500 miles from the steppes of Kazakhstan (and its sighting, only the third of the species ever in Britain, drove the birders wild). But Saturday 26 April was the moment the weather changed: it was the first warm day of spring. When Seb and I went for a morning bike ride along the Thames towpath from Richmond to Ham we found, in the sunshine, a short-sleeved society. People had sprouted summer clothes like the trees were sprouting leaves. The horse chestnuts were out, iridescent in their greenery, and so were the oaks, with the plane trees and the sycamores just starting to burst their buds, and the opening willows hazily green along the riverbank. The blossom was spectacular: it was the blossom day of the year. In gardens there was electric-blue ceanothus and clean white choisya; on house fronts **55** were the azure grape-bunches of wisteria and the creamy petals of clematis; and along the road to Twickenham Bridge were cherry trees with boughs bending under the blossom load, alternately white then pink, white then pink, reminding me of something I couldn't grasp until I realized it was childhood ice cream.

When we got to Ham, we crossed the river with our bikes on Hammerton's Ferry (me pointing out Mick Jagger's house and Pete Townsend's house on the distant crest of Richmond Hill), and then we cycled back along the Thames on the Middlesex side. On the water were mallards chasing each other furiously and a great crested grebe resplendent in chestnut ear tufts ('Look at that!' cried Seb), and by the thundering river race of Richmond Lock there were a pair of grey wagtails, bouncing balls of yellow and purple. All along the towpath there were crowds, adjusting to the new warmth, unfolding and opening out like the leaves above them, smiling like the sunshine.

It was warm still when evening came, and we set out on our expedition. I think it's fair to say we had a sense of adventure, although it was hardly Colonel Fawcett up the Amazon: we went by Volvo rather than canoe, and the log of our journey was somewhat more mundane. We drove through Kingston upon Thames and, for the record, took the A3 as far as the A243, and followed that down past the Chessington World of Adventures theme park to cross the M25; then we skirted Leatherhead to take the A246, the road that leads to Guildford, with the spreading village of Bookham 4 miles along it. It was archetypal edge-of-London commuter territory, not quite town, not quite country, a prosperous mix of clean air and green fields and hairdressers and Italian restaurants, where Waterloo station is the daily destination for thousands, and house prices will for ever figure in the conversation when two or more residents assemble.

Yet when we drove on to the common itself and took the bumpy track through the oakwoods to Ian Swinney's cottage, we left all that behind. We found ourselves in a different Surrey, a wilder world with its own ecological rules. A sign of this, a blessed one, as soon as we **56** got out of the car: the cuckoo was calling, my first of the spring.

Ian had three nightingales, he said: three singing males. One had arrived the previous Sunday, and two more late in the week, with the warmer weather. The year before he had a total of five. At the start of the 1980s there had been only one, but since then he had managed the habitat for them and they had increased: numbers had peaked with fourteen singing males in 2000.

The important part of the habitat, he explained as we walked out over his kingdom in the evening sun, was the scrub, the dense bushes of blackthorn and hawthorn, interspersed with young willow and birch. 'Birds need cover. There's nowhere in a young oak tree, say, for birds to nest: predators can get them. It's common sense. Only certain species of birds are in holes. All the rest are in the bushes, somewhere where magpies and jays can't get them from above, dogs and foxes from the side, stoats and weasels from below. Think in three dimensions.'

He pointed at a blackthorn bush. 'See? They want a big cage of scrub, a cage of thorns. Fairly impenetrable cover.'

Nightingales in particular needed a mix of scrub, he said – mature scrub to sing from, higher up, and young scrub to nest in, nearer the ground – and that required management constantly. It was work not always appreciated by the public. 'People like trees. They don't like scrub. It's thorny, in their way for walks. They think it's rubbish. But it's the protection the birds need.'

The cuckoo was still calling. We surprised a roebuck, to Seb's delight: the deer stared at us boldly from 20 yards away before bounding off. And then we came to the amphitheatre, the circle of scrub right in the common's heart.

'They like to sing here,' said Ian. 'It echoes really well.'

'What, nightingales?'

'Everything. But what the nightingales often do, they compete with the other birds in the evening chorus, and then an hour after sunset they start up again.'

Seb said, 'So do nightingales sing in the day as well?'

'Sure,' said Ian. 'You can hear them singing in the day. You can **57** see them, too. You see like a slim robin with a cream chest, and you realize you're looking at a nightingale.'

Competing with the evening chorus: it was an engaging idea, in human terms, at least. *I don't just do this at night, you know.* And so we waited, the three of us, as the sun went down and the light began to fade and the aforesaid chorus swelled to a climax, the blackbirds and the song thrushes, the robins and the chaffinches, and other birds too – woodpigeons roo-cooing, and a green woodpecker detonating its yaffle, its half-dozen laughing notes – until eventually, to use a military metaphor, amid all this small-arms fire there was a burst from a heavy-calibre weapon and Ian Swinney cried, 'There!'

It rang out from a flowering clump of blackthorn on the far side of the clearing, a sudden sharp explosion of song with a staccato *jug-jug-jug* in the middle of it. 'Nightingale!' said Ian, and I felt a shiver of excitement, a definite case of hairs-on-the-back-of-the-neck. I was alert then, straining to pick up the tiniest sound, and twice more in the next twenty minutes the brief burst of fire broke out, cutting through the symphony of birdsong surrounding us.

But the night was what we had come for, and so to wait for its arrival we went to the Windsor Castle, a pub-cum-restaurant in Little Bookham; it was packed, but we found a table. I asked Ian how he had got into conservation, and he laughed and said, 'I ran away to the woods.' He had trained as a commercial forester in his late teens, but was much more interested in wildlife; he was 51 now, and had run Bookham Commons (as the site is officially known, for there are three commons altogether) for nearly thirty years. He was fascinated by landscape history, especially by the idea of the wild-wood, the natural forest which developed after the ice retreated, and which came to cover all of Britain, and he saw his own site in histor-ical terms: although the Bookham woodlands were now dense, with a thick understorey, or lower foliage layer, as grazing had long since ended, the great wide-spreading oaks that were scattered throughout were evidence of how the woods had once been kept much more open by the animals under the trees. 'When they come up together,

58

the oaks, they come up tall and thin; but when they've got room they come up big and wide.'

He told us, as we munched, the history of the common, how it had been saved from development by local people in 1923. He told us the ecology, and how the London Natural History Society had been surveying it continuously since 1941 and had recorded nearly 500 species of flowering plant and a staggering insect fauna (more than 1,100 species just of flies). And he told us of the management and its challenges, of how he tried to manage the common for variety in an ecological sense, while allowing for the special needs of species such as nightingales – which, by then, with the sun long since set, it was time for us to seek in their proper context.

When we left the Windsor Castle, commuter Surrey was going to bed. It had eaten its Saturday-evening dinner and drunk its Cabernet Sauvignon and its Chardonnay, and now it was closing down operations. But we had the other Surrey there awaiting us, the untamed Surrey, and as we drove again over the threshold of the common and plunged into the woodlands – this time in the darkness – it felt like the children escaping through the back of the wardrobe into Narnia.

At Ian's cottage we got out of the car and breathed, and looked, and listened. There was no moon, and the darkness was thick and enveloping. There were scents on the night air. The evening chorus was long since over, and the common was resting now and still, and swathed in quiet – except that after a couple of seconds I realized something was chipping away at the corner of the silence. A lone bird was singing in the distance.

'That's him,' said Ian.

I felt my heart quicken. Here it was.

The sound was distant but it was unmissable, because it was unceasing, the song phrases rolling on and on without a pause, and we set out towards it in the darkness, treading the path through the woods. Seb was excited and asked to hold the torch. I stumbled against grass tufts and stones and tree roots. Once I fell. Ian knew **59** the way intimately, and strolled. And as we moved forward, the unrelenting sound got steadily stronger and I was briefly reminded of walking to a football match, Seb and I going to Craven Cottage to watch Fulham play, and if you were late you could hear the crowd roar several streets away and the roar got more thunderous as you got closer and set your anticipation on fire – but this was different again. As you approached, it took hold of your mind even more. It didn't need to be of giant dimensions. It was something far more hypnotic, a single sharp crystal river of sound flowing through the silence and the blackness directly into your ears, ever more strongly, and I had a sense of being hypnotically drawn towards it down the pitch-dark woodland path – closer and closer, with all your experience telling you that as you closed with it, as you came upon it, round a corner, over a hill, behind a tree, you must finally discover what was making this sound, you must finally see what it was.

But when we got there – it was at the edge of the amphitheatre – there was nothing to see. There was only The Voice, the amazing voice on the soft night air, deep in the scrub right next to us, pouring its song out unendingly, fortissimo.

Seb whispered, 'Wow, it's *loud*.'

It was. I remembered a legend that a village somewhere was free of nightingales because a bird had once disturbed St Thomas à Becket at his devotions there, so he commanded that none should sing in the village ever again, the miserable, begrudging sod. (I looked it up later: it was Otford in Kent.) Ian murmured, 'I can hear them in the cottage half a mile away, with the windows closed and the curtains drawn and the TV on.'

The bird was releasing a cascade of sound, fluting and bubbling, long yearning notes interspersed with rattles like gunfire, with every few phrases the characteristic triplet, *chook-chook-chook*, or *jug-jug-jug*, and then, with a faint pause beforehand, a succession of melodious, deep piping notes that went straight to the heart.

Seb, listening hard, said, 'It's like a man whistling.'

60   'Liquid, it's liquid,' said Ian.

The song bounded back up: it was striking how the bird could go instantly from low to high and back again, *cheep-cheep-cheep-cheep chup-chup-chup-chup cheep-cheep-cheep*, striking indeed the range of its invention, from long sweet sounds to clattering trills.

Seb whispered, 'It's like a man playing lots of different whistles.' It was just so.

As we listened, another bird began to sing on the far side of the amphitheatre, and then, after a minute or so, another one still, further away. Our first bird seemed to respond: it sounded even quicker and more forceful, and Seb suddenly said, 'It's like a scat singer.' I was taken aback. I said, 'How d'you know about scat singers?' He said, 'From last summer in America,' and I remembered we had been to a music festival while on holiday in Cape Cod, and a scat singer had performed with a jazz band.

The comparison made me think: was it improvisation that was so special about the nightingale? How much of the song was improvised and how much was learned? I didn't know. But something else struck me, as we stumbled across the common in the dark, with Ian guiding, to listen to the more distant birds (he thought there might be four, or even five; I could distinguish only three). It was this: the role of silence in the nightingale's song. We were listening now to the furthest bird, right underneath it: the voice was so loud and continuous it seemed to occupy the whole world. With open eyes, I could see nothing. I could hear nothing else. All that there was in existence was this song, and I realized then that it was a duet with silence. Silence was its background; silence moulded it; silence made it perfect, as it filled the world entirely. And for some reason I suddenly wondered if it was midnight and I switched on the torch to check my watch, and in the sideways light of it I saw Seb as he too listened motionless, and I caught my breath for there it was, written unmistakably upon his face: the sense of wonder.

Who is to know what part of us it reaches? Only that it does. We may cast around for explanations as long as we like: they will not come. Reason and science fail us. It cannot be understood with the head, the way it touches us, this sound; it can be understood only **61** with the heart, and so it is hard if not impossible to convey to others. But if it does touch us, properly, we are suddenly at one with the poets who have gone before: we understand that John Keats was not filled with a fury to write, for no reason.

Once everyone in southern England knew it, during the six weeks when it is audible in April and May, the sound of the most celebrated of all the spring-bringers, which today for most people has retreated into myth and legend and popular fantasy. That Seb now knew it too left me thrilled and proud, although anxious in a way a father can be about imposing his views or feelings on his children. We listened for a full hour altogether. Seb never said, 'Can we go now?' and I felt that it must have meant something to him, but I wanted to let him have the experience and own it for himself, uninfluenced by me, so I was loath to ask him. Being a boy with a kind heart, he might have said yes just to please me.

At least he's heard it, I thought, the real nightingale. It's got to have gone in there somewhere. But I didn't know for sure until we were leaving, having made our goodbyes to Ian with the birds still singing in full voice, and we bumped down the track through the woods and left Great Bookham Common behind and came back out into the street lights, the lights of conventional Surrey, the Surrey of golf and tennis and BMWs and catching the morning train to Waterloo.

Seb said, 'Could we have stayed there all night?'

'Well,' I said, 'I think they pack up in the middle of the night, although they sing again just before dawn. But we've got to get some sleep, haven't we?'

And then, quite unprompted, 'Dad, that was so fun.'

A rush of relief, on my part. Then the insecurity following it to the surface.

'Honestly? It was OK?'

The voice was sleepy, but not too tired to reassure.

'It was brilliant, Dad.'

We were 19 miles from Berkeley Square. It wasn't that far away. But it was far enough.

FOUR

Unlocking the Soundscape

Sedge Warbler

Self-deception comes very easily, as does self-congratulation, but it did seem to me, looking back, that with the nightingales which sang while the rest of Surrey slept, Seb and I had perhaps got near to the heart of things, to the essence of one of the spring-bringers; and I found myself eager to go further into birdsong, now so lost from our lives, and seek out what else the spring migrants brought to it. And so, like Eliot Howard a century before, but with a different aim in mind, I sought out the warblers.

This was the only occasion on which I looked for a cluster of species rather than a single one, but it seemed appropriate, for the warblers hung together as the largest migrant grouping: there were ten of them which came from below the Sahara, and two more which migrated a shorter distance from North Africa (the chiffchaff and the blackcap); in effect they constituted a third of the total of thirty-three land birds arriving to signal the change of seasons. They were all small, very active, insect-eating birds, and warblers they were called for their most prominent characteristic, their singing ability. **63**

If the nightingale was The Star of birdsong in springtime, it wasn't too fanciful to see the warblers as The Chorus.

They were also united by something which struck me as odd, in considering what they added to the world: their cultural obscurity. The contrast with the nightingale was extreme. There are no warblers in the Bible, for example, even though the Holy Land lies on a major migration route which millions of warblers annually pass along, and many other migrants are mentioned. There are no warblers in Greek mythology, none dispatched as messengers by the gods (they'd have done the job with perfect competence, if perhaps a little primly), no warblers supplying similes in Homer, none in Aristophanes' *The Birds*, none flitting through Virgil's Eclogues, in fact not really any in classical literature, unless we count a possible sedge warbler in Aristotle. Most surprising of all, there are no warblers in Shakespeare. No major poet ever mentioned birds more, and Shakespeare's ornithological interest is clear and his knowledge capacious – he mentions separately, for example, all seven members of the crow family in Britain (raven, chough, rook, jackdaw, crow, magpie and jay) – and he instances many songbirds, finches and buntings, swallows and martins, starlings and sparrows, larks and thrushes, but never, in all that great corpus of vivid reflections of his own natural world, never a warbler – never a one (and leafy Warwickshire in the May-time of the 1570s, when he was growing up, must have been warbler-crammed). Until relatively recently, these birds were as subdued and unremarkable in reputation as they are in plumage – but therein, perhaps, lies the explanation.

The Old World warblers, as they are generally known, consist of more than 350 species of songbirds of Europe, North Africa and Asia, many of which look so similar as to be undistinguishable in the field, being generally a dull brown or browny-grey or olive-green or greeny-brown. Western Europe holds about thirty species. While nothing else really looks like a robin or a wren or a cuckoo – and so robins, wrens and cuckoos were long ago given identities which enabled them to figure in literature, folklore and myth – several things look very like a reed warbler, and a reed warbler doesn't look very special anyway. It was not until proper scientific ornithology came along, starting about 200 years ago, that the different warblers began to be separated out and seen, and indeed named, as individual species; previously they were stages on an identity-continuum, blurring into one another. And you can't build a legend around something that has no name (apart from characters in spaghetti westerns).

Yet there is an evolutionary reason for their closeness in appearance, and it is ultimately what governs their fascination for us today: these are creatures which have abandoned the distinguishing values of colour and pattern, when playing the mating game, in favour of the distinguishing values of sound. Two different species may look alike, but they do not sound alike. Within species, it is not the quality of the tail, say, that matters when it comes to attracting a partner – warblers are at the opposite end of the spectrum from the peacock – it is the quality of the song. Never mind my tail: listen to this. In the world of the Old World warblers, song is everything.

It is fascinating to compare them with their counterparts across the pond, the New World warblers, which are not related, but occupy much the same ecological niche, as small migratory insectivores; their journeys stretch from their North American breeding grounds to wintering grounds in Central and South America. Colour for these birds is much more significant – perhaps because they generally winter in deep dark tropical forest, whereas the Old World warblers mainly spend their African sojourn in open savannah and scrub – and one of the pleasures of being an American birder is to watch Connecticut or Massachusetts fill up in springtime with these brilliant diminutive bundles: the myrtle warbler, the magnolia warbler, the Kentucky warbler, the black-and-white warbler, the black-throated blue warbler and the dazzlingly patterned golden-winged warbler – this last being an improbably spectacular confection of dove-grey, black, white and golden yellow. In February 1989 a golden-winged warbler, all 4½ inches of it, somehow managed to cross the Atlantic and was spotted in the car park of a Tesco **65** supermarket in Maidstone, Kent, by a well-known birder called Paul Doherty, who was on his way out to post a letter. He released the news to Birdline, a fledgling bird-spotting pager alert service, and the next morning Britain woke up to the phenomenon of mass twitching – the determined pursuit of the sight of rarities by unconscionable numbers of people – when 3,000 birders, armed to the teeth with expensive optics, descended on the Tesco car park.

But a chic package of dove-grey, black, white and gold in the middle of Kent is a one-off. It is mainly sound which distinguishes British warblers, and one way of getting a handle on them, on where they fit into the scheme of things, is to compare their groupings by song complexity. To go briefly into bird-guide mode: Britain has fourteen warbler species: two residents (Cetti's warbler and the Dartford warbler) and the dozen migrants, the latter being split between four genera. Leave one genus aside entirely, the *Locustella* or grass warblers, of which Britain contains two species, the grasshopper warbler and Savi's warbler. As their generic name ('little insect') signals, these birds, hidden deep in foliage, make long continuous whirring sounds like those of a grasshopper or cricket in summer evenings, fascinating in themselves, but not really what we think of as birdsong. It is the other ten species which provide that in plenty.

The genus with the simplest songs is that of the *Phylloscopus* or leaf warblers: the chiffchaff, the willow warbler and the wood warbler, which are very small, olive-green above and whitish or yellowish below. A genus with more complicated song is that of the *Sylvia* or scrub warblers: the blackcap, the whitethroat, the lesser whitethroat and the garden warbler, which are attractively patterned variations on a theme in grey (apart from the garden warbler, irredeemably subfusc, with the plainest plumage of any British bird, as was brought home to me in the ringing station on Gibraltar. It is a feathered Methodist). The genus with the most complex song of all is that of the *Acrocephalus* or swamp warblers: the reed warbler, the sedge warbler and the marsh warbler, which are brown, with **66** either plain backs (the reed and the marsh) or streaked (the sedge).

And these take birdsong to heights which, until very recently, were entirely unappreciated, and which I did not appreciate myself when I set out in May to try to discover the essence of them all.

How I was to do that had occupied me for some time. I knew a certain amount – like most non-specialists interested in birds, I knew the chiffchaff's song, the first sound of spring in southern England, and the willow warbler's, which follows it – but there were many gaps in my knowledge, and in wanting to see and hear warblers in the round, compare them against each other and grasp the sum of them, I finally conceived of an uncommonly specific outing: to go warbling, like one might go fishing, or swimming, or shopping. I would need a guide, and the number of people who can take you warbling is clearly limited, but when I asked my friend Mark Cocker if he could show me ten warbler species in a day, he laughed and said, 'That shouldn't be a problem.'

Ah, the terrifying expertise of birders. Mark had as much of it as anyone, but he also had much more. He was a writer-naturalist, or a naturalist-writer, and it was impossible to tell where one passion began and the other ended, with his expertise so matched by his eloquence, except that birds were his principal focus. On the chilly moorland hills above his home in Buxton in Derbyshire he had begun as a boyhood birdwatcher in the 1970s, a decade after I had done the same on the marshes of the Dee, but whereas I had left birds behind, Mark had gone on with unslackening ardour and burgeoning skill into the years when birdwatchers transmuted into birders, and what had been a hobby for one generation became a way of life for the next.

It was a minor phenomenon of social history, facilitated by the triple transformation of optics, mobility and information – vastly improved binoculars and telescopes, the spread of mass car ownership, and the beginning of electronic alert services – and it was the culmination of the unstoppable boom in popular interest in birds in Britain from the sixties onwards, a growth reflected in the soaring membership of the Royal Society for the Protection of Birds. The **67** figures are astounding: from 10,000 in 1960 to 50,000 in 1969, and then a vaulting leap to 200,000 in 1972; then 300,000 by 1980, 400,000 by 1986, 500,000 by 1987, 860,000 by 1994; and then in September 1997 membership reached the magical mark, the apotheosis: 1 million. Imagine – a million members! In France, a country with just the same population as Britain – 60 million – the direct equivalent of the RSPB, the LPO (La Ligue pour la Protection des Oiseaux), has 38,000 members: twenty-six times fewer.

In this upsurge of zeal which the shift from birdwatching to birding denominated, Mark Cocker was not only a central figure: he became its chronicler. For birding gave birth to a curious subculture with its own rules and heroes and legend and indeed language – 'dipping' (missing a bird one had travelled to see) and 'suppressing' (keeping the news of a rarity to oneself), 'long-stayers' (visiting rarities which remained in place) and 'blockers' (birds which the observer continually failed to see, so preventing his tally from moving forward) – and eventually Mark laid it all bare for the non-birding public in his 2001 best-seller *Birders: Tales of a Tribe*. When I read it I was gripped. It was the most original book on birds I had ever encountered. (It still is.) It opened my eyes to an ardent life I might have been part of, had I gone on; it was like realizing that, had you stayed in the army, this was the campaign you would have been marching in.

It was when Mark had written another, even more successful, book, *Birds Britannica*, that I got to know him. This was a compendium of avian folklore whose model was the groundbreaking *Flora Britannica* of Richard Mabey, Britain's leading writer on the natural world, a book which was entirely original in that it was not a botanical flora, but a cultural one, gathering together the sheaves of legends that clung to Britain's native plants. It triumphantly caught the imagination of a public that mostly appeared to have lost interest in wildflowers: the size of a doorstep, it sold 100,000 copies. Richard Mabey intended himself to write the sequel devoted to birds, but he became ill, and the task fell to Mark. He produced a masterwork, as forceful and encyclopaedic a statement of the cultural importance of birds as it was exquisitely written.

I went to see Mark to write about *Birds Britannica* myself and we became friends, and, having opened my eyes already to the tribal customs of the world of birding, he then opened them to something more profound: his landscape. His adopted landscape I should say: Mark had exchanged Derbyshire for Norfolk, the hills for the flat-lands, and he lived in the Norfolk Broads.

Throughout most of my life I had thought of the Norfolk Broads as a joke. Try as I may, I cannot recall any other landscape whose mention triggered mirth, but this complex of shallow lakes (the broads) and winding rivers behind the coast always seemed to me irresistibly comic, probably because its principal purpose appeared to be the fostering of a peculiarly English summer ritual: the boating holiday. Not the sort of vacation afloat which nowadays takes place off somewhere like southern Turkey, with bronzed bodies, chilled rosé and a keel sweeping through the sea: this was an altogether more cautious affair of cardigans and ham sandwiches in a craft called a cabin cruiser – a damp version of a caravan – which chugged from broad to broad with Dad at the helm in a sailor's cap. Not sweeping, but chugging. Pretend-adventure. It seemed to encapsulate the timorous smallness of English life in the 1950s and '60s, when thousands upon thousands of families went safely a-chugging in these 150 miles of lock-free waterways. I still find it hard to believe they never made a *Carry On* film about it all: *Carry On Boating* or, more probably, *Carry On up the Broads*.

Mark had left the Peak District at 18, when he went to the University of East Anglia in Norwich, drawn to Norfolk by the incomparable birding opportunities on its north coast around the village of Cley, the British birders' Mecca; and when eventually he went to live with his wife, Mary, and their two daughters in the valley of the Yare, one of Broadland's principal rivers, he had of course seen the environmental reality rather than my ignorant tourist stereotype. Never mind the cabin cruisers: here was a wetland of **69** stunning wildlife richness. As he first walked over the threshold of their cottage, he looked up and saw in the sky a marsh harrier, one of England's rarest and most charismatic birds of prey – how was that for an omen? – and he began to feel his way into this world where the water so mingled with the land that it was hard to say which predominated.

By the time I met him he knew it like his back garden and adored it, and when I went out into it with him he showed me its complexity and its richness. He unlocked the landscape. It ceased to be a joke; it was full of surprises. I remember him taking me to see cranes, the mysterious long-legged, long-necked waterbirds which had returned to breed in England, in the Broads, after an absence of 400 years. He led the way to one of the few high points for miles around, set up the telescope, and said, 'Look for sheep.' I had no idea what he meant until eventually his own keen eyes found them, nearly a mile away, and in the telescope eyepiece, with their necks bent down grazing the grass, the birds' bulky oblong grey bodies looked like sheep for all the world.

Recently Mark had dug even deeper into Broadland, through his extraordinary study, his obsessive pursuit even, of the rooks which in the evening came to roost in the woods fringing the Yare valley in enormous numbers – massing armies of the night, tens of thousands strong. *Crow Country* explored and explained this uncanny phenomenon. But, in exploring and explaining, Mark only made the landscape more mysterious: the more he looked, the more there seemed to be to find, and after reading his book I knew I would never see the Broads as commonplace again.

There was a third enlightenment Mark had provided for me besides birders and the Broads, or rather there was the beginning of one, and that was to do with birdsong. I had begun to see dimly that it was a special world of its own, as a result of a walk we had made with other friends in the valley of the Derbyshire Wye in the Peak District's heart. Much less well known than its great Welsh-borders namesake, this Wye is nonetheless a thoroughbred of a river, exuding power and character in the way some smaller watercourses can without the need for great dimensions, such as the Helmsdale in Sutherland or the Bundorragha in County Mayo (famous fishing rivers both). The wildlife of its limestone valley is as rich as its fishing, and in the course of a two-hour ramble, downstream and then back up, we had encountered a lot of birds, and heard most of them before we saw them. Mark identified, by song or call, every single one. They ranged from goosander to common sandpiper, from dipper to bull-finch, from raven to willow tit. He heard them and told us; then we beheld them – there they were. Jaw-dropping? I'd never witnessed anything like it. More than that, I'd never realized such extensive knowledge was there to be possessed, and I began to feel this implied more than something about one individual's proficiency, startling though that was. It implied some sort of bigger truth about birdsong and the world, which I was unable to discern. At the time.

Yet what was crystal clear was Mark's matchless birdsong skill, and so it was with real eagerness that I eventually set out with him into the Yare valley, and into the world of warblers. It was 14 May, a day whose firm sunshine and spirited east wind made the air as invigorating as an unexpected glass of champagne and brought the landscape to life. The Yare is the biggest of the five main Broadland rivers, and its tidal length drifts unhurriedly from Norwich to the sea at Great Yarmouth, 20 miles away, embanked through a steadily widening flood plain of grassland and grazing marsh edged with willows and woods. This day, with its greens and browns flecked with the pale petals of ladies' smock (the cuckoo flower) and the bright yellow buttons of buttercups, the valley seemed to be putting its living inhabitants on show, for within fifteen minutes we had seen two fox cubs outside their earth in a combat of tumbling playfulness, a Chinese water deer lolloping away from us, the first of the spring dragonflies, the hairy dragonfly, buzzing about us on patrol, and in the distance a hobby, the most debonair of the falcons, dashing about the sky in pursuit of the dragonflies, or perhaps the St Mark's fly, a big black insect whose legs hang down like the undercarriage of **71** a landing jumbo. And the cuckoo was calling. 'It's a great time to be in the countryside,' Mark said. 'Everything is desperate to find food, so things are doing things.'

I felt that too. It was a terrific time.

We entered the valley at Rockland St Mary, a hamlet possessed of a staithe – a landing place, or tiny port. Once it had been bustling with wherries, the old Broadland sailing craft, taking the black-glazed roof tiles which were made at Rockland up to Norwich for sale; now it had dwindled into a small marina surrounded by hedges, connected by a channel to nearby Rockland Broad and, beyond, to the Yare itself. The staithe was sheltered from the wind, and at once I realized the trees and hedges about it were full of birdsong. Being on warbler alert, the first thing I heard was a chiffchaff. That was appropriate. The warblers start with the chiffchaff, it seemed to me, in more than one way. The song of the tiny green leaf warbler is the earliest song of spring, heard from mid-March onward, and it is also the most rudimentary, being merely a prolonged alterna-tion between two short notes: *chiff-chaff-chiff-chaff-chiff-chiff-chaff*. Yet people are very fond of it, as the alarm bell of the changing year; and it is more than just a metronome, as Edward Grey – he of the dimming European lights – pointed out in *The Charm of Birds*: 'Ill-disposed persons may say that it is nothing more than chirping: against this assertion I should protest. There is a spirit in the notes of the chiffchaff which suggests the same motive as song, and there is something more than the reiteration of two notes. The sound suggests industry, as of the passage of a shuttle to and fro . . .'

Mark, who knew how to hear in ways which I will never attain, pointed out immediately that a willow warbler was also singing. I got it after a few seconds. That seemed appropriate too, for I had always felt the willow warbler was the second of the tribe: after the chiffchaff (which it resembles very closely) the next to be heard, and the next up in complexity of song – a simple series of descending notes.

Simple; yet this song is of a different order entirely in terms of its allure. It is one of the sweetest sounds of spring, a silvery falling cadence, dropping plaintively down a full octave, *Seep-seep sip-sip sep-sep sap-sap sup-sup*, and regularly repeated. I have stood in a clump of hawthorn bushes surrounded by willow warblers singing and it felt like being caught in a sound shower. Mark loved it, partly because it had alleviated the ruggedness of the landscape of his boyhood. 'In the northern uplands, that's the sound of summer,' he said. 'In Derbyshire, North Staffordshire and Shropshire, you don't get chiffchaff and blackcap. In the Derbyshire moorland, you would come down to a bit of sallow or birch scrub and you would just hear willow warbler. In some parts of Scotland it's the only summer bird-song. It brings that bit of softness to a harsh landscape.'

There were other birds singing about us, and with Mark's help I gradually started to pick them out – robins with twittering warbles, wrens with angry trills, chaffinches with a descending cadence of their own (harsher than a willow warbler's, though: more of a rattle with a flourish at the end) and a loud blackbird. Then suddenly Mark started. He thought he had caught, in his words, 'a little shot of nightingale'. We listened intently, but it was not to be repeated. Instead the blackbird sang out sweetly over the staithe. Mark said, 'You do get something very dramatic with nightingale song – pauses, silence, then the machine-gun delivery of the sound. But the blackbird is so gentle. It's the gentleness of it which I love. You can't get lousy blackbirds. They get better as the season goes on.'

We walked out on to the dyke that lined the channel to Rockland Broad and the distant Yare, and the handsome valley opened before us in the splendour of the spring morning – and the warbler count went up. Next was a whitethroat, which we caught sight of, bouncing up out of a bramble patch then dropping back down – its song flight. Not exceptional, the song: brief and dry, like the Sardinian warbler's in Gibraltar (they're closely related). 'It's a scratchy ditty,' said Mark – 'short and scratchy. Hardly deserves to be called a warbler. Should be called a scratcher.' I enjoyed it all the same. But the song that followed, from within the trees that lined the dyke, was a very real pleasure, a short aria of high, sweet flutings: it was **73** a blackcap. As Mark pointed out. This was one of the gaps in my knowledge of which I was somewhat ashamed, for the blackcap is fairly common and famous for its song – it's sometimes called 'the lesser nightingale' – but I did not know it. Now I listened intently to what Mark called its 'very pure high liquid warbling, its high, light sweet piping' and I knew that I loved it and that I would not forget it.

That made four warblers. There were quickly two more. The first was the Cetti's warbler, not one of the spring-bringers, but a resident bird and a fairly recent colonist of Britain from the European continent. It specializes in sound explosions, and from deep within the adjacent scrub it opened up with an electric burst of song, accurately captured in the mnemonic Mark had for it: *bet you will see me no you won't no you won't*, ending as abruptly as it began. Say it quickly at the front of your mouth; that's just what the bird sounds like. He had an even better mnemonic for the reed warbler, the next and perhaps the most typical of all the Broadland birds, found wherever there are stands of phragmites, or common reed, with a long song full of stuttering hesitations. Mark's version of it was *I-I-can't-can't-quite-quite-get-get-my-my-words-words-out-out-out*, which got it just right; but my problem, I told him, and another major gap in my knowledge, was that I couldn't distinguish reed warbler from sedge warbler, its fairly close relative. The songs to my untutored ear had always seemed pretty similar, but Mark said, 'It's really straightforward. You'll do it by the end of the day.'

I wondered.

We had reached the edge of Rockland Broad now, and to my amusement I beheld a living example of my Norfolk Broads stereotype: a cabin cruiser was moored at the side, containing a middle-aged couple smoking and listening to the radio. *Enjoy it*, I thought. *There's room for you too.* But all about us was birdsong, and with great gratification I realized that willow warbler, whitethroat, blackcap, Cetti's warbler and reed warbler were all singing at once, and that I could identify them. This was going warbling indeed.

Mark also took great pleasure in it. He was animated not just by the performances, but by what they meant. Song was vital to the birds' lives, and he heard the meaning as much as the music. 'That reed warbler is saying, "I don't need to feed. I'm so good I can sing and keep all the males out of my territory."' He grinned. 'It's saying to the females, "I've got the Mercedes in the drive."'

As we sat and listened to the warbler chorus, a cloud of small flies drifted by us from the edge of the broad. 'See the biomass of insects?' he said. 'That's protein to be converted into music. That's the ecology of song – it's about abundance. If you don't have that biomass, you can't sing. The birds themselves can only sing if they have a huge surplus of food that enables them to take time out. Singing denotes a sense of luxury, of peace with yourself.'

The chorus continued. Mark said, 'All these birds singing are not on feeding activity. They're going, "I don't need to feed: I've this surplus time, this energy, which I can devote to vocalizing." The more you sing, the more the female says, "Christ, he's got big territories."'

'That's the importance of sound in birds' lives. But it's also an addition to our experience. That's why they're so important to us. We can enjoy the physical appearance of birds, but they're so much more special because they provide us with the soundscape.'

'The what?'

He gestured around us with his arm. 'The soundscape.'

Of course. I suddenly saw it; I suddenly understood. Each bird singing was not in isolation. They all came together as part of something bigger, a whole layer of existence, of which I had been ignorant. We usually apprehend the earth through vision, but we can also apprehend it through hearing. Not always – August, Mark pointed out to me later, was the most meagre season for sound – but in spring, when birds are such a prominent part of the opening world, and focused on breeding, and singing in order to breed, something massive is taking place which vision alone cannot fully encompass.

It felt like stumbling through a door into another dimension. There was that humbling feeling of suddenly seeing there was more **75** to the world than you had previously acknowledged, and it had all been going on in complete disregard of you, and was indifferent to whether you knew of it or not – and how much more, you think, do I not know? – but there it was. The soundscape.

As soon as you realized it existed, you began to see comparisons which illuminated it. That just as the lesser celandine, the bright yellow star with the heart-shaped leaves, was the first spring flower, scattering gold about the landscape in March, so the chiffchaff was its exact aural equivalent, injecting brightness into the soundscape at just the same time. And just as the primrose followed the celandine a month later, splashing the landscape with a more intense beauty, so exactly the same was done for the soundscape by the willow warbler, a few weeks on. But of course there were more than 200 species of breeding birds in Britain, and together they made up a whole world of sound, and when I asked Mark about it I realized that people could enter it as well as birds – once they had unlocked it, or it had been unlocked for them, as Mark had unlocked it for me.

He said, 'The soundscape is where many birders live. I suspect other naturalists too. If I'm honest, I spend a lot of time attuned to the sounds in landscapes. Most of my birding is by sound. If birds didn't or couldn't fly, I could cope with that. And if they didn't have bright colours, that would be OK. But if they didn't vocalize, I don't really think I'd be interested.'

Then he led me into the soundscape further.

We set off down the channel from Rockland Broad to the river, to tackle the difference between reed-warbler song and the song of its sedge-warbler cousin.

'Hear the chatter?' said Mark.

'That's a reed warbler?'

'Yes it is.'

'So how d'you tell the difference?'

He said, 'The reed warbler has a narrower range of sounds; it can't seem to capture the range that a sedge can. It's slower, more pedestrian, kind of trugging, chugging – just sort of chugs along. It sort of sings to itself. It's sort of "I feel very nervous about my song."'

We listened to the stuttering mantra: *I-I-can't-can't-quite-quite-get-get-my-my-words-words-out-out-out.* I said, 'I see what you mean about it sounding nervous.'

He said, 'The sedge is so much more ebullient and extroverted. It hasn't got hesitancy. It's more strident and dramatic. We'll find one in a minute.'

We did, halfway down the channel; it was singing in the reeds on the other side. We sat down to listen and watch, and the bird flew up into the air, and flew back down again. 'That's something else: the sedge warbler does a song flight,' he said. 'It parachutes down. The reed warbler never does that.'

Another sedge warbler began to sing, on our own side of the channel this time, quite near us, in a patch of brambles among the reeds. 'See?' said Mark. 'Very fast: *dee-dee-dee-dee-dee-dit-dit.* More accelerated and confident. Don't listen for notes, listen for the quality. It's an accelerated, confident, bubbling, upbeat displaying song. And the other thing is, it does mimicry.'

'Mimicry?'

'It mimics the calls of other birds.'

'Does it?'

'Yeah. Perfectly. Lots of them. Listen. Hear that?'

'What?'

'That.'

There was a call I didn't know.

Mark said, 'That was a blue tit.'

'It was a blue tit?'

'It was the sedge warbler mimicking a blue tit.'

'Was it?'

'There it is again. Listen. Now hear that?'

There was a whistle.

'That's yellow wagtail. Now it's doing yellow wagtail.'

We listened. It changed again.

'That's whitethroat contact or alarm call.'

'That the sedge warbler is doing?'

'Yep.'

This was completely new to me. I was a bit bewildered. I said, 'Why do they mimic other birds?'

'To extend their call range. It's predominantly the Acros [the *Acrocephalus* warblers]. The sedge warbler mimics more than the reed warbler. But the marsh warbler mimics most of all. That's yellow wagtail again. It's doing yellow wagtail. The bramble in phragmites is perfect for sedge.

'That's blue tit.

'That's linnet. That's the linnet mimicry. Hear it? The high trilling sweet note?'

We listened.

'That's starling.

'That's swallow. It's good, this sedge. That's a swallow alarm note: *perchink, perchink*. If a swallow is being chased by a hobby, that's what it does.'

I was bemused. I took Mark's word for it that there in the thicket in front of me the sedge warbler was imitating all these other bird species. But not knowing their calls and songs myself – although I wouldn't for a moment have doubted him – I had no way of appreciating it personally.

Then something strange happened. A greenshank called. The three unmistakable clear liquid notes rang out, *tyew–tyew–tyew*, and I cried, 'Greenshank!' and turned involuntarily towards the flood plain to spot it, moved as I always am by the call, taken instantly back to my boyhood and filled with the wildness of the Dee estuary under the great skies, and I saw that Mark was grinning.

I said, half-hesitantly, 'Hear the greenshank?'

'Yeah, I did.'

'Why are you laughing?'

'' 'Cos that was the sedge too.'

'What?'

'That was the sedge warbler.'

'That greenshank was the sedge warbler?'

He nodded.

I felt weird. For a moment I felt – hyperbolic though this may sound – that the ground under my feet was shifting, that reality was dissolving. I struggled to comprehend what had happened: that I had just been moved to the core of my being – by ventriloquism.

By ventriloquism by a bird.

By a bird ventriloquist.

Truly, once unlocked, the soundscape was a dimension full of marvels unimagined. I did not doubt the mimicry any more. I merely said, still amazed, 'Why do they do it?'

'To mate.'

'Explain.'

Mark said, 'Mimicry functions as a sexually selective advantage. The sedge warbler is saying, "I'm very clever, I can master all this stuff. I've got a large voice, a big, big territory. Come and sleep with me." It's like the peacock's tail, in sound.'

'Does it work?'

'It's been shown, experimentally, that the birds with the biggest mimicry repertoires find mates first.'

Birdsong operated at levels I had never dreamed of. Yet there were more levels still, which I began to discern as soon as I asked the question, Where did the sedge warbler learn? Where did it learn its mimicry, the other songs and calls? From its encounters with other birds, Mark said. But where did these take place? It could be here, in the Yare valley, he said, or it could be in Africa, or anywhere in between. 'Somewhere in its life, it's spent time with greenshanks.' Yet the question then arose, are they always learning direct from other species, or are they sometimes learning from each other? It was possible, he said, that it might just have heard another sedge warbler, and perfectly copied a greenshank from that. So the real greenshank behind the mimicry could have been one that landed **79** here this morning, or it could have been hundreds of years ago, and the imitation could have been passed on, from sedge warbler to sedge warbler, down through time.

'At any event, these are ancient sounds,' he said. 'The birds being imitated have been heard here through the Holocene. You think you're hearing now, now, now – but in fact you're hearing the past. You're hearing the aural history of the bird and its relation to this landscape. You're hearing the history of the landscape itself.'

I was gripped by the idea. Down among the brambles, this biscuit-sized bit of bones and feathers was giving a presentation of the landscape in sound, and I listened avidly now, with Mark as audio guide, as its mimicry switched from yellow wagtail to swallow, from linnet to whitethroat, then to a fresh species, wood sandpiper – *chiff-iff-iff, chiff-iff-iff* – and then to greenshank again, which I ruefully recognized. And as we sat with our ears focusing hard on the sedge and its landscape-encompassing song, the cabin cruiser from Rockland Broad came chugging down the channel past us, chug-chug-chug, the middle-aged couple still smoking and their radio playing pop, they with their listening, we with ours.

We sat at lunch outside the pub opposite Rockland staithe, in the breezy sunshine. I was still affected by the greenshank that wasn't, still bowled over by having been moved by the mimicry, full of wonder at the sedge warbler and all its works. But Mark pointed out that even the sedge was eclipsed by its cousin the marsh warbler, in whose extraordinary repertoire the songs and calls of no fewer than seventy-six other species had been identified, half of them purely African birds, which it heard and imitated on its wintering grounds and then brought to Britain in the spring. So in listening to the marsh warbler in England, you could be hearing the soundscape of Africa. 'It's astounding,' he said. 'It's like a nightingale on acid. Within the matter of a few seconds the mimicry can be ten species.'

We wouldn't find it in the Broads; although common in eastern Europe, it was one of Britain's rarest birds and there were only a handful of breeding pairs, occasionally in the Severn valley in Worcestershire (Eliot Howard country), and occasionally in Kent.

Then he suddenly said, 'You know, the bird I really hope you get to see is the wood warbler, which we won't see here either.'

'Why's that?'

'It's the leaf warbler I'm most attached to. It's the most special of the Phylloscs [the *Phylloscopus* warblers], much rarer than either of the other two [the chiffchaff and the willow warbler]. It's physically the most beautiful, and it has this amazing, explosive song – as it sings, it throws its head back and quivers its wings. It's just fantastic. I'm really hoping you will get to hear it.'

It was still common, he said, in 'the arc of the western woodland', the belt of Atlantic oakwoods on the western fringe of Britain, from Devon, through Wales and through the Lake District to Scotland, but it had gone from East Anglia.

Nevertheless, the Broads had been rich enough in warblers, I thought. If you go fishing and catch seven fish, you might be pretty satisfied. We had gone warbling, and found seven species in a morning. (And after lunch we found two more: the garden warbler, which is almost as musical a singer as the blackcap, and the Dartford warbler, which is more on the level of the whitethroat. For all Mark's determined efforts, the lesser whitethroat eluded us; but we still found nine out of ten.)

I say 'we', but it was Mark who found them. The expertise of birders might be terrifying; it was also wonderful. Mark said, 'There are birders who can identify several thousand species on call. I never will. I find going to the tropics a bit of a nightmare for that reason. It's like reading, but reading a book where you don't even know the script, let alone the language.'

I said I thought his ability was special enough. He smiled and said, 'I've loved being sharp about birds and the sounds of birds. I don't want to lose it. I'm 48. You get aged and you lose things. **81**

I hope that doesn't start; it would be like losing a limb. I haven't had to face that.'

I hoped so too, thinking of what his ability stood for: human understanding of the natural world, at more than a trivial level. It had found me a basketful of skittish songbirds in the course of a morning, and given me a taste of them I would not forget – especially the sedge warbler – and a grasp of them in the round. But, more than that, it had provided a way of comprehending them in their terms as well as ours.

For the soundscape really was another dimension, another layer of existence, and once you were aware of it much more of the earth made sense. It struck me that it was like entering into the world of smell in which most wild mammals exist – you might call it the scentscape – but humans are simply not equipped to step into that. Yet we are equipped to step through the door into the world of sound, once the key has been turned and our ears have been opened; and once inside, with a group of birds like the warblers . . . perhaps you did get somewhere near to the heart of things. At the least, you apprehended fully the virtue of these small passionate creatures, singing as though their lives depended on it – as indeed they did. You could recognize what song meant to them, but you also saw and at last had a means of recognizing and articulating just what they gave to us in their singing, on their miraculous springtime return from Africa – scattering life and newness and brightness about the soundscape, every bit as much as the landscape is brightened by spring flowers.

FIVE

The Spirit of the Place

Wood Warbler

A nd there was one more of the warblers, Mark Cocker had said, which I must not miss.

Driving over the border, driving deeper into the hills, my pulse rate rose and my anticipation mounted, but it was not at the thought of a bird. All my life Wales has moved me, not only with the loveliness of its upland landscapes, which would move anyone, but also with something I cherished personally: its sense of forcignness, its sense of complete difference, very near at hand.

Where I grew up on the Wirral peninsula, then in Cheshire, now in Merseyside, I could see Wales from near my home; I could see the distant peaks of the Clwydian range, crowned by Moel Famau, the Hill of Mothers, and I knew, and was strangely excited by the fact, that in the valley on the other side of those hills, in the tiny town of Ruthin, a mere 25 miles from the city of Liverpool and its Merseybeat that was steamrollering the world with the Beatles and the bands that came after them, they spoke another language.

Scotland defines its nationality with institutions: its legal system, its education system, its currency, and now its parliament. Wales **83** proclaims its identity with Welsh. I spent several years, from my early teens onward, having a go at this tongue far older than English, and although I gave it up before mastering it properly, I did get far enough to be able to chat to the locals in the Anglesey dialect – 'Sut mae, hogia? Sut mae'r petha'n mynd?' – 'How do, lads, how are things going?' – when I became a volunteer warden on a nature reserve in Anglesey in the late 1960s, at a period when anti-English feeling was fairly widespread.

I never minded anti-English feeling – 'Saison allan!' – 'English out!' I was glad they were proud of their country. And if I left the language behind, I never lost the sense of excitement at Wales's difference, the sense of it being far more than just a hilly version of England. Always, getting to the border, my senses quickened and a sort of animated restlessness began, as it did again this day in late May when spring was turning into summer as I passed Monmouth and Abergavenny, headed up to Brecon, skirted the Brecon Beacons National Park, and rolled over the foothills of the Cambrian Mountains to the old cattle drovers' town of Llandovery, where I found Mark Avery sitting in the bar of the hotel, nursing a pint. We grinned at each other. I said by way of greeting, 'I'll have a large gin and tonic.'

A large one seemed appropriate. Mark was a large man, robust in every way, and he had offered me a singular favour: to help me find the wood warbler. The bird whose praises the other Mark had so enthusiastically sung, outside the pub at Rockland staithe, and whose voice was missing from the chorus of warblers jamming round the Cocker corner of England, was also known and loved by Dr Avery, to accord him his proper honorific, and he was unusually well positioned to locate it, being Director of Conservation for the Royal Society for the Protection of Birds, the world's biggest bird protection club, with 200 nature reserves under his hand covering more than 300,000 acres across Britain. He was also an old friend, and he had said, 'I know just the place.'

I had begun to pick up some of the mystique that attached **84** to *Phylloscopus sibilatrix* ('whistling leaf-lover' would be a direct

The Spirit of the Place

translation). Not in cultural history – as with the other warblers, there was virtually none of that. And not with the general public, either – this was not generally a well-known creature at all. But among birders, I had started to realize, the wood warbler was regarded with reverence, as very special, almost like a cult band in the rock community. More than any other bird in Britain, it seemed to have an underground reputation. And doesn't that always prick your interest?

Gilbert White had first properly identified it, in Selborne Hanger, the wood of noble beech trees on the chalk hill above his Hampshire village. He had separated it out from the other two, strongly similar, leaf warblers, the willow warbler and the chiffchaff, first by song and later by close comparison of shot specimens. (No binoculars then, remember.) White referred to all three leaf warblers as 'willow-wrens', and in a letter to his fellow naturalist and correspondent Thomas Pennant on 17 August 1768, he wrote, 'I have now, past dispute, made out three distinct species of the willow-wrens, which constantly and invariably use distinct notes.' In an earlier letter he had already distinguished the chiffchaff ('the smallest willow-wren' or 'the chirper') and the willow warbler ('the middle willow-wren' or 'the songster'), and now he set out the details of the third species: 'a size larger than the two other, and the yellow-green of the whole upper parts of the body is more vivid, and the belly of a clearer white'.

He went on:

I have specimens of the three sorts now lying before me; and can discern that there are three gradations of sizes, and that the least has black legs, and the other two flesh-coloured ones. The yellowest bird is considerably the largest, and has its quill feathers and secondary feathers tipped with white, which the others have not. This last haunts only the tops of trees in high beechen woods, and makes a sibilous grasshopper-like noise, now and then, at short intervals, shivering a little with its wings when it sings.

85

Habitat, song, behaviour, all in one sentence: the parson had it spot on. What a chap, eh? If the wood warbler had remained obscure to the non-birding world in the 240 years since he so precisely picked it out, that was probably because it wasn't at all easy to see. In contrast to its close relatives which could be found in scrub, on bits of waste ground, in suburbs or even in your garden, it was a bird of deep woodlands and forests – in its winter quarters in Africa as much as in its breeding habitat in Britain.

Now, as Mark Cocker had said, it had largely retreated, to the woodlands on the western fringe of Britain: the Atlantic oakwoods. These constituted a very specialized habitat, sometimes described as 'temperate rainforest' because of their humid climate and their abundance of lower plants, mosses and lichens, fungi and ferns. They were ancient, unusual places, and you might have to go a long way to find them – I had driven nearly 200 miles from London. But once you got as far west as somewhere like Llandovery, you were knocking on their door.

I was pleased to be back in the pint-sized, lively town, which had fascinated me on an earlier visit because of its associations with Owain Glyndŵr, the rebel who in 1400 began the last Welsh revolt against English rule, conquered the country, instituted the first Welsh parliament, and disappeared from history about fifteen years later, still a free man. (Shakespeare anglicizes his name to Owen Glendower in *Henry IV Part 1* and makes him a Welsh windbag. I resent it, but I still laugh. It's unfortunately very funny.) Owain stormed through the area more than once, but in 1401 Henry IV stormed his way back and captured one of Owain's principal lieutenants, Llewellyn ap Gruffydd Fychan, and in the market place of Llandovery, with that barbarous cruelty which was as characteristic a trait of the Plantagenet kings as their love of courtly splendour, he had him hung, drawn and quartered. The story went that the English soldiers cut his stomach out and cooked it in front of him.

Learning this had only increased my animus against Henry IV, the princely thug who had deposed his artistic cousin Richard II.

(Richard represented the best of the Plantagenets, and if you want to see the difference between the cousin-kings at a glance, look at their effigies: the wooden carving of Richard in Westminster Abbey displays a slim face of acute sensitivity, while the alabaster tomb of Henry in Canterbury Cathedral shows a beefy bullyboy bursting out of his robes.) Now the townspeople of Llandovery had erected a statue to the martyred Llewellyn, an empty cloaked and helmeted figure in stainless steel about 15 feet high, which struck me as having something of the monstrous about it – it reminded me of the Ringwraiths in *The Lord of the Rings* – but certainly made its point.

Such was the hold Wales had on my imagination that thoughts such as these were occupying my mind entirely until I met up with Dr Avery under the old oak beams of the bar of the King's Head, and the focus returned to birds. Naturally, Mark had a different take on this part of the world. To the ornithological community, mid-Wales had been special throughout the twentieth century as the last stronghold of one of Britain's rarest birds, the red kite, a stunning chestnut-and-white raptor with long feather-fingered wings and a deeply forked tail. It had once been ubiquitous (and is often mentioned by Shakespeare), but had been persecuted to the brink of extinction by egg-collectors and trigger-happy gamekeepers and for decades was doughtily defended in its last abode. The Cambrian Mountains north of Llandovery were long thought of by birders as 'red-kite country'.

However, a reintroduction programme in the 1990s had been a great success, and now red kites were flourishing in England and Scotland as well as Wales – they were joyously visible in their aerial grace from the M40 motorway from London to Oxford, as it cut through the chalk scarp of the Chilterns – and so birding attention in mid-Wales had shifted to a group of the area's songbirds which were also regarded as out of the ordinary, the migrants of the oakwoods. Four of the spring-bringers in particular came back from Africa to the oak-clad valleys – the pied flycatcher, the tree pipit, the redstart and the wood warbler – making up a small, specialized community **87** that was very attractive, and the RSPB had several reserves catering for them. Mark had one of them in mind.

He was one of the most powerful figures in conservation in Britain (and he looked the part: 6 foot 3, built like a battleship, a fierce black moustache with the first few grey hairs in it), and he ran a department that carried real influence in public affairs: the RSPB had played a major role, for example, in forcing the abandonment of plans for a new airport at Cliffe on the Kent coast and a giant wind-farm on the Isle of Lewis in the Hebrides, successfully making the case each time that the damage to wildlife would outweigh the economic advantages. It had also been a prime mover in the successful campaign to outlaw the trade in wild birds right across the European Union. In policy terms the society had moved far beyond its origins as a birdwatchers' club and campaigned to protect the natural world on issues from marine pollution to agriculture to climate change.

But although he was now a policy general, Mark had remained at heart the birding footsoldier he started out as, the 1970s teenager cycling from his home outside Bristol to Chew Valley Lake in Somerset to seek out common sandpipers, black terns and whatever else might turn up. Thirty years on and more, he still went birdwatching every week in his own time at the gravel pits near his Northamptonshire village, and enthused about it: every visit, he said, was different and fascinating in its own way. Wherever he went he carried with him a notebook for writing down the birds he saw and a pair of battered binoculars, Zeiss 10x40s which were his eighteenth-birthday present from his parents 'on 29 March 1976', the date tripping off his tongue. They hung around his neck on an old bootlace, and he swore he would never replace them even though they were, in his own words, 'distressed', with the black coating peeling off to show the silver of the metal casing underneath. He said, 'I've seen every species of bird I've ever seen through these. They're slightly scratchy, but prisms and lenses don't really wear out. If I had a new pair I feel I'd have to start birdwatching all over again.'

That was the foot soldier; but the fact remained that he was a general now, with an empire of nature reserves under his command, all of which he knew very well, and when I mentioned my quest for the wood warbler and asked him for advice on where to find it, he pinpointed a place at once. And he enthused about its beauty: it was timeless and unchanging, he said, and when you got there it felt like a sanctuary far away from modern life, and it never disappointed. I was intrigued; I said, Yes please. It turned out he would be on sabbatical at the time I wanted to go, so we agreed to go together.

After meeting in Llandovery, we set out the following morning up the valley of the Towy. That was another of the town's attractions: it sat on a super river. At 70 miles, the Towy (Tywi in Welsh) was the longest river running entirely within the principality and, although it was no giant, it was a broad-shouldered striding watercourse celebrated for its fishing, for its salmon and still more for its sea trout, known in Wales as sewin (say 'seven' with a w instead of a v, and you've nearly got it). Llandovery was the point where its character changed: below the town it was a big solid stream whose broad valley had an air of pastoral tranquillity about it, all the way down to the sea beyond Carmarthen, but above Llandovery was increasingly a rushing hill river of rocky gorges and tree-shaded pools, the further you penetrated into the enclosing Cambrian Mountains. It was one of the few natural routes through the great empty fastness, and Owain Glyndŵr marched down it in 1403 as he took his revolt south.

We were going the other way. I was surprised at how pretty the valley was, even on a cloudy day: still with the fresh green of April on its hills and meadows, hedges and trees – the bloom of youth in plant terms, which by now, at the end of May, had dulled in England. No doubt the western rain was responsible. And as over the next few miles the valley narrowed and its topography became more stagy, with the hills starting to loom over it, it grew prettier still, for it was edged with deciduous woodlands – the Atlantic oakwoods, **89**

I realized – which gave a far softer feel to the landscape than the dark spiky harshness of the planted conifers which now bestubble so much of the uplands in Wales.

By the time we came to our destination, a conical hill covered in woodland which seemed to sit in the valley's centre (but actually divided it), I was beginning to grow entranced by a sense of place; with its soft green hills and woods and tumbling river, the valley about us was simply too lovely for words, the beauty so remarkable that it left you shaken, almost. And it came to a climax under the oak trees.

The hill was called Dinas. It was an RSPB reserve, with a small car park, and there Mark and I met the young warden, David Anning, who knew exactly what his reserve held that day in terms of the birds we were interested in: 30 pied-flycatcher territories, 15 redstart territories, 5 tree-pipit territories and 13 wood-warbler territories. His mention of the last brought me back from the landscape to the bird: with a tingle of excitement, I felt that the creature with the underground reputation was now just around the corner. And as we chatted the rain began – not a deluge, but a steadily pattering warm spring drizzle.

When you enter Dinas, you first meet a long stretch of alder carr, or wet woodland, lining the banks of a clear stream that runs down to the Towy, and we were led over its boggy pools and flaring yellow marsh marigolds by a wooden boardwalk, with on either side of us pied flycatchers flitting through the trees, black and white glimpses darting in and out of the nest boxes attached to the alders, feeding their young. The oakwood began where the boardwalk ended, on the slope of the hill.

To enter it was like entering a church – a great green church, hushed and still. Everything was bathed in dim green light as if from green stained-glass windows; in fact it was light reflected down from the young green oak leaves and back up from the woodland floor, which was carpeted with plump green mosses from which pale-green bracken stems elegantly uncurled. There was one other colour, powder blue, from the swathes of bluebells which flowed down some of the slopes, but otherwise it was an enclosed universe of green, and the lines of Andrew Marvell, from 'The Garden', came straight into my mind:

> *Annihilating all that's made*
> *To a green thought in a green shade.*

Distant lambs were bleating; a blackcap was singing; there was the faint and far-off boom of the river. It felt like a long way from anywhere, this place, so uncommon was its beauty, as if beauty and distance were somehow linked – as if beauty were the reward for travelling this far – and I remembered what Mark had said and realized he had not exaggerated: timeless and unchanging, a sanctuary from modern life, and if you returned, it never disappointed you.

There couldn't be many places like Dinas.

And did it hold the wood warbler? I thought. Would I hear it now, would I see it, the bird that was the birders' secret, the creature whose specialness only they knew?

Not immediately. Mark and David were ahead of me, walking slowly and stopping, listening and looking, and there was birdsong enough – the blackcap had been joined by a chaffinch and a willow warbler – but no sign of *Phylloscopus sibilatrix*. We scanned the high branches of the oaks, trying to catch small movements, but we were confused by the rain, which was not heavy enough to drum solidly on the canopy, but enough to flick a leaf every few seconds. Flick. Flick. That? There? No, it's the rain.

It was when Mark and David cocked their ears and then smiled at each other that I realized we might be in luck. I moved up alongside them. What were they hearing? They made a sign to listen. I caught the whispery drizzle and the faraway roar of the river; nothing else. But then, just half heard, was a faint dry trill, and Mark and David smiled once more and Mark gave the thumbs-up sign. I listened: there it was again, more distinct this time, from somewhere high in **91** the branches – a short accelerating trill, like a string of beads being dropped vertically on to a parquet floor.

The wood warbler at last.

We were motionless and listening.

Then a quite different bird called, five deep sweet notes with a haunting edge of melancholy to them, *pioo, pioo, pioo, pioo, pioo*, for all the world like the long low notes of the nightingale, and I wondered what on earth that was, and I saw that Mark and David were smiling yet again, and they explained: this was the wood warbler too. It was a bird with two songs, so utterly unalike that they seemed to come from two completely different species; but the same handful of feathers produced both.

Would we see it?

We scrutinized the woodland for movement, on the branches, among the leaves, in the air. Nothing. We moved slowly forward through the oaks, their dark trunks lightened with grey lichens, as the rejuvenating rain dripped down on to the mossy floor and the bluebells; then, to the side of us, something was flying. We turned: there were three small birds chasing each other through the trees. They were wood warblers, giving a call note, a short liquid *pioop!*, as they flew, but too quick to hold in the binoculars for more than a second, tearing after each other in some unfathomable fuss of competition and disappearing as suddenly as they had come – except for one. This bird, we saw, landed on the low branch of an oak tree about 50 yards away and was clearly visible. We moved towards it, gingerly; when I had got to within 30 yards I chanced my luck no further, squatted down on the moss, and raised my bins to my eyes.

Beauty came sharply into focus. I saw a bird with a vivid green back and head, the latter bisected by a bright-yellow eyestripe; it had a lemon-yellow throat and upper breast above a belly that was so pure white it appeared to have been freshly laundered. As it moved its head, the light caught the yellow throat and the white belly in turn, contrasting them handsomely with each other and with the green back above; it was as if a willow warbler had been worked on by a team of picture restorers and emerged with sparkling new colours. And as I watched, it dropped its wings down by its sides, threw back its head with its lemon throat to the sky, opened its beak, and gave its trill, its string-of-beads-on-a-wooden-floor trill, shivering its whole being as it did so.

I was knocked out. It was like watching an amateur tenor going for a high note, dropping his arms and clenching his fists as he reached the top. It was the epitome of exuberance. Why did the bird do it? What was the evolutionary advantage of shivering? Did the best shiverer get the best female? I couldn't see it. It seemed to me, as over the following minutes I watched it again and again, that it was simply an adjunct to performance, it was simply letting rip. *Here comes my trill, baby – oh yes! Get down and boogie!*

I had a perfect view and couldn't take my eyes away; I was glued to the bird, this terrific bird, so arresting in both its colours and its behaviour, and so hard to find, so hidden away in its western woodlands. I felt a sort of triumph just in viewing it, and I lost the sense of time passing, until eventually, with no warning, it flew, and the branch was empty. I looked around; David was sitting a few yards away; Mark was higher up the slope; we were all wet by now, as the rain had begun to penetrate the canopy. Dr Avery in particular appeared to be soaked. With his bins on their bootlace, his tatty green Barbour open and dripping, and his black hair plastered over his forehead, the Director of Conservation looked like a ragamuffin, but all he'd been interested in was the bird.

Yet there was more than one; the wood held thirteen wood-warbler territories, David Anning had said, which potentially meant twenty-six birds or more, and, after David had left us, Mark and I began to catch their songs. They seemed to be concentrated at the far end of the wood, near the gorge of the Towy, which surges down one side of the hill, and as we approached the river and its roar the tiny trills became more frequent, floating down from the oak-leaf canopy, from the unseen shiverers high above. Occasionally we glimpsed them flitting about, and one bird that we had in our binoculars **93** suddenly flew directly towards us at head height, its throat and upper breast so prominent that for a split second it appeared to be entirely yellow and Mark and I let out a cry of surprise simultaneously. But mostly we heard them, the trills dropping all about us, the lightest rain of sound, as the river thundered below.

Dinas and its environs were so alluring that we stayed on, ignoring the wet, and spent the afternoon hunting for the other spring-bringers which belonged to the western woods. We had the least luck with the gaudiest, the redstart (blue-grey back, marmalade-orange breast and tail, black face): the most we could manage was a glimpse in a distant hedgerow. We did better with the tree pipit, skylark relation, migratory first cousin to the meadow pipit, and to me virtually indistinguishable from it, although David Anning had said he was a tree-pipit enthusiast ('Great bird – subtle yellow breast with very pronounced black streaks and bubblegum-pink legs' was his description): we watched one soar in its song flight from hawthorn bush to hawthorn bush down a hillside. And we enjoyed an abundance of pied flycatchers, decorating the woodlands with their splashes of black and white. Two further summer-migrant species also graced us with their presence: a pair of common sandpipers, spirited small waders bobbing skittishly about the river, and a spotted flycatcher, the pocket-sized insect predator normally found in gardens and farmland, which this day had taken up station on a stone in the middle of the Towy, as a base for swoops against passing mayflies – something neither Mark nor I had ever come across before.

All those birds added to the wooded valley's potent appeal; yet it was the wood warbler which gave me most to think about as we left Dinas and rolled back down the river to Llandovery. I knew it was the most special, but now I wasn't quite sure why. I had come all this way to see it, and had not been disappointed – just the opposite – yet there was something about it that I couldn't quite put into words, something lurking around the edge of my consciousness, something about seeing it . . . where we had seen it.

I think I had not envisaged that its habitat would have as big an impact on my feelings as the bird itself. I had started out seeking an exceptional creature, but in finding it I had found an exceptional landscape too, and now I was somewhat confused, about . . . what? Which took precedence? Which I liked more? I was confused about what I was confused about.

Mark began to put my feelings in order over a beer in the King's Head, before he shot off (he was driving overnight to Northumbria; I was staying another night). He said, 'But the two things come together.'

'What do?'

'The bird and the landscape.'

'In what way?'

'Well,' he said, 'it's a bird of a place, isn't it?'

'How d'you mean?'

'If you told someone, on the phone, say . . . if you told someone you were listening to a wood warbler, they might have a better stab at knowing what the landscape around you looked like than with almost any other species.'

I started to see it.

'If you listen to the song, as you can on a CD, I think that takes you back to the place quicker than looking at a photograph in a book. And that place is the place you will always think of when anybody says 'western oakwoods'. The bird sort of belongs there. It's the expression of it. If you went back to that landscape in January, it's waiting for the wood warbler to come back. You could say that's what winter is, there: waiting for the wood warbler to come back.'

This was such a novel idea that I struggled with it for second, but then I saw the woodland frozen hard in a mountain January – bare and wood-warbler-less – and a door began to open in my mind. I nodded. 'And you said yourself . . . the place is timeless. It's natural. It's always been like that . . .'

Mark said, 'Well, you do kind of feel that these western oakwoods have been pretty much like that for thousands of years, and there have been wood warblers doing what we saw them do for all of that time. Sitting in a Welsh oakwood like Dinas, you do feel that Owen Glendower could have sat somewhere rather similar, and got wet, and listened to a wood warbler, just like we were doing.'

I felt I had the beginning of an understanding; and when Mark had gone I thought about it a lot more, wandering around Llandovery in the still evening with the rain now ceased, looking at the river, and the Norman castle keep, and the monstrous empty stainless-steel statue of the martyred Llewellyn ap Gruffydd Fychan (monstrous in an acceptable way). And I decided to go back to Dinas in the morning, to see if I could bring my understanding to completion.

When I did so the weather had cleared; the blue sky was dotted with cotton-wool white clouds; the sun was strong. The upper valley of the Towy, so soft and appealing in its contours the day before, even under skies of grey, was soft and appealing still but now washed in vibrant colours, and the oakwood also was transformed. The green haze of its interior had lost its dimness and was sliced with sun-beams; the young oak leaves were iridescent emerald; the bluebells seemed to have taken on an electric charge and now flowed like a lilac smoke over the woodland floor. It took my breath away. The beauty of it all seemed newly minted and perfect; it seemed to be the most intense beauty that the earth had to offer.

In the clear air the birdsong too seemed even fuller and livelier than it had done the day before – although that may have been because I was alone and concentrating – and I realized with pleasure that I could deconstruct the soundscape myself: I picked out willow warbler, blackcap, song thrush, wren, chaffinch and even the croak of a raven, and then in the distance the five long mournful notes, *pioo*, *pioo*, *pioo*, *pioo*, *pioo*, and I smiled, for I knew now what that was. I walked on further, towards the river, listening hard, and eventually it crept to my ear, the first of the accelerating trills.

First the one, then another, and another, and another, dropping down lightly from the canopy as the spring rain had yesterday; and eventually I caught sight of a bird on a branch, in a shaft of sunlight. In the binoculars it appeared brilliant silvery-green, and it matched the young oak leaves so perfectly it could have been one of them as it raised its lemon-yellow throat, dropped its wings, and shivered out its whole soul. And in that moment I understood.

It was a bird of a place, Mark had said, and it was. But it was more than that. It was the bird of an exceptional place, an exceptional landscape, and it matched that landscape in specialness. All the reborn spring beauty of Dinas flowered in the young oak leaves and the bluebells, when they came back; but it flowered most of all in the wood warbler, when that came back too, for the bird bloomed not only in its beauty, but also in the vividness of its life. Mark was right: you could define winter, here, as the wood warbler's absence. It was more than the bird of the place: it was the spirit of the place.

Maybe, I thought, this is what the birders saw, without really articulating it: they understood instinctively that, in the places where it was found, this bird was truly the *genius loci*, it was at the heart of things. It was almost, you might say, their mystic knowledge. You had to come a long way to find it, this jewel of the western woods, but when you did you found a landscape unequalled in loveliness, and then you found a bird which brought that loveliness to crowning and unforgettable expression.

SIX

A Promise of Lazy Days

Turtle Dove

J ust as there were landscapes that were special in seeking out the spring-bringers, there were days that were special too, and the best of them all was a day in mid-May which really belonged to high summer. It was immaculate in its colours, in the radiant blue of its skies, the unsullied green of its fields and woods, and the gold of its sunlight; it was poised and calm in its stillness and rich in its warmth; and most of all, what I remember and will always remember, is that it was decorated in white by the may blossom, the flowers of the hawthorn. The countryside was criss-crossed by hawthorn hedges, and every one seemed to have been garlanded in white as if for a wedding. The landscape seemed to sing for joy.

There was never wildlife abounding as on this day. On every field there were hares, chunky, loping and eminently visible, as well as partridges, the red-legged and the much rarer grey, now on alert, now running. There were lapwings and oystercatchers, curlews and stone curlews, all birds which these days would crown a country walk in many parts of Britain if seen singly. Down a narrow track, two
98 cock pheasants in bright uniforms fought angrily, springing up and

battering each other with their wings, ignoring the human observers close at hand. A muntjac deer trotted past unhurried, like a pig in the low-slung way it carried its body. And over it all the skylarks sang, numberless and unceasing, showers from a clear blue sky.

It was an exceptional landscape, of course, and I had encountered it at an exceptional moment: there are few days like that one in any year. I was there seeking the turtle dove, the spring-bringer from the Bible, the bird whose voice was heard in the Song of Solomon, denoting the shift in the seasons, and I was seeking it with the same aim as I had had in seeking out the nightingale – to find the real creature under a heavy load of legend.

Once again I had had the strong impression that here was a bird familiar in fable, but virtually unknown in feathers and flesh, certainly to a great part of the population. Very few people, especially in towns and cities, would seem to be aware of what the turtle dove looked like, especially as it was getting rarer every year (and is often confused with the collared dove, a bird which could be found in suburbs and even in towns); still fewer would have any idea that it flew here from Africa every spring, and was our only migratory pigeon. Where everybody did know it was in the carol 'The Twelve Days of Christmas', in which the present from the true love on the second day is two turtle doves, following on from the partridge in a pear tree on the first. But I never heard anybody remark that this was odd because at Christmas turtle doves have all disappeared.

The carol, in fact, had become the cheap-and-cheerful last resting place for the bird in popular culture, just as Berkeley Square had become the cheesy sepulchre for the nightingale. Yet for many centuries, until really quite recently, the turtle dove had enjoyed a far-reaching, deeply influential and profoundly serious symbolic reputation as the avian icon of fidelity.

It seems impossible to say when it began, this idea of the turtle dove as the emblem of romantic affection that is devoted and true, but it is very old, and may be one of the oldest metaphors of civilization, perhaps dating back to ancient Egypt. It seems to have

99

particularized out of a general perception that there was an exceptional quality, something peaceful and gentle perhaps, about the doves and pigeons as a family. The terms 'dove' and 'pigeon' are interchangeable – in Britain the increasingly common bird now called the wood pigeon used to be called the ring dove – but the scruffy reputation of the feral pigeon, street scavenger of our towns and cities, has attached a certain opprobrium to the p-word, while the d-word still denotes elegance and refinement. In reality, doves and pigeons are all members of the family Columbidae, and in the Near East, in ancient Israel, in Greece and in Rome, these birds were widely seen as pure, even sacred, and especially suitable for sacrifice.

The first surviving explicit statement about their alleged fidelity seems to be in the *Natural History* of Pliny the Elder, the literary admiral killed trying to rescue the citizens of Pompeii during the eruption which buried the town in AD 79 (while his nephew Pliny the Younger was recording the scene from the other side of the Bay of Naples, having told his uncle he didn't, er, really fancy the trip, if that was all right). The *Natural History* is a gigantic encyclopedia in thirty-seven books dealing with the whole of the natural world: birds are the subject of Book 10, and in Chapter 52 of it Pliny talks about the habits of pigeons and doves in general, saying, 'their chastity is extreme, and adultery is unknown amongst them; although they live together with others, they do not break the marriage bond.'

By the early Middle Ages, this virtue was being ascribed to the turtle dove in particular, as we can see from medieval bestiaries, those monk-illuminated manuscript compendiums of animals and birds with moral lessons attached; and when we get to the late fourteenth century, and the age of Chaucer, the connection has become axiomatic. The turtle dove features prominently in Chaucer's dream-fantasy *The Parliament of Fowls*, written about 1380, and the very first reference in this is to 'The wedded turtil, with hire herte trewe'. (The word itself is taken from the French equivalent, *tourterelle*.) Later in the poem the dove makes a passionate plea for constancy which is so charming it is worth quoting in the original Middle English:

100

'Nay, God forbede a lovere shulde chaunge!'
The turtle seyde, and wex for shame al red,
'Though that his lady everemore be straunge,
Yit lat hym serve hire ever, til he be ded.
Forsothe, I preyse nat the goses red;
For, though she deyede, I wolde non other make;
I wol ben hires, til that the deth me take.'

('No, God forbid a lover should change!'
The turtle dove said, and blushed for shame.
'Though his lady be cold to him evermore,
yet let him serve her always, until he is dead.
Indeed, I do not praise the goose's argument [that you should
not bother loving someone who did not love you];
For even if my lady died, I would have no other mate;
I would be hers, until death took me.')

By the time we reach the Renaissance, and Shakespeare arrives, the symbolism is rock solid. Not only is it the focus of his stand-alone (and difficult) allegorical lyric poem *The Phoenix and The Turtle*, but there are numerous references throughout the plays. In one of the earliest, for example, in *Henry VI Part 1*, the Dauphin of France is described as fleeing the sack of Orleans with Joan of Arc:

Like to a pair of loving turtle-doves
That could not live asunder day or night.

In one of the middle plays, *Troilus and Cressida*, Troilus tells Cressida how faithful he will be when they are separated by the Trojan War, and says that 'true as Troilus' will replace tired old similes like as true 'as sun to day, as turtle to her mate'. (Pity about Cressida.) In one of the very last plays, *The Winter's Tale*, Florizel, the disguised prince, leads Perdita, the lost princess, to the dance with the words

Your hand, my Perdita: so turtles pair,
That never mean to part.

And at the end of the play Shakespeare uses the metaphor once more to give a poignant speech to Paulina, the fearless truth-teller who had striven to limit the earlier tragedy and paid with the loss of her husband Antigonus – last seen, you may remember, about to comply with Shakespeare's most singular stage direction: *'Exit – pursued by a bear.'* Noting how everyone else has found happiness, Paulina says:

I, an old turtle,
Will wing me to some wither'd bough and there
My mate, that's never to be found again,
Lament till I am lost.

(But she gets a new husband, just in time for the play to end.)

Countless poets used the image: for loyalty in love, for true devotion and trustworthiness, the bird had become virtually a universal symbol. It had become an ingrained part of the culture of the English-speaking world – so ingrained, in fact, that eventually the symbolism spread to America, where the turtle dove does not exist.

We can see this clearly in the most extraordinary bird book ever produced, John James Audubon's *Birds of America*, the collection of 435 giant, lustrous, stunning images of the avifauna of the New World which the long-haired, Franco-American frontiersman painter took to Britain to be published as hand-coloured engravings between 1827 and 1838 (the necessary expertise being unavailable in the US). In their beauty and drama and vigorous life, they have never been surpassed; if you are lucky enough to gaze upon them, in the rare-books cabinet of a museum or the house of a very rich man – there are 119 complete sets still in existence, but not one on permanent public view – you will never forget the experience. To accompany the plates, Audubon wrote a handbook entitled

102 *Ornithological Biography*, and it is fascinating to consider the entry for the species which is now known across the North American continent as the mourning dove, *Zenaida macroura*.

This is one of the commonest and most widespread of American birds – its population may be in excess of 500 million individuals – and is one of the most widely hunted, with as many as 70 million shot annually. Everybody knows it. Yet Audubon called the mourning dove something else – 'the Carolina turtle dove' – and he painted two pairs of the birds (in the one image), both in what might be called amorous situations.

He wrote, 'I have tried, kind reader, to give you a faithful representation of two as gentle pairs of Turtles as ever cooed their loves in the green woods. I have placed them on a branch of Stuartia, which you see ornamented with a profusion of white blossoms, emblematic of purity and chastity.'

One pair is at the nest; the female is receiving food from the bill of her mate 'and listening with delight to his assurances of devoted affection'. The other pair is on the branches above, where, Audubon says, 'a love scene is just commencing,' and he describes it:

> The female, still coy and undetermined, seems doubtful of the truth of her lover, and virgin-like resolves to put his sincerity to the test, by delaying the gratification of his wishes. She has reached the extremity of the branch, her wings and tail are already opening, and she will fly off to some more sequestered spot, where, if her lover should follow her with the same assiduous devotion, they will doubtless become as blessed as the pair beneath them.

Never mind the language, which now seems cloying to a degree (although the image does not). The significant thing is that Audubon is calling this bird a turtle dove, even though it is in an entirely different genus – *Zenaida* – from the real thing, whose scientific name is *Streptopelia turtur*. *Zenaida* is a strictly New World genus, with seven species; *Streptopelia* is a resolutely Old World, mainly African, one, **103** with nearly twenty. It is as if the fidelity symbolism were so powerful that Audubon was determined to have a turtle dove in America, even if the creature itself were missing. Indeed, the symbolism persisted strongly down the years, especially in American popular song, and seems to have reached a peak in the early years of rock and roll in the 1950s and '60s when turtle doves became extremely common as similes and metaphors for love, and the phrase 'turtle dovin'' was frequently being used, not least because it was a handy rhyme with 'lovin''. In 1956, for example, Gene Vincent, the first major rock star to follow Elvis, had a global hit with 'Be-Bop-A-Lula' and on the B-side recorded 'Woman Love' in which he wants his lovin' baby to call him 'turtle dove'; in 1958, Buddy Holly, the most creative of all the early rock and roll pioneers, silenced at the age of 22 with Richie Valens and The Big Bopper in the notorious plane crash of February 3, 1959 ('The Day The Music Died') had one of his biggest hits with 'That'll Be The Day' in which he refers to his girl giving him all her lovin' and all her turtle dovin'; and in 1959, the Canadian rocker Jack Scott, who is hardly known on this side of the pond but had a string of hugely successful singles, had his own biggest hit with 'The Way I Walk' in which he asks his girlfriend to c'mon and be his little turtle dove. And if you want a home-grown British example, you only have to turn to Cliff Richard's biggest-ever hit, 'Bachelor Boy', of 1962, in which the ageless crooner warbled that his wife and child would be his turtle doves, when he eventually got married.

It is only in recent years that the image has finally run out of steam: there is no place for what the turtle dove was said to stand for, in the age of rap.

From the outset I never thought that getting to the heart of the turtle dove would be about the romantic fable, although I was aware of something remarkable – that we now had ways of telling whether or not it was based on fact. In the previous thirty years huge advances had been made in the understanding of bird behaviour, especially in the area of sex and reproduction, and it had become clear, since the development of DNA fingerprinting in the late 1980s, that very many species of birds, even ones where males and females have only a single 'official' mate, engage in copulation outside the pair bond – adultery in human terms, 'extra-pair copulation' in non-judgemental biological ones. Promiscuity, to use the word in a purely scientific way, occurred in males and females both. This resulted in an astonishing amount of extra-pair paternity, which genetic fingerprinting had now revealed – large numbers of chicks in nests had been fathered by a male other than the one who is helping their mother feed them. It had been found with species after species after species, especially in the passerines, the songbirds, where it seemed close to being the rule rather than the exception.

Does promiscuity occur in pigeons and doves? According to Tim Birkhead of the University of Sheffield, the leading British authority on the subject, extra-pair copulation has been observed in feral pigeons, but extra-pair paternity has not yet been proven. (It takes a lot of work to do it.) With the turtle dove, neither extra-pair copulation nor extra-pair paternity has yet been shown. So, while probably less likely than it was before we knew what birds really got up to when their partners' backs were turned, it is still just possible that the legend has a basis in truth; or to be more precise, as Professor Birkhead himself put it to me, 'With the idea of the turtle dove as a model of fidelity, the jury is out.' The whole idea probably began, he said, in early observations that pigeons and doves seem very affectionate towards each other, preen and feed each other as part of courtship behaviour, and go everywhere together – although we have come to understand now that male birds assiduously accompanying females everywhere are usually trying to prevent them being inseminated by rivals.

However, seeing the turtle dove as one of the spring-bringers, as the Song of Solomon poet had seen it, was to see it in a quite different way from the love legend. I felt that its essence would be located in **105** its ecology, about which I knew a certain amount, although I should shamefacedly admit – and this was a prime reason I was so keenly interested – that I had never seen the bird myself. It had always been a species of the south and east of England, and there were no turtle doves in the Wirral in England's north-west – none, at least, that I ever encountered – when I was a boyhood birdwatcher there.

The key ecological fact was that it was a seed-eater, and yet it migrated, which is almost a contradiction in terms. The overwhelming majority of migrants are insectivores, heading north to take advantage of the profusion of insects in the high latitudes in the summer, which disappear until the following spring once winter comes. To be a seed-eating migrant is very rare, and in *The Palaearctic–African Bird Migration Systems* Reg Moreau pointed out that out of the 187 species which annually leave sub-Saharan Africa for Eurasia, only 7 were 'wholly or mainly seed-eating', while in western Europe the total was down to just 5: the short-toed lark, Cretzschmar's bunting, the ortolan bunting, the quail and the turtle dove. (It is this peculiarity of behaviour, by the way, which makes the ortolan the most prized, and now most unlawful, of all gastronomic delicacies in France. Since migrants are programmed to fatten themselves before their journeys, and the ortolan is a seed-eater, it can be trapped in late summer and fattened further in captivity with grain, before being drowned in Armagnac and served to you whole as a single fat-packed morsel, to be eaten with a towel over your head, as the former French president François Mitterrand did at his final dinner with friends, entirely illegally, a few days before he died of prostate cancer in 1996. Imagine, if you care to put yourself in the position of the bird-trapper, how you would fatten the other migrant songbirds, which are insectivores. Where would you find the insects?)

No one seemed to know why the turtle dove should choose to leave Africa every spring to find seeds to eat in Europe, when the rest of its close relatives in the genus *Streptopelia*, the laughing dove, the ring-necked dove, the vinaceous dove and several others, found no reason whatsoever to do so. I put the question to Britain's leading expert on migration, Professor Ian Newton, who had just published the most comprehensive account of the subject ever written in English, *The Migration Ecology of Birds*. This is 976 pages of the clearest and most accessible science you will ever meet with, a masterpiece of deep learning and explanation with the lightest of touches – if you want to know more about migration, this is the book – yet when I asked him about it over lunch, he screwed up his forehead in intense thought for ten seconds, then burst out laughing and said, 'I just don't know.'

However, it was not the reason for the turtle dove's migration which most had caught my interest: it was the famous reference to the bird in the exquisite English of the Authorized Version: 'For, lo, the winter is past, the rain is over and gone; the flowers appear on the earth; the time of the singing of birds is come, and the voice of the turtle is heard in our land.'

The Song of Solomon is one of the most intriguing books of the Old Testament, if not in some ways the most unusual of all. It is certainly the loveliest. Although it sits naturally with the rest of the so-called 'wisdom literature', especially the books of Proverbs and Ecclesiastes, of which Solomon himself was traditionally the author, the open eroticism of its love poetry – now a woman is speaking, now a man – is so at odds with the tone of the rest of the Bible that you can find fundamentalist Christians who will denounce it as having been slipped in by the Devil. Certainly, commentators have long have to jump through complex allegorical hoops to square its frankly sexual imagery with a message from the Lord: 'Thy breasts are like two young roes that are twins, which feed among the lilies . . .'

Much of the imagery is taken from the natural world, which gives the poem its ravishing freshness of tone, and this is the case with the invocation of the spring in its Chapter 2. It might be the Bible, but this is direct observation. It is one of the earliest and clearest references to the role of the migrant birds in announcing the change of seasons – it may date to 900 BC – and from my own point of view it immediately prompted several questions.

What was 'the voice of the turtle'? Was it a cooing, like that of other pigeons and doves?

Why did the poet – indeed Solomon, if it were he – feel impelled to single it out from the rest of 'the singing of birds'? What was so special about it?

I had to confess I had no idea. I didn't know what the song, or the call, of a turtle dove sounded like, but I badly wanted to find out, and so I began to search for someone who might show me. Although books had been written about the wood pigeon, and even the feral pigeon (*The Public Life of the Street Pigeon*, by Eric Simms) there was no modern monograph on the species, and at first the answer was by no means obvious. I mean, who knows all about turtle doves?

The man who did turned out to be working at a desk on the fourth floor of an office block in Cambridge, worrying about the fate of the yak in Tibet and the cao vit gibbon (the world's rarest ape) in Vietnam. He was Stephen Browne, the Asia-Pacific programme manager of Fauna and Flora International, the British conservation charity, and in fact when I first emailed him he was away in Cambodia, worrying about the fate of the Siamese crocodile (one of the world's rarest reptiles). But he said he would be happy to help on his return.

Stephen was 38 and had been involved with FFI and with Far Eastern wildlife for two years, but before that his career had been in bird conservation in Britain. He had spent four years studying the turtle dove for the Game Conservancy (now the Game and Wildlife Conservation Trust), trying to work out why its numbers were tumbling. The results of his research became his doctoral thesis, and this had been the only in-depth study of the bird for nearly forty years.

He had been a boyhood birder in Norfolk, coming from a village on the outskirts of Norwich. The attractions which drew Mark Cocker to the county were there for Stephen from the start – 'Living out in the sticks in Norfolk, everywhere you go is a birdwatching adventure,' he said – and while doing his first degree, in environmental science, **108** he had been bitten by the ringing bug. He was badly infected, like most people seem to be, and after his MSc he got a job as a researcher with the BTO, the British Trust for Ornithology, which is not only the UK's leading bird research organization, but is Ringing Central – it administers all ringing activities, issuing licences, supplying rings, co-ordinating training, and collating ringing records.

When Stephen joined the BTO at its headquarters in Thetford, Norfolk, he at once ran into the character who had dominated the bird-ringing world in Britain for many years, Chris Mead. An outsize figure in physique, personality and reputation – he had the hair and beard of an Old Testament prophet – Chris Mead personally ringed more than 400,000 birds of 350 species in 20 countries, headed the National Ringing Scheme, and became a leading authority on migration as well as on ornithology in general. Stories about him were legion – he was said to have eaten a washing-up bowl full of cornflakes as preparation for a long day in the field, and to have carried on birding wearing only a curtain after falling into the sludge of a sewage farm. A stroke in the mid-1990s meant he had to cut back on fieldwork, and he became the BTO's media spokesman and in effect its voice – a memorable voice, deep, mellifluous and masterful, familiar to many through his radio broadcasts – and he gradually assumed the mantle of father figure of British ornithology. When he died of a sudden heart attack in 2003, at the age of 62, there was an outpouring of grief from the birding world.

Stephen had met him a decade earlier; and not long afterwards he also met Chris Mead's daughter Harriet, doing temporary work at the BTO while she got her career as a wildlife sculptor off the ground. They became an item, and set up home together in a cottage in the Norfolk village of Hilborough. Harriet's widowed mother Verity, known as Vee, also lived in the village, and in Vee's outbuildings Harriet had her workshop, where she spent hours every day in a face mask, wielding a white-hot welding torch: she created her sculptures out of scrap metal.

You may have seen scrap sculptures before; sometimes you struggle before you recognize the subject and say, 'Oh yes, I see, it's a   **109** hedgehog'. With Harriet's work there would be no hesitation: she had an absolutely unerring eye for line and form, for what birders refer to as the 'jizz' of a creature, the property that allows for an instant recognition from the briefest of glimpses (the word may come from aircraft recognition techniques in the Second World War and refer to 'general impression, size and shape'). Outside her workshop she had a pair of boxing hares, just finished: they were made up of dozens of individual pieces of metal, but the result was quite perfect. (Harriet was very fond of hares.) Now she was working on the giant head of a shire horse.

It was a Sunday evening in mid-May when I went to see Stephen and Harriet on my turtle dove quest; Stephen had a brief window of opportunity in Norfolk before going off to Chengdu in China to supervise the launch of FFI's programme to help the herders of the Tibetan plateau restore their rangelands. Today turtle doves; tomorrow yaks. Meeting them at their cottage, I thought that their situation was idyllic, and I told them so. They seemed surprised. It was just home, they said, but later Stephen told me they had discussed it and thought perhaps they were taking it for granted; they agreed they lived in an exceptional place.

For Hilborough sat in the heart of one of Britain's most unusual landscapes, the Breckland. Its key characteristic was sand, windblown into the area thousands of years ago, which made the soil poor and hard to cultivate. In the nineteenth century, attempts had been made to stabilize it by planting belts of trees uncommon in southern England, Scots pines. Their dark cragginess combined with substantial areas of gorse-covered heath and scrub to give the countryside a wild and untamed look, more akin to somewhere like Russia than to the normal patchwork-quilt mildness of southern England.

The Brecks (as people refer to the area) had a specialized flora and fauna, with scarce birds such as the stone curlew, but they were very rich in wildlife generally, Stephen explained to me, because the area had always consisted largely of aristocratic estates which, because of
the poor soils, were used for shooting rather than agriculture; they

had been managed historically to maximize the numbers of wild game. 'They've been managed almost like nature reserves,' he said, 'for deer, ducks or whatever, so there's a wide range of habitats and species, and not many people.'

On these big Norfolk estates, Stephen had followed his turtle dove study with a study of the grey partridge, Britain's most rapidly declining gamebird, so he knew the estates well and was welcome on them, and he had no doubt that in their midst he would be able to show me turtle doves (although I wanted to hear them as much as see them: I kept wondering, What was the voice of the turtle?). And the next morning he drove me out into Breckland in his Land Rover.

This was the day that stood out: the most splendid day of the whole spring. I loved the landscape at once. It was not the very wildest part of the Brecks – it was farmed – but the fields were interspersed with patches of rougher pasture, and there was none of the ruthlessly controlled feel of intensive agriculture. There were woods dotted around the horizon as in the background of an eighteenth-century landowner's portrait by Gainsborough, and the wildlife was, as Stephen had said, abundant everywhere – superabundant even, every field with its hares: no wonder Harriet was so fond of them. I had never seen anything like it in England; it made me think of an African game reserve.

But the true magnificence was in the day itself. Hot, clear, still, it did not really belong to spring, it was an interloper from mid-July, with unfettered sunlight poured upon the face of the earth until everything seemed to glow – most of all the may blossom, which turned the hedges into great white ribbons streaming across the land. In Britain, battered as it is by Atlantic depressions, there are only a handful of days like this each year, when the sky and the sun and the air combine in such poised perfection that you start to think that there must be something greater behind it all. That I should meet such a landscape at such a moment seemed to me a spectacularly fortunate combination. Whenever Stephen stopped the Land Rover **111** and we got out, we were showered with skylark song. 'Sometimes you can't hear yourself think, there's so many skylarks singing', he said.

His first stop, his first likely turtle-dove location, was the top of a slight hill that was covered in hawthorn scrub with a few tall trees; he told me how scrub was a key turtle-dove nesting habitat, just as Ian Swinney had said of the nightingale on Great Bookham Common. 'Most farms have taken out all their bits of scrub because of the need for more production,' he said. 'I mean, for most farmers, scrub is just rubbish, isn't it? But in this landscape there are these pockets of scrub everywhere you look.'

We began to look, and we began to listen. There was a pair of stone curlews, all knobbly knees and bug-eyes, in the next field, which soon flew off; larks were carolling invisibly above us; in the scrub, the falling cadences of willow warblers made a continuous chorus, silvery and sweet.

When I first heard it, I wasn't sure I was hearing it, until Stephen signalled to listen harder. It was a faint purring, *purr-purrrrrrrrrr*. Faint, but undeniably penetrative in the warm still air.

A pause. Then again: *purr-purrrrrrrrrr*.

'There it is,' said Stephen.

This was the voice of the turtle.

It was quite unlike the roo-cooing of wood pigeons or domestic pigeons: it was higher pitched, tenser, almost hypnotic. We scanned the trees to try to pinpoint its origin, and after a few seconds Stephen spotted the bird, silhouetted on a branch a good distance away. I couldn't pick out its colours, but as we were watching it took off on its display flight, soaring up and then gliding down in descending circles with its wings spread and its tail fanned out – a wedge-shaped black tail edged all around in white, clearly visible. It landed in a tree that was nearer, in the sun this time rather than silhouette, and I suddenly had a view of it: breathtakingly beautiful. The back was a sandy orange, scalloped with black spots, and it seemed to glow in the sunlight, while the breast was rose pink, with a black-and-

white mark on the neck which for some reason made me think of an army officer's collar badge. It was a bird of great elegance, definitely dove – if we employ our old linguistic prejudices – as opposed to pigeon. One wouldn't want to be fattist, but if you thought that the street pigeon tended to plumpness, and the wood pigeon – now, with warmer winters, one of our commonest birds – did a lot more than tend, you saw a bird which in its slender lines was much more pleasing to the eye: it was slight, almost gamine.

Yet it had not found fame from its appearance: it was the call which had made the impression on people, and had given the bird its name in many languages, with a *t* being used for the sound instead of the English *p*: *turr-turrrrrrrrrr*. It was not only *tur* in the original Hebrew, in the Song of Solomon: it was *turtur* in Latin, *tourterelle* in French, *tortola* in Spanish, *tortora* in Italian, *turteltaube* in German, *zomertortel* in Dutch, *tuturduva* in Swedish, and so on. What was it about the call? Why had the Song of Solomon poet singled it out?

Stephen and I began to talk about this after our bird flew and we drove over the Brecks looking for more, stopping every so often to listen, while the temperature began to rise into the high 70s, perhaps even touching 80, mid-May feeling like the peak of the summer. We saw bird life in profusion, from yellowhammers to shelducks – I marvelled at it – but not *Streptopelia turtur*, so Stephen decided to try another special spot a couple of miles away, a dewpond overlooked by an old willow tree in which the birds often sat and sang.

I asked him if he actually *liked* turtle doves, besides being an expert on them.

'They're fantastic birds,' he said at once. 'So beautiful, and now getting so rare. But then I'm captivated by the pigeons as a family.'

'Really?'

'It's very easy in Britain to think, "Oh pigeons, millions of them, they're just a pest," but if you go a bit deeper you find stunning species, threatened species . . . The dodo, that was a pigeon. Classic example of how man can obliterate a species. The passenger pigeon, in America, that was another. In the middle of the nineteenth century there were 5 billion of them; by 1914 it was extinct.'

113

We were sitting in the Land Rover with the windows down and the doors open to ease the heat, overlooking the dewpond; no sign of turtle doves as yet, but Stephen pointed out a pigeon-like bird which dropped down to the pond's edge to drink, softly and subtly plumaged: grey-blue with a hint of pink on the breast.

'There's another bird people think is just a pigeon, but is very beautiful,' he said. 'A stock dove. People don't even notice them, but they're a species I'm very aware of.'

As we waited, I asked him what he thought about the turtle dove's call.

He said, 'It's very unusual, isn't it? It's a bit like a grasshopper warbler. So unusual, it stands out.'

'But what is it that's special about it?'

Stephen thought and said, 'Well, it's a summer sound.'

'How d'you mean?'

'It's a long, hot summer's day call. I immediately associate it with long, hot summer days, when most things have gone quiet, and you hear that purring away. A sound that penetrates through the stillness, in the heat of the day.' And then he cried, 'There one goes, on cue!'

It floated through the air to us: *purr-purrrrrrrrrr*, and again: *purr-purrrrrrrrrr*, slight, soporific and dreamy, but carrying unfailingly through the baking heat.

I began to see. This was where it belonged, that call: on a day like this. This was what it was part of, at least for people. It was a true summer sound – the sort that sleepily nudges the ear, like the cries of distant bathers, or the hum of bees, or the purr of a lawnmower in the evening. Yet you heard it suddenly in the spring, when the winter was past, the rain was over and gone, the flowers had appeared on the earth, and the time of the singing of birds had come. When the voice of the turtle was heard in our land it was its promise that was special about it: it was full of the promise of summertime to come.

No wonder the Song of Solomon poet rejoiced when, on an April morning 3,000 years ago, he heard it drifting drowsily out of the vineyards and the olive groves: he heard a promise of lazy days

114

when it was too hot in the afternoon to do anything, and the grapes and the olives and the crops were ripening, and the mornings were crystal and the evenings were golden. No wonder he singled out the voice of the turtle: of all the spring-bringers, this was the one which promised everything. And in the Brecklands of Norfolk I understood that too, hearing the voice of summer with the may blossom all about me.

SEVEN

What's so Special about Swallows?

Swallow

Writing in Jerusalem, the Song of Solomon poet – perhaps King Solomon himself; perhaps another; perhaps even a woman, it's been suggested – chose the turtle dove. But in about 500 BC a vase painter in Athens was invoking the spirit of spring in a different way, with a different creature. His name was Euphronios, and he worked in a style which had just been developed known as red-figure, where the figures are pale-terracotta-coloured on a black background (earlier Greek vases were painted in black-figure style, where the colours are reversed).

On a small vase no more than 15 inches high – a pelike, which is an amphora-shaped container with open handles and a bulbous belly – Euphronios set down a scene which shows a bearded man, a younger man who is clean-shaven, and a boy. All three are looking upward and pointing, the bearded man twisting round in his seat to do so, and their pointing fingers combine with the inward slope of the vase's sides to draw the eye ineluctably towards a diminutive object just below the neck: it is a bird. Look closer, and the wing shape and sharply forked tail make its identity obvious. But putting the matter beyond doubt are comments in Greek script issuing from the characters' mouths. *'Idou chelidon'* – 'Look! A swallow!' – says the younger man. *'Ne ton Heraklea'* – 'Yes, by Heracles!' – exclaims the bearded man. *'Autei'* – 'There she is!' – cries the boy. And in the air about them floats the caption that draws the whole scene together and makes its point: *'Ear ede'* – 'Spring already!'

This tiny and enchanting drama, which now resides in the Hermitage in Leningrad but occasionally emerges for display in the outside world – it was shown at an exhibition at the Courtauld Institute in London in 2006 – illustrates unforgettably that, while the turtle dove may have symbolized the change of seasons for the Israelites, for the ancient Greeks this was signalled by another bird altogether, in a tradition which has flourished in western culture to this day.

There are only four references to the swallow in the Bible, and only one (Jeremiah 8:7) associates it with the coming of spring, but classical Greek literature is full of them, from Hesiod (active *c.* 700 BC) and the beginning of lyric poetry onward. In fact something about swallows seems to have appealed to the Greeks from the start of their civilization. The Minoans, predecessors of the classical age by more than a millennium, painted them on the walls of the houses at Akrotiri, on the volcanic Aegean island of Santorini (or Thera), before the settlement was consumed in the gigantic eruption in about 1600 BC which probably brought Minoan civilization to an end. The huge fall of ash preserved the frescoes at Akrotiri, just as it did in Pompeii, and over the last thirty years they have been uncovered: in one, swallows are flying about between lilies in a rocky landscape, and a pair of the birds are 'kissing', rising vertically towards each other and touching beaks with their tails outspread, in a quite stunning image (though what it may well represent is a parent bird feeding a fledgling).

The Greeks adored swallows. They had a 'swallow song', originating in Rhodes, which was sung by bands of children going from house to house at the beginning of spring and begging for treats in the name of the arriving bird, very much in the manner of Christmas **117** carollers: the young people carried a wooden swallow on the end of a staff, and the song was performed on 1 March in many parts of Greece until relatively recently.

Yet the symbolism of swallow and spring spread far beyond Hellas itself to cover the whole classical world: for the Romans too the bird was the season-switcher par excellence, and there are references to it as such in most of the major poets, including Virgil, Ovid and Horace, this last telling his billionaire backer Maecenas that he will return from the coast to see him in the spring, '*cum zephyris . . . et hirundine prima*' – 'with the west winds . . . and the first swallow'. The admonitory proverb which we may think of as particularly English was common even then to both cultures. In Greece they said, '*Mia chelidon ear ou poiei*', while in Rome it was '*Una hirundo non efficit ver*': one swallow doesn't make a spring.

The symbolism endured in later European culture. We may remember Shakespeare's lovely reference in *The Winter's Tale* to 'daffodils that come before the swallow dares', but the image was used continent-wide. The Victorian naturalist Charles Swainson, in his encyclopedic compendium *The Folk Lore and Provincial Names of British Birds*, published in 1886, lists pages of obscure traditions and old rhymes from various parts of France, Germany, Italy and Russia, as well as from Britain, associating the arrival of the bird with the coming of the new season (and with good fortune in general) and states as simple incontestable fact 'The swallow is universally considered the herald of spring and summer.'

But why? Nearly 200 species of birds arrive in Europe as the winter ends (more if you count those which don't cross the Sahara). What is it about this particular bundle of feathers which sets it apart and gives it pride of place? Why not the nightjar, the pied flycatcher or the yellow wagtail, all of which risk just as much on the odyssey from Africa, and bring their own distinctive appeal? Why not the hobby or the honey buzzard? Why not the wheatear? Why not the corncrake? Why should the status of spring-bringer supreme be accorded, down the centuries, to the swallow?

118

Seeking to get to the heart of it, I knew once again that only someone who knew the species profoundly could start to provide an answer, which was why on a warm, muggy day at the beginning of June I found myself in a swallow-adorned farmyard in a Nottinghamshire village with the British expert on the bird, Angela Turner.

It was a privilege to be with Angela with her enormous knowledge, lightly worn, but I am sure she would not mind me saying it was even more of a privilege to be close at hand with swallows. I had forgotten how exhilarating it was, just as you can forget how exhilarating it is to swim in the sea. The air seemed to be full of them. We were standing at the entrance to a big barn where they were nesting, and they were swooping around us, the curves and parabolas they were tracing so swift that your head had to move to follow them. Each was a long-tailed glossy dark-blue blur, hurtling past, and I found myself wishing that English had an intensified verb to describe what they were doing, as 'adore' is more intense than 'love', or 'slay' is more intense than 'kill'; I mean, if 'fly' was what blackbirds, robins and blue tits did, what was this higher version of the activity going on around us? Watching them was a pure, sweet pleasure sufficient unto itself, like smelling jasmine or tasting ripe pears. I felt I would happily pay for it – 'Watch The Swallows, £5' – and I started to realize the nature of their appeal, at the most simple level: it was visual. Nightingales, warblers and turtle doves all signalled the spring with their songs, but that was not the only way. These were creatures which did it for our eyes, with the sheer surpassing exuberance of their flight.

Yet there was clearly more to it than that, and Angela began to decode it for me, in an ecology masterclass in a farmyard. We had come to Barton in Fabis, a pretty pantile-roofed village in the flood plain of the river Trent just outside Nottingham, where she worked at her day job, as it were, as editor of the journal *Animal Behaviour*, based at Nottingham University. She had been studying swallows for thirty years, beginning with a doctorate at the University of Stirling in the late 1970s, after a zoology degree at London's Royal

Holloway College. In 1989 she wrote *A Handbook to the Swallows and Martins of the World*; in 1993 *The Swallow* (a short paperback); and in 2006 she produced *The Barn Swallow*, the first full-length study of the species in English for a well over a century, since *A Monograph of the Hirundinidae or Family of Swallows* was produced by Richard Bowdler Sharpe, a famous Victorian ornithologist in charge of the bird collections of the British Museum, between 1885 and 1894. Angela's own monograph documented recent discoveries about the swallow's way of life, some of which were remarkable, not to say startling.

But first a few biological basics. The swallow is one of a big family of streamlined songbirds, the hirundines, or the swallows and martins (from the Latin for swallow, *hirundo*), and all are aerial insectivores – that is, they make a living solely by catching flying insects. No nuts or seeds or worms for them. Angela's 1989 handbook recognizes seventy-five hirundine species, and the most widespread one is our own swallow, *Hirundo rustica*, which spans the globe and is increasingly referred to by the name used for it in the United States, the barn swallow (although I shall keep it simple).

In Europe, this bird is joined in its summer visits from Africa by four close relatives, the house martin, the sand martin, the crag martin and the red-rumped swallow, the last two being birds nesting mainly in the Mediterranean countries. But the swallow itself, the house martin (which has a navy blue back with a white rump) and the sand martin (which has a brown back and a brown chest band) cover the whole European continent, from Sicily right up to northern Norway.

Were these three species all in competition for the same haul of flying insects? No. They had evolved to occupy separate niches in the aerial ecosystem, so that there is enough food for them all. They divided the air, Angela explained to me, into layers. Swallows were at the bottom, sand martins were slightly higher up, and house martins were at the top. Swallows fed on the big, fast-flying insects found

near the ground, such as hoverflies buzzing in and out of flowers, bluebottles and house flies hanging around farmyard manure heaps, and horseflies and other biting insects which were pests of cattle. (That's why livestock farms were their favourite places). Sand martins and house martins both took much smaller, weaker-flying insects such as midges, small flies and aphids, found in the air at higher levels.

As the swallow had the most difficult prey to catch, it had evolved to be the fastest and most skilful flyer, and was a more determined and rapid mover through the air than either of the other two. This became quite obvious when you watched swallows and house martins in an area together, as Angela and I were doing now. The house martins from the village were not only higher up – they liked to fly over the tops of trees – but they spent much of their time gliding with outstretched wings, flap flap glide, flap flap glide, something the swallows did far less frequently. The swallows' flight seemed powered, as if they were highly tuned racing cars or jets, simply incapable of moving slowly.

So swallow flight was spectacular (chasing the big fast insects), and swallow flight was low (because the big fast insects were near the ground). The next key point was that swallow flight, when we encountered it, was usually very *close* to us. This was because the swallow, like the house martin (but unlike the sand martin), nested among people. Both species had adapted to human habitations in a way that very few others had managed to do, save the swift (of which more later), the starling and the house sparrow. They had done so because both had found substitutes in human structures for their original nesting habitats, which were caves (in the case of the swallow) and cliffs (in the case of the house martin). 'A swallow nesting in a barn thinks it's in a cave,' said Angela. 'A house martin thinks the wall of a house is a cliff.' (As sand martins nested in colonies in long burrows, they had been unable to adapt in a similar way, and were usually to be found in riverbanks or sand quarries.)

Nesting among us had always given the swallow singular status; for one's barn or shed or stable or outbuildings to be chosen by the birds as a breeding site had long seemed (to all but the most curmudgeonly) a **121** privilege, a blessing, a sign of good fortune. But what it meant in terms of our encounter with swallow behaviour was that wherever the birds were to be found, they seemed to be almost within touching distance, if ever we could reach out fast enough to touch them. Add to this one other point of swallow breeding biology. The birds needed to feed their chicks frequently, and so confined their insect-hunting to within a short distance of the nest – usually, said Angela, to within about 200 yards – so they were never away for more than a minute or two. This means that they were not only close; they were *constantly* close.

Put it all together. Ever-present; near; low; superfast. Here is the outline of the swallow experience, as we might say, for anyone lucky enough to meet with it. Occupying the ground-level insect-hunting niche as they did, *they were in our line of sight*. The sand martins were away feeding around their riverbank; the house martins were high overhead; but where swallows nested they were visibly and vividly present, and were the most spectacular flyers, and did their spectacular flying low down, and did it all around us, and did it constantly. No wonder the air around the barn seemed to be full of them. Out of their ecology, deconstructed for me by Angela, came this heart-stopping, unrivalled display.

None of Europe's other spring-bringers, for all their many attractions, quite did this; and there was a further factor bolstering the swallow's pre-eminence, which was its sheer physical beauty. It was not just the colours, lovely in themselves – the lustrous navy upper parts, the chestnut forehead and throat, the creamy breast – it was the stunning elegance of form, the streamlining of sharp wings and sleek body culminating in a forked tail so delicately elongated it seemed to be almost a fashion accessory, to be purely for show as much as for anything else – as indeed it was, Angela told me, in an even more revealing account of what being a swallow meant.

We had come to the far side of the village, to the home of a life-long Barton in Fabis inhabitant, Angela Plowright, whose father had **122** owned the farm where the swallows were nesting in the barn (it now belonged to a relative). This other Angela lived with her husband, Paul, and 13-year-old daughter, Harriet, in an old blacksmith's forge, and swallows had bred in its outbuildings, in either the shoeing shed, the wood shed or both, for all the twenty-five years she had occupied the property. So far this year the birds had not begun nesting, but they appeared to be engaged in the preliminaries in the wood shed, dashing in and out continually.

As we sat in the garden, myself and the two Angelas, relishing a spectacle no bird table could provide and talking about what it meant to have swallows on your property, we noticed a pair perched on the telephone wire by the gate: one with a longer tail than the other. It was a male and a female, Angela Turner pointed out.

'The males have the longer tails?' I asked.

'They do. But actually much longer than is necessary.'

'Why's that?'

'Well, swallows' long tails help them manoeuvre in flight, they help them change direction quickly when they're chasing insects. But the optimal length for foraging is actually the length of the female's tail.'

'So why do males have even longer tails?'

'Because female swallows prefer long-tailed males.'

I was intrigued. And Angela went on to explain that, in the fiercely competitive business of finding a mate, if you were a male swallow, possession of a very long tail – that is, one with noticeably elongated outer tail feathers, or streamers – was everything. 'It's showing the females that you're a good-quality male. It probably takes a lot of energy to grow a very long tail in the winter during the moulting period, and it impacts on your foraging.'

'You mean it makes it harder to forage?'

'Yes.'

'So, if you can catch insects even with a very long tail . . .'

'It's a sign that you're pretty successful. Whereas if you're a weak, sickly male, you can't grow it, and you wouldn't be able to feed adequately with it anyway, and you're stuck with a short tail.'

But was it a real sign of quality? It was, said Angela, and that was why female swallows preferred it. 'There's a lot of evidence to show that males with long tails are better. They have a more efficient immune system and they tend to live longer, they survive better over winter and on the migration route, and they tend to be the first ones back on the breeding grounds in the spring. They're also more resistant to parasites such as mites and things. Good qualities such as parasite resistance are heritable. So their sons will all have long tails and be healthy males who will live a long time and be successful.'

'Which is why the females want them to father their chicks?'

'That's right. The males come back first in the spring, and then the females come and look around and see who's got the longest tail. And it's not just the tail length, it's the symmetry [having the tail streamers of equal length]. Various experiments have shown that males with the longest and most symmetrical tails are most likely to get mates first.'

It seemed tough on the others, I thought. What happened to them? Angela explained that short-tailed males could take a long time to find a mate, or might even not find a mate at all. They were definitely second-class. 'The females that come back too late to find a long-tailed male, they just pair up with a short-tailed male, if that's all that's around.'

But then, she said, for the short-tailed ones it got even tougher. Because the long-tailed males came and cuckolded them.

Until twenty-five years ago, swallows were seen as another personification of conjugal fidelity, rather like turtle doves, not least as a nesting pair of the birds would constantly be seen swooping around together, the male attentively at the female's shoulder, considerately concerned for her welfare – or so it seemed. Then in 1984 the geneticist Sir Alec Jeffries at the University of Leicester discovered DNA fingerprinting, and the study of bird reproduction was turned upside down. Promiscuity, it was suddenly discovered, was everywhere.

As mentioned earlier, DNA fingerprinting may eventually show that fidelity in turtle doves is a myth. But it had already shown it – decisively – with swallows. The figures were extraordinary. 'About one-third of swallow chicks in a given nest are fathered by an extra-pair male, not by the male that's at the nest feeding them,' said Angela. 'DNA fingerprinting has shown us this. Extra-pair copulation is a normal part of swallow life.'

The long-tailed males, Angela said, got their own females on eggs, then went off and look for other females to mate with. 'And *these* will be the ones that didn't find a long-tailed male because they came in too late. They ended up with a shorter-tailed male, but they didn't *want* a shorter-tailed male to father their offspring, so they're happy to mate with a long-tailed male who just comes calling. They work for what they can get; but when offered something better, they take it.'

I asked Angela what view she took of the long-tailed males' behaviour. 'I take a purely scientific view,' she said. 'But don't just blame the males. The females are looking out for themselves as well. They don't go out and actually solicit the extra-pair copulations, but they will display to another male who comes into their territory, to show that they're receptive.'

It all meant that the old image of swallow fidelity was entirely illusory. What the seemingly caring and considerate male was doing while he is swooping alongside the female everywhere, in twosome togetherness like a Georgian couple out for a morning walk, was 'mate-guarding' – he was merely preventing other males from copulating with his partner at the vital time when she was fertile, before she had laid her eggs. Once she had, he was away. Angela said, 'As soon as he's got the female on eggs, the male will go off and find another female.'

'Sounds like a typical man to me,' said Angela Plowright, who had been listening, as fascinated as I was.

'Well, yes,' said Angela Turner, not entirely comfortable with anthropomorphic judgements. But then in spite of herself she said, 'Once, when I was ringing swallows, I came to a female that was incubating, and I had her off the nest just for a few minutes really. **125**

In that time, the male came back and flew around, couldn't see her, and came back a couple of minutes later with another female. He had found another female in just that time.'

A thought occurred to me. 'Is there any of this stuff in *A Monograph of the Hirundinidae or Family of Swallows* by Richard Bowdler Sharpe?'

'The book has next to nothing on behaviour and doesn't mention anything about monogamy or sexual habits,' Angela Turner said. 'It just classifies the various types of hirundines.' She grinned. 'Ornithologists in those days had no idea what birds got up to.'

'And when the male goes off,' said Angela Plowright, still concerned, 'does no one come and feed the poor old female on the nest?'

'With house martins the males help incubate, but swallows don't do that,' Angela Turner said.

'Somehow I thought they would be quite good parents,' the second Angela said, shaking her head, somewhat dismayed. 'People just go and have a bit on the side, eh? I didn't know any of that. Swallow affairs, basically. Well, well.'

She had loved her swallows for all the time she had lived in the old blacksmith's house, and I was keen to talk to her about the experience of being . . . what? The phrase that leaped to my mind was 'a swallow owner', like a dog owner, a cat owner or a car owner, all those categories that figure in consumer surveys; but of course, as she herself pointed out at once, there was no owning when it came to swallows. 'You can't pluck your swallows out of the air. You can't go down to a garden centre and get them. You don't choose to have them. They choose you.'

What was the phrase, then, for a person who had swallows nesting on their property? A swallow host, perhaps. How had she found being a swallow host?

'All these years, they've given me pleasure. It's that great feeling that summer's arrived, when you see your first one. They're such beautiful birds, wonderful in their livery, and so acrobatic, swooping, chattering around. They're a lot of fun. So are the house sparrows, but they're not such aerial acrobats.'

Yet they inspired more than just enjoyment, she said. 'When you think of the migration, what they've gone through . . . it makes you feel . . .'

'What?'

'Reverence, really. The huge trek they've been on, it makes you feel small. I'm always worried for them while they're lining up on the wires, and when they go, I really miss them, I really miss hearing their chattering sound. Then, come the next April, you hear them again and it lifts and cheers you up at once, and you feel so privileged that they've chosen you again. Such a privilege to have the birds nest so close to where you live, such beautiful birds You're always worried that they won't. But they always have, so far.'

Two of them flashed through the garden. She glanced up. 'These have been prospecting in the wood shed. Although they haven't started nesting yet.'

If they didn't?

'For the first time in twenty-five years? I would be mortified. I would also feel . . . I was letting them down in some way.' She sought the words. She said, 'They fly in . . . money can't buy them. Even if you built the best swallow habitat in the world, there's no guarantee they would use it.'

She looked around, at the garden, the house. 'That would be the most valuable thing about it for me. A lot of people might think, "Oh those bloody birds." An estate agent came to have a look and said, "You haven't got a garage. You've got these outbuildings – why don't you make them into a garage?" He couldn't see any of the charm. Just into floor space and how many bedrooms. I said to my husband, we would never buy anywhere to match this place. One of the things would be the swallows. How could we match the swallows?'

Have other people thought like this, I wondered, down the centuries: so loved the swallows that had blessed their dwellings, and **127** feared to lose them? They must have done, and in numbers, when so many more of us lived in villages and small settlements where the birds could abide. In our cities, we had forgotten now. But that was how they brought the spring: not by shooting past as some glimpse high in the sky, but by arriving at your home one April morning and proceeding to fill your air with flight, decorating your outside space more flamboyantly than any gardener ever could.

Trust the Greeks, I thought, to latch on to them first. Seeing as they latched on to poetry first, and theatre, and history, and politics, maybe swallows were a minor consideration in the great scheme of things, but the Greeks did get there first as well. Their love of beauty led them there, and, thinking of their love of male beauty in particular, I fancied they would find nothing shocking or even inappropriate in the idea of the male with the longest tail carrying all before him: it would seem like the natural order of things. But it was more than beauty itself, great though that was, which appealed to them so deeply. It was beauty which was given to us intimately – miraculously appearing on the doorstep.

Nearly 4,000 years ago they spotted that swallows were special; and they were right.

EIGHT

Understatement on a Fence Post

Spotted Flycatcher

To go from the swallow to the spotted flycatcher was on the face of it like going from satin to sackcloth, from brilliance to deepest obscurity. Here was a bird without a hint of glamour or glory about it, a bird which carries off first prize for being inconspicuous: it was, in birderspeak, a classic LBJ – a little brown job. The contrast between its featureless feathers and the swallow's smart outfit of navy, chestnut and cream was acute: it wasn't even spotted, for heaven's sake, the palish breast under the plain grey-brown back being streaked or striated. (At least the scientific name got it right: *Muscicapa striata*.) And it was modest not only in size and appearance: the song was one of the weakest of all the passerines, just a thin, reedy, barely audible *tseep*.

The cultural contrast with the swallow, too, could not be greater. Its unexceptional characteristics meant the spotted flycatcher had been resolutely ignored by European folklore, literature and art. While swallows and other species, from peacocks to hoopoes, sweep and strut through the mosaics and frescoes of the ancient world, and then the paintings of later centuries, no spotted flycatcher observes them **129** from the side of the scene; no *Madonna of the Flycatcher* flowed from the brush of Raphael, as did a *Madonna of the Goldfinch*. No legends grew up around the bird: Greece and Rome, the Bible, and medieval, Renaissance and Romantic literature ignored it equally. It did not even seem to have had a standardized name in English until the late seventeenth century. Gilbert White, as ever, was the exception, and wrote about it on several occasions, but otherwise the spotted flycatcher was a bird, as used to be said of a virginal woman, without a past.

Yet it had a present. People really liked it. I liked it, and I knew that I would include it in any quest to seek out the spring-bringers, even at the expense of migrants which were ostensibly much more attractive, such as the redstart or the yellow wagtail. It was partly the vigorous life so manifest in this little brown job – not just the fact that it trekked to Europe every May from right down at the bottom of Africa, but the way it went about its daily business of catching flies and other aerial insects. It was a 'sit-and-wait predator'. In contrast with species such as warblers, which would actively search out insect prey all the time, gleaning small caterpillars from leaves, say, *Muscicapa striata* would perch on a fence post, a gate, a branch, a TV aerial or even a tombstone, and patiently wait to see what flying insects would happen along, occasionally flicking its tail or its wings the while. And then it would sally. Oh yes. It would sally forth.

A good word, 'sally', both as a noun and as a verb (via the Old French, from the Latin *salire*, 'to leap'). It perfectly describes the springing bound with which the bird took off from its perch after a passing butterfly, and the swift, sometimes acrobatic, pursuit which followed, until it returned almost immediately to its station, with prey or without, and resumed its upright watchful stance. The stance was very characteristic, as was the head of the bird, which seemed just a little too big for its body: it was the size it was to accommodate a bill with a considerable gape, so that large insects could be captured the more easily.

These sallies were enchanting. I had loved watching them since I was a boy. They were small explosions, moments of sudden drama, and in essence it was the same drama as a peregrine falcon stooping on a pigeon, except that it was miniaturized, and the prey was the size of your fingernail – a fly or a moth or a bee or a wasp. (They dealt with bees and wasps by battering them on the perch to get rid of the sting, and they could perfectly distinguish them from hoverflies, which to human eyes look almost identical, but are stingless – and the flycatchers swallowed these whole). What somehow made the performance most attractive was the fact that the sally was a discrete, closed episode, and after every one the flycatcher flew back to its perch and stood to attention. Almost all small birds that fly from a perch fly away, but this one came straight back, and the out-and-return loop – as if the bird were on a piece of elastic – made for a jizz so distinctive it could be spotted from hundreds of yards away.

Sitting-and-waiting as they did, they tended to have a small hunting range, usually near the nest, so if you found one, you would be able to watch it for hours. But more importantly from their point of view, it meant that they were crucially dependent on a stream of aerial insects passing their perch. This was why they were generally one of the last of the spring-bringers to return, arriving in late May, when the warmer weather tended to assure an insect supply. Though originally a bird of hedges, orchards and woodland edges, an increasingly favoured habitat was gardens, especially the big overgrown gardens to be found in country houses and villages, and a favourite nesting place was a creeper or vine on a wall, sometimes right next to a door. So, although spotted flycatchers were not automatically thought of as birds associated with human settlements, like swallows, house martins, swifts, sparrows and starlings, in fact their connection with people was often intimate and strong.

This was impressed upon me when, in trying to work out how I might find my way to the essence of the bird, I discovered the only book which seemed to have been written about it. There was no scientific monograph, and I initially thought there was nothing whatsoever, until in a chance conversation at the BTO someone said, 'You know, there is a book called *The Spotted What!?*'

I said, 'The spotted *what?*'

'No, that's it. *The Spotted What!?* That's the name of the book.'

It took a week to track down, via the publisher. A major imprint – Oxford, Cambridge, Harvard University Press – it was not: it turned out to be Plum Tree Publishing, of Worcester, and when the £5.99 volume eventually slid from its envelope into my eagerly waiting hands I found it to be a slim softback of 80 pages, with, in place of the elegant image normally gracing a bird monograph, a cartoon on the front cover.

Somewhat garish, this showed a red-faced, balding and white-moustached old buffer, the elderly proprietor of what was obviously a country house – it had a large stone entrance portico, and a stag's head and a fox's head could be seen behind him on the wall of the hall – answering the door to a diffident-looking chap wearing binoculars and carrying a curious pole-like device, which close inspection revealed to be a mirror on the end of a stick. In the mirror, the reflection of birds could be seen; they were chicks in a nest atop the portico, from which an adult bird was flying away. The old buffer was clad in a luxurious dressing gown with a towel over his arm, and was dripping from the bath or shower he had obviously just left to answer the door to his importunate caller. He held a bulldog by the collar, and, in response to what was clearly a question from the mirror-on-a-stick man, was barking, 'The Spotted What!?' with an exclamation as well as a question mark.

What on earth was this about? It quickly became clear. The scene encapsulated the event at the heart of the publication – the education and mobilization of a rural community in support of a bird – and I realized with delight as I began to read the book that it was largely concerned with the very aspect of the spotted flycatcher I was concerned with myself, which was the human response to it.

It had been published in 2005. The author, John Clarke, a nature conservation adviser working for an estate in Worcestershire, had organized a spotted-flycatcher survey in some of his local villages, invited people to join in, and then been overwhelmed by the scale of the reaction. A large number of householders eventually came together in what he referred to as his 'flycatcher gang' to help find, monitor and protect the nesting birds in the village gardens. The book was an account of four years of the survey, during which time 182 nests were located at a total of 72 properties, although 120 households actively supported the study, which provided scientific data about the birds' breeding status and success, and a fund of lively anecdotes about their behaviour.

But even more interesting to me was the behaviour of the members of the flycatcher gang. Some were ignorant of the bird at first ('The spotted what?' was heard more than once), but virtually everyone contacted became enthusiastic when they realized the birds were nesting among them; and, once involved, they became deeply involved, putting themselves out, changing their domestic plans to facilitate nesting and help it succeed, and becoming desperately upset – tears were common – when, as frequently happened, breeding failed, often as a result of predation by animals such as grey squirrels, or by other birds such as jackdaws and magpies.

I was intrigued by the intensity of the response which John Clarke's initiative had triggered. Just what was it about these creatures which so touched the men and women who became engaged with them? My initial thought, bizarre as it may seem, was that it was something to do with the way the birds behaved and Englishness. I at once dismissed it as ridiculous, as imagination running riot, not least because *Muscicapa striata* spent the best part of nine months of the year in tropical Africa. Yet the thought persisted, for these people, it should be said right away – and John Clarke freely admitted it – were a particular group. (The cover cartoon spelled it out.) The villages they lived in, which he did not identify, were very beautiful, epitomizing an old-fashioned idea of England; each had its medieval church surrounded by cottages of honey-coloured Cotswold stone, half-timbered or thatched houses, or really substantial properties with names (as he said himself) like The Manor, The Court, The Vicarage or The Grange – all with extensive gardens. He admitted that these were also, now, costly places **133** to live in, so the householders were generally (although not exclusively) very affluent. But, more than that, they themselves tended to epitomize an old-fashioned idea of formal Englishness: like the buffer with the bulldog, they could have been characters from a Miss Marple story. Some were retired business people; others, retired officers from the services. Not a few were old English county families from what used to be thought of as the natural upper tier of society. Like all who are affluent, they were concerned for their privacy and their security, and one of John Clarke's more notable achievements was to win their trust to such an extent that they allowed him unfettered access to their properties at any time of the day, to wander around looking for flycatcher nests in the creepers on their house walls with his mirror on a stick (which was a quick and painless way of checking whether a high or difficult-to-access nest held eggs or chicks).

In return for their trust, he kept the names of their villages confidential in his book. Well, I agreed I would do so too, but I will be more precise than he was about their location. When I discovered it, I was once more forcefully struck with the idea of Englishness, for they were situated in what had a better claim to be thought of as the heart of England than anywhere else in the land.

If the line of the Cotswolds is a rampart along the horizon, Bredon Hill is an outlying fort in front. It stands out solidly above the orchards and meadows of the flood plain of the Avon – Shakespeare's Avon – flowing to join the Severn at Tewkesbury. Although Bredon Hill is in Worcestershire, A. E. Housman made it the theme of one of the best-loved poems of his archetypal English collection *A Shropshire Lad*, a slight but deeply melancholy song of a love affair cut short by death, usually known by its opening lines:

> *In summertime on Bredon*
> *The bells they sound so clear.*

Several English composers had been inspired by it – Ralph Vaughan
134 Williams, George Butterworth, Julius Harrison – and looking across

to Bredon from a hotel terrace high on the Malvern Hills, where I sat with a cup of coffee, it occurred to me that if you had to locate the geographical centre of what used to be thought of as traditional Englishness, it would be here somewhere, with the Cotswolds and their perfect honey-stone villages as a backdrop, Shakespeare's Stratford just over the horizon, the landscapes beloved by Elgar – the most English composer of all – on your left hand and behind you, and in front of you the Vale of Evesham, the Garden of England, with Housman's Bredon rising from its centre. That was the very heart of it.

The villages where John Clarke had carried out his flycatcher survey were at the base of Bredon Hill, ringing it like a necklace; and when I visited them I was even more intrigued by the idea, which continued in my mind despite its improbability, that there might be something in some of the people who lived here in the heart of England which responded to this bird in a particular way.

John too lived in one of the villages, with his wife, Pamela, in a cottage encased in flowers down a shady and sleepy lane near the church. At 66 he was a tall and imposing man – he was 6 foot 3 – but he had been very ill the previous year and was still struggling to some extent with poor health, although he readily agreed to see me, in late May, and to take me out on flycatcher patrol, and perhaps to talk to some of his flycatcher gang.

He was not himself from the heart of England, not a Worcestershire native. He had grown up in Farmoor, near Oxford, and for seventeen unfulfilling years had worked for what was then the motor industry giant British Leyland. He said, 'I was a very bad engineer in a very bad company.' Always interested in the natural world, his life changed when he met Pamela, and an enlightened and nature-minded land-owner offered the couple a cottage in return for work integrating forestry, farming and wildlife on his estate; they slipped sideways into conservation. In the mid-1980s they moved to Colonsay in the Hebrides, but in 1994 they returned to conservation work on **135** the estate, which was on the Bredon Hill slopes; John managed the estate's conservation trust.

He had appreciated spotted flycatchers since 1979, when, taking his first steps in wildlife activism, as it were, he put up a series of nest boxes in woods near his home. In a small copse he fastened a half coconut shell in the ivy around a tree, his nest box manual having informed him it would attract pied wagtails. A pair of flycatchers moved in at once, and he had been charmed by the birds ever since (and very aware of coconut shells' attractive powers).

The reaction to the survey he began in 2001 had taken him completely by surprise. Its initial aim was to gauge the numbers of birds in four villages in which, John had noticed, they were quietly nesting. Beginning with a few posters in local shops and articles in four parish magazines, the survey had mushroomed, taking in more and more people, until what he termed 'the tidal wave of support' dragged in five extra villages and he was averaging more than 220 nest visits in the three-month breeding season, which he found hard to cope with. John was the surveyor; the flycatcher gang were his eyes and ears. From mid-May they were all on the lookout, and if a bird was spotted flicking from pillar to post around a particular property, he would get a phone call and set out with his stick-mirror to locate the nest, record the number of eggs, go back to record the number of chicks, and eventually record the number of chicks which fledged (successfully left the nest) – or record the failure of the whole enterprise, which was a regular event.

He had got to know the flycatchers' habits very well, especially the way they would immediately start to build another nest elsewhere if the original one failed, and so you had to be quick to locate it, as once it was complete the birds would be much less visible. Sometimes they had to try three times before they succeeded. Grey-squirrel predation was a major problem – and the adult birds would attack the squirrels fiercely, sometimes driving them off, sometimes in vain – but the chicks could also die from hypothermia or starvation if the English summer turned cold and wet and insects were not on the wing for more than a day or so. 'Sometimes you can find dead babies below the nest,' he said. 'I've found different sizes. They throw them out as they die. It's awful.'

Over the course of the survey, about thirty pairs of flycatchers had nested on average each year in the nine villages; when I visited John on 27 May he and his watchers had, up to that point, located only thirteen pairs (one of them building in the jasmine by John's own back door – in a coconut shell) and he took me out with him on his daily inspection round to try to locate more. It was quite a sight: the Flycatcher Man, as he was known locally, striding into property after property, gated, gabled, ivied, half-timbered, thatched, gravel-drived, with his mirror on a stick peering into things – the affluent house-holder's nightmare, unless you knew who he was, and everyone did.

We began with his own village, something of a flycatcher hotspot, and to my great pleasure we caught sight of the birds at once on phone wires and fence posts, sitting and watching, sometimes flick-ing their tails. It struck me forcefully, now I was concentrating on them, just how unobtrusive they were, and how easily they could be missed. In John's van, we moved on to neighbouring villages and found a number of nests, several of which had been predated, in one case the whole nest having been pulled out and cast on the ground, but we also found healthy clutches of eggs in creepers and climbing roses, tiny greyish-blue spheres spotted reddish-brown. And then we met his flycatcher gang – or rather two members of it, who had agreed to speak to me.

What was remarkable about the two women I talked to – both well-dressed county ladies, you might say – was that, while John had told me lots about the spotted flycatcher's ecology and its behaviour, they both, quite independently, wanted to talk about something subtly different: its character.

Can a bird have a character? Is not the idea just anthropo-morphic, sentimental nonsense? Many scientists might well tell you so. But science doesn't account for all of life, and people can sometimes apprehend the phenomena of the world, or other living creatures, in non-rational ways which can capture profound truths. At any event, these women had perceived something in the behaviour of this bird which had moved them not just to an aesthetic, but to a moral approbation.

They thought there was something admirable about it.

Mary Doney, whose husband designed showjumping courses, lived in a sizeable house in a neighbouring village; their extensive and gorgeous gardens – the herbaceous borders were quite spectacular – had at one time held four pairs of the birds. 'I think they're wonderful,' she said. 'There's something so personable about them. They're individuals. You can almost tell the difference if you've got more than one pair. For many years we've had them nesting outside the front door, which is lovely, just lovely. And when the young are hatched and they're hunting so much, you're almost part of the territory they're working around. You can be having a barbecue and they're around you and they take not a blind bit of notice of you. They take no notice of you whatsoever.'

One particular incident had impressed itself upon her – when a bird flew into the house and became trapped. She said, 'A flycatcher flew in – one of the pair at the front door. It was in the front hall, just sitting there. Sitting on a flower vase, looking out of the window. It was so calm, it was unbelievable.

'My first concern was that it shouldn't go into the rest of the house or we would never get it, so I shut all the doors except for the front door. It went on to the sofa and just watched me, and eventually it just flew out and went back to the nest.

'When it happens with other birds – swallows, blue tits, pigeons, crows – they panic. But the flycatcher knew it was in the wrong place, and it knew where it wanted to be. Yet it didn't flinch. It was amazing.'

Ros Long, who worked for one of the local landed estates, lived in a small but very pretty cottage in a village in the opposite direction, and was concerned that no flycatchers had yet arrived. She was missing the *tseep*. 'I have not seen one or heard that lovely sound,' she said. 'It's quite high-pitched, almost like a little squeak, and they flick when they do it. When I was in my cottage at the top of the village, it was one of the sounds of spring. How wonderful! They've arrived! You could see them in the trees, going backwards and forwards. I haven't seen a single one this year.' She turned to John. 'So how many pairs have you got?'

He said, 'Thirteen, so far.'

'But it was thirty something once, wasn't it?'

'It got up to forty pairs one year.'

Ros said, 'I've been keeping my eyes open and especially my ears. The top of the village is a very special place, with the stream. I've spread the word, encouraged other people. I'm very flycatcher-aware.' She said to me, 'I thought it was a really interesting thing to do, just individuals going round, not massed groups of twitchers – people just going round quietly, with a mirror on the end of a long pole, doing their very best not to disturb the birds at all. Though they're not easily disturbed by human beings: they tend to operate round, say, a lunch party in a garden. Yet one worries about them so terribly because they are so vulnerable to the weather, and every loss now is a disaster.'

But they always carried on building, I said.

'Yes,' she said. 'It just carries on, very elegantly, and then it goes back. It doesn't do anything in a hurry. It doesn't harm any other bird. It's not aggressive. It's very independent. It just comes here, and if people mess about with it, it will move on and try again. It's a stoic sort of bird.'

Was it her worst year for flycatchers, I asked her.

'Oh gosh, yes,' she said.

What exactly was it that they had seen, both these women, which struck such a chord with them? They had clearly sensed a quality in this most unspectacular bird which was special, which was not to be found in other birds they saw daily in their manicured gardens – robins or blackbirds, sparrows or starlings. And as I thought hard about it, the word which came into my mind was 'understatement'. **139**

In formal terms, of course, understatement is merely a literary technique, the opposite of hyperbole: the deliberate underplaying or undervaluing of something, often with ironic intent. But in English society it has been much more powerful than that: it has been the dialect of the elite, finding its most vivid expression in the higher Civil Service. Not having been born into the elite, I did not grow up speaking it; but, being interested in language, when I came across it I set about learning it, with as much keenness as I had done with Welsh as a teenager.

I met it when I began to shadow closely a major government department, the Department of the Environment, as environment correspondent of *The Times* in 1989, and found myself becoming engrossed with the culture of Whitehall, which was famously secretive and not easy for journalists to penetrate. In sharp contrast to journalistic practice in Brussels or Washington, say, the idea that you might ring an official directly was greeted with horror, and if you did so you would be referred in short order to the press office. But if you were taking a genuine, long-term and serious interest in policy, senior officials might gradually become willing to engage with you, if only to prevent misunderstandings in your reporting. And if you asked them out to lunch they might accept and, finding that their confidences were not betrayed, would later pass on the word that you were OK to lunch with, and other invitations would be accepted, and slowly it became possible to tunnel into that world and comprehend its very particular ethos.

For example, I knew from the outset that if you became the head of a ministry, the Permanent Secretary, Grade 1, you could expect a K – a knighthood. You would be dubbed Sir William Buggins (and, perhaps even more important for your domestic happiness, your wife would become Lady Buggins, and could give one in the eye to her sister). But I learned subtler things. If you only made it to Deputy Secretary, Grade 2, you could in the normal course of events expect a CB – you would be made a Companion of the Order of the Bath, an

order of chivalry which dates back to 1725, and you would become

William Buggins, CB, and although your friends and neighbours might not appreciate the significance of this, your colleagues most certainly would. And even if you only made it to Undersecretary, Grade 3, you would then automatically qualify for *Who's Who*. There would be an entry for Buggins, William, Undersecretary, Dept of Widgets, and you could list your family and your education and your interests in gardening and the theatre, and you could have hours of delicious pleasure when the rest of the family had gone to sleep leafing through the volume (which of course you had bought), confirming and reconfirming what you knew anyway: that no one else at all from your class at school was in the great, fat, fabulous red tome, and you were Something and they were all most assuredly Nothing.

But it was the language of the officials which really fascinated me. It was in effect a private code, which I thought of as 'dynamic understatement'. It seemed to have arisen as a means of expressing strong disagreement between gentlemen without lapsing into incivility, so certain words which might appear anodyne became charged with sharper meaning. A good example would be 'unhelpful'. This expressed dissatisfaction, irritation, even real anger, in the guise of a sort of rueful acceptance. I once left a senior official momentarily lost for words when he said to me, 'That piece you wrote was unhelpful,' and I replied, 'It wasn't meant to be helpful. It was meant to be true.' It was as if, by being literal, I had switched languages.

This drawing the sting of expression extended to both praise and blame. I marvelled at the form of words used for the highest acclaim, which in the outside world would be 'fantastic', 'tremendous', 'sensational', 'wonderful', 'world-beating', whatever. In Whitehall it was: 'rather impressive'. Once, and only once, I had 'rather impressive' used of something I had written; I glowed for weeks afterwards. Conversely, the means of expressing the harshest criticism was similarly defanged: an action which the world at large might consider 'catastrophic', 'terrible', 'appalling', 'disgusting', 'the pits' would in Whitehall be termed 'unfortunate', or on very rare occasions indeed, **141** 'most unfortunate'. Again, once and only once, I saw 'most unfortunate' used directly to an individual about his conduct, and it sent a chill down my spine: I never wanted it used of me.

The underplaying made the true meaning all the more forceful. And such a technique needn't involve just individual words: it could be used to construct complex expressions involving whole sentences. The supreme example in my own experience was the resignation speech of Sir Geoffrey Howe in the House of Commons on 13 November 1990, which led directly to the end of Margaret Thatcher's premiership. Howe had been Thatcher's Chancellor, Foreign Secretary and deputy, but he had fallen out with her decisively over the issue of European Monetary Union, and in his speech he not only revealed the extent of their previous disagreements, he ended with a clarion call for her political assassination, in final words of enormous power. What he *meant* by them was for Thatcher to be directly, and indeed precipitously, thrown out of office. What he actually *said* was 'The time has come for others to consider their own response to the tragic conflict of loyalties with which I have myself wrestled for perhaps too long.' You could hear a pin drop in the chamber. Everyone looked at Thatcher. And then everyone turned and looked at Michael Heseltine, the long-haired assassin-in-waiting, now being summoned to wield the dagger – which he duly did.

Yet understatement was in essence far more than a rhetorical trick, or even a private language. It was an attitude of mind. It was a rejection of that favourite pastime of the sixties, letting it all hang out, and an affirmation that there was something inelegant – no, that's not quite it: perhaps we should say, something debasing – about expression of feeling which was not subject to control, or at least to a controlling intelligence. Understatement was the manifestation of that intelligence. It involved subtlety. Above all, it involved self-possession. It grew out of the English ruling elite's long-standing belief in self-possession, now thought by many to have been fatally caricatured as 'maintaining a stiff upper lip'.

Yet caricature is an undependable window through which to view the world, as one person's lampoon is another person's set of values; and the values which understatement might be said to represent were still held by some of those, for example, who lived in the villages at the foot of Bredon Hill. It seemed to me that understatement was one way of describing what Mary Doney and Ros Long found to admire in this most unshowy and unspectacular of birds, this little brown job with no colour in its plumage and no song to speak of, so inconspicuous that European culture had passed it by completely, but which nevertheless to them had something unusual, something you could describe only as character. It did not make a fuss. It did not shout and scream. It did not panic like other birds did, Mary Doney said. After loss, it just got on with things, said Ros Long. It was a stoic sort of bird.

Self-possession on a perch. Understatement on a fence post. Is it all fanciful? Had they really perceived something about the spotted flycatcher which got to the heart of it? Something which ecology could not account for? Who can say? All that was certain was that their admiration was sincere, and it was ardent.

After leaving Ros Long's cottage we continued on John Clarke's nest inspections, a garden here, a house wall there, and after about twenty minutes his mobile phone rang. I heard him say, 'Hello? Really? Really? Great. That's great.'

He turned to me. 'That was Ros.'

'And?'

'A few minutes after we left, she looked out of the window, and there was a flycatcher on the wire opposite her cottage.'

'Is she pleased?'

'She's overjoyed.'

NINE

The Wildness Within

Swift

When, in the darkness, the black curtain at last is lifted, the sight is entrancing. But first there is the climb.

It begins at an iron-bound wooden door in the cloistered marble gallery, quite unmarked, with nothing to show it leads anywhere. Once opened, the door reveals a narrow stone spiral staircase which rises in the medieval fashion, clockwise – so the defender could have his sword arm free – for fifty-one steps. Up you puff, into a room lit by arched windows. There follows another spiral stair – of metal this one: thirty-seven steps – which winds up into the dark, so that when you get off it the only light is from a glowing red bulb and you have to wait for half a minute to get your night vision. A ladder is next. Its twenty nearly vertical rungs have to be taken gingerly in the blackness, as does the business of easing yourself off it on to the wooden landing. Then there is the final ladder of another dozen steps – gently does it – and you are there, in the top of the tower.

Around you, on each of the four sides, you can just make out sets of double boxes, set at chest height into the sloping roof, with **144** a faint aura of daylight around them. You are bidden, by torchlight, to approach. A hand reaches for what you suddenly realize is a piece of black cloth on the end of a box, acting as a curtain, and as it is raised you see a piece of glass, and behind it, a foot from your face, a swift.

The most mysterious of all our birds. The most unapproachable, because the most aerial – never hopping, perching, or pecking; never coming for scattered crumbs; never on the lawn, the branch or the bird table, let alone the upside-down coconut; not even on the telephone wire; inhabiting only the sky. A young swift will launch itself from its nest and spend the next three years on the wing – that is, *all* of the next three years, until it begins to try its hand at breeding, during which time it may make two journeys from Europe to Africa and back, without touching down. The sky is where it lives. The sky is where it hunts and feeds. The sky is where it bathes. The sky is where it sleeps – far, far above the surface of the earth – and the sky is where it *mates*. The only thing a swift cannot do in the sky is nest, and it spends precious little of its time doing that, perhaps as little as ten weeks in a given year. The rest of the time it exists above us, in the way we once thought only angels did. It forces us to rethink radically our idea of what habitat means, for though there may be scrub for warblers, forest for woodpeckers, farmland for turtle doves, and marshes for snipe, for the swift there is only the air – only racing through the high, unbounded air. Until here, perfectly still and quiet in an intimate closeness you could not have dreamed of, sitting on the nest.

How elegant the curve of the head and the streamlined dark-brown body, the white throat patch visible as she – I assume it's she, but it could be the male – squints up at our presence beyond the protecting glass. Can she see us clearly in our darkness? Can she see us at all? We can certainly see her, in a way that swifts are rarely if ever seen, the arrowhead silhouette in the summer blue here in tranquil repose. It's like glimpsing a completely new bird.

Edward Mayer comes up behind me, peers over my shoulder, and whispers, 'Gorgeous.'

We had come on a pilgrimage, Edward and I, to the nearest thing to a temple to swifts: the tower of the Oxford University Museum of Natural History. For sixty years, these most mercurial of all the spring-bringers have not only bred inside the top of the tower, in substantial numbers, encouraged by the provision of nest boxes, but have also been watched and studied intensely there, and eventually understood – in a way which, rather than lessening their mystery, has only reinforced it.

Edward knew the tower well. He had climbed it before. In fact he had been to the haunts of swifts in many parts of Europe, for he loved them to such an extent that he gave them most of his time. A retired senior civil servant – he had been manager of the Tate Gallery – he was now a champion of swifts and their welfare, constantly campaigning for the recognition of a great threat to the birds in Britain: the modernization of buildings, which was depriving them of nesting places all across the country. As the focus of his activities he ran a website, 'London's Swifts', but much of his time was spent raising awareness of swifts and their needs, and offering advice on swift conservation to local authorities, private companies, individuals and indeed anyone who wanted it. His speciality was swift boxes: self-contained nesting boxes which could be easily fixed to a building. Edward had managed to get them installed across the capital in sites that range from London Zoo to the 800-foot tower at Canary Wharf, Europe's tallest office block. (They have started to nest at the zoo, but not yet at the Wharf.)

In seeking to understand swifts myself, I found myself coming across Edward's name more and more, and eventually I went to see him. At 60, he was a jovial man, and someone in whom, as I discovered when we began to talk at length, boyish enthusiasms had never died, one of which I found I had shared: plane-spotting. Does any boy enjoy this now? Hard to believe. Virtual planes, perhaps. But in the 1950s, when we grew up, many pimply youths were plane-spotters, buying their annual editions of *The Observer's Book of Aircraft*, and, especially, building their plastic scale models of fighters and bombers from the Second World War and beyond, made by a company called Airfix. And sitting in Edward's flat in West Hampstead, discussing in detail swift nest boxes and building regulations and suchlike, I was suddenly and bizarrely having an Airfix conversation – the first for many decades.

'So did you make the Hurricane?' I found myself asking.

'Yes.'

'And the Spitfire?'

'Yes. And I also made the Supermarine floatplane, which won the Schneider Trophy.'

'. . . and was of course the Spitfire's predecessor? Designed by R. J. Mitchell?'

'That's right.'

'And did you make the Messerschmitt Me 109?'

'Yes.'

'And the Me 110?'

'No. Although I did make the Focke-Wulf FW 190.'

'But you didn't make the Me 110?' (Sensing superiority!)

'No.'

'You see, that was twin-engined. With twin tails. That was hard.'

Edward said, 'Well, the one that completely defeated me was the Supermarine Walrus. Biplane flying boat. You had to mount the single engine between the wings in the middle of a sort of X-strut. That was absolutely impossible.'

I began to realize that the plane-spotter in Edward had never died. He went to air shows, and had just had his first gliding lesson ('That was absolutely smashing'), and it was clear that not a little of his empathy with swifts was based on their outstanding aerial abilities. 'It's the aerobatics: you don't see any other birds do that. OK, you sometimes see starlings do that clouds-of-starlings thing, but swifts! It's like "The sky is ours! We're going to zoom all around it!" It's a bit like the Red Arrows plus.'

It was true: the swift had evolved the potentialities of flight to greater extremes than any other species – so far, in fact, that not **147** much was left of its legs, which were short and weak, so that young swifts which suffered the misfortune of falling to earth found it impossible to take off again. Even adults found it hard. The swift's scientific name was *Apus*, Latinized Greek, meaning 'without feet'. Useless on the ground; but its mastery of the air made it absorbing to observe, perpetually jinking and dodging, making lighting-fast course corrections as it scooped up 'aerial plankton', tiny flying or floating insects and spiders, in its gaping mouth: as many as 20,000 creatures in a day. Aeronautics researchers had recently discovered that the swift's long, narrow sickle-shaped wings were constantly 'morphed' in flight, changed in shape from extended to swept-back positions, like some military jets, to enhance flight performance and perform turns with what might seem an impossibly high G-load (and Edward knew all about G-load).

The bird had not been completely cold-shouldered by western culture like the spotted flycatcher and the warblers, but it had long been characterized as one of the swallow's poor relations, as a second-class hirundine. That was understandable. It looked and behaved like a member of the swallow family: it was the same general shape (if larger), it rapidly pursued aerial insects all day long just as the hirundines did; and like them it had adapted to human habitations, exchanging its original nesting places in tree and rock crevices for the greater security from predators to be found in the roofs of buildings.

Yet the resemblances were merely the result of convergent evolution, of natural selection producing similar appearance and behaviour in species which shared the same ecological niche, as high-speed aerial insectivores, but were entirely unrelated. On the evolutionary tree, the swift did not even belong to the great order of the Passeriformes, the passerines or songbirds, in which the hirundines roosted, along with more than half of all bird species. Instead it belonged to a quite separate order of its own, the Apodiformes, literally the footless ones, and its closest relatives were the hummingbirds.

People had no idea about that, of course, until very recently. All they could go on was appearances, and thus the swift was lumped in with the hirundines and more or less ignored. Why? Well, it was streamlined and handsome, but it was not pretty, like the swallows and martins. Furthermore it was . . . strange. It was dark-coloured – so sooty-brown as to be almost black – and a widespread old English name for the swift was 'devil birds'; John Clare called it the 'deviling'. Not hard to understand why – little black birds flying around looked little black devils flying out of people's mouths in medieval illustrations. It was less familiar than the hirundines, because it was harder to see – it flew higher, and its nest was much less accessible. Swallows' nests were on the beam of a barn; house martins' nests were on the outside wall of a house: swifts' nests were inside the house itself, on the beam the roof rafters rested on, or under the roof tiles. So, although swifts too were among our principal spring-bringers, flying out of southern Africa to cavort in the sky all over Europe, their specialness was not recognized before the twentieth century – except by one man, and of course it was Gilbert White.

The curate of Selborne had an eye which missed nothing in his parish or further afield, and he cast it over *Apus apus* with surprisingly fruitful results. Among his many casual and mixed observations of the natural world, he wrote four much longer essays on what he considered the four hirundine species – house martin, swallow, sand martin and swift. These 'monographies', as he termed them – nowadays they would be scientific papers – are very impressive, and the one on the swift is the most impressive of all, considering that White only had his unaided eyes for observation. What he managed to do, in a letter to Daines Barrington dated 28 November 1774, was to set down for the first time most of the breeding biology of the bird. He realized it is quite different from the 'other' hirundines, being single-brooded instead of double-brooded – it had only one brood of chicks per summer, whereas the swallows and its cousins had two. It had only two eggs, while the others had four or five. He realized that it gathered tiny insects together into a 'bolus', a nut-sized ball in its throat, which provided a very long lasting meal for chicks, and so they did not need to be fed nearly so often as swallow chicks, and the swift could forage much further afield (the reason why it could successfully live in cities).

These major differences and others – not least the anatomy of its feet – caused White to suspect that the swift was indeed not a hirundine, and he mentioned the supposition to this effect of 'a discerning naturalist', identified as 'John Antony Scopoli of Carniola, MD'. That was pretty clever. But most astonishing of all was Gilbert White's realization that the swift mated on the wing, behaviour still to this day found in no other bird, and the excitement and pride in his discovery comes through even in his measured prose.

'As I have regarded these amusive birds with no small attention,' he wrote, 'if I should advance something new and peculiar with respect to them, and different from all other birds, I might perhaps be credited; especially as my assertion is the result of many years exact observation.'

He went on, 'The fact that I would advance is, that swifts *tread*, or copulate, on the wing; and I would wish any nice observer, that is startled by this supposition, to use his own eyes, and I think he will soon be convinced.'

He explained, 'If any person would watch these birds of a fine morning in *May*, as they are sailing round at a great height from the ground, he would see, every now and then, one drop on the back of another, and both of them sink down together for many fathoms with a loud piercing shriek. This I take to be the juncture where the business of generation is carrying on.'

Modern observation has confirmed what White recorded. It was an amazing discovery, and today a scientific paper based on it would feature prominently in *Nature* or *Science* and be reported all over the world. Yet, even though *The Natural History of Selborne* was a colossal success, it did not succeed in bringing swifts out of the obscurity in which they had always languished, because White's 'monography' was subsumed in the rest of the book, which was seen by its readership as a whole as picturesque rather than scientific – an evocation

150   of the timeless values of the eighteenth-century countryside.

To come into the light, to get their due, swifts had to wait another 180 years, for someone every bit as original a thinker about birds as the Hampshire parson.

David Lack, the man who gave Reg Moreau his job at the Edward Grey Institute in Oxford, was a reserved, bespectacled don who played a crucial role in the key mid-twentieth-century development of zoology in general and ornithology in particular – the move away from classification and anatomy, to the study of the behaviour of living creatures in the wild. The son of a prominent ear, nose and throat surgeon in London, Lack was a passionate boyhood birdwatcher at Gresham's School in Norfolk (where he was three years behind W. H. Auden), although he qualified in zoology at Cambridge without head-turning distinction. However, after graduating, he got a job as a teacher at Dartington Hall, the Devon school then famous for its progressive education values, and with the ample free time he was allowed he began a detailed study of the behaviour of robins, which was to result in one of the classic natural-history books of the twentieth century. The first detailed behavioural study of a British bird, *The Life of the Robin*, published in 1943, turned a popular image on its head. It showed that the Christmas-card image of the friendly little red-breasted chappie symbolizing seasonal peace and goodwill is an illusion: robins are among the most aggressive and belligerent of all songbirds and will instantly attack any intruding robins on their territories, which they will defend if necessary to the death.

The Life of the Robin, with other work including studies of the finches on the Galapagos islands which had first prompted Charles Darwin to think about natural selection, established Lack's credentials as a brilliant scientific ornithologist, and after the war, which he spent doing secret work on radar, he was a natural choice as the new director of the EGI, which he ran from 1945 till his death in 1973.

Looking for research subjects for himself and his students, Lack decided against his beloved robins, because their nests were too hard to find, and instead began intensive work on the great tits of **151**

Wytham Woods, the lovely stretch of ancient woodland just to the west of Oxford; the tits would readily use nest boxes, and so could easily be studied. (The study has now continued without interruption for more than sixty years.) But great tits nest in April, and he realized there was another bird, which nested in June, which could also be studied without work overlapping, and that was the swift. He began work on a colony of swifts in an Oxfordshire village, where the birds were nesting in the roofs of the cottages.

All the time, swifts were cruising in numbers around Oxford itself; they were nesting in the tower of the University Museum of Natural History. This building, sometimes described as a cross between a French Renaissance chateau and a medieval cathedral, was one of the monuments of Victorian Gothic, and had been the scene of one of the most famous scientific disputes in history. On 30 June 1860, just after it had opened, it hosted the argument over evolution between the Bishop of Oxford, Samuel Wilberforce, and Thomas Henry Huxley, Darwin's defender. *The Origin of Species* had been published six months earlier, with its implication – devastating for Christianity – that man had not been created by God, but had naturally evolved from the apes. At the meeting of the British Association for the Advancement of Science in which the debate took place, Soapy Sam (as he was known) reportedly asked Huxley whether it was on his mother's or his father's side that he was descended from an ape, and Darwin's bulldog (as Huxley was nicknamed) replied that he would rather be descended from an ape than from a clergyman who used authority to stifle truth. (The exact words are disputed.)

Eighty-five years later, swifts were nesting in numbers in the ventilator shafts of the tower of the museum, which was empty; but it did not occur to David Lack that they might be accessible, until in 1946 he paid a visit to the Swiss village of Oltingen, in the Jura, where the schoolmaster, Emil Weitnauer, had fitted swift nest boxes to his house. The birds had occupied the boxes, and Weitnauer had begun to study them. Lack realized that this could be done in the museum tower, and by the spring of 1948 nest boxes had been installed in the forty ventilator shafts; when the swifts returned for the summer, they began to use them.

For the next eight years Lack spent his summer months climbing up a series of wooden ladders, the longest being nearly 30 feet, into the hot, pitch-dark, cramped wooden womb above the museum, observing the swifts at close quarters, on their nests, through the glass backs of their boxes. Talk about patience. But patience which paid off. The result was *Swifts in a Tower*, published in 1956, the first study of the birds since Gilbert White 182 years earlier, and the first proper monograph on the species.

An admired critical success, the book did for even more for the swift than *The Life of The Robin* had done for its subject: it put the bird firmly on the cultural map. In admirably lucid English, Lack spelled out for the first time quite how extraordinary were the lives that swifts led, firstly in the cramped and unseen confinement of the nest. He revealed, for example, that adults would have fights over nest-box occupation, two birds gripping each other with their feet for sometimes five hours or even longer, and that the young would prepare for their first flight by raising themselves on their wings in exercises which were for all the world like press-ups. Some of the most startling discoveries concerned the way the birds were adapted to cope with periods of cold and wet when insects were scarce: the adults could delay their egg-laying, while the chicks could drop their body temperature and go into a torpid state in which they could survive without food for as long as three days. In similar circumstances chicks of other species – spotted flycatchers would be a prime example – would quickly succumb.

Secondly, Lack made crystal clear the swift's complete aerial mastery, stressing that this had 'not received the admiration that it deserves'. He set out in full the bird's astonishing life in the sky, confirming its ability to copulate in the air and showing that many swifts, especially young non-breeders, flew higher as dusk fell and spent the night on the wing, almost certainly sleeping in the air

153

(breeding adults spent the night in the nest). One of his most startling revelations was of the way swifts interacted with weather systems – to avoid storms they would fly around depressions in temporary journeys which could be as long as 1,000 miles – while one of the most moving was his account of the nestling's first flight, its abrupt, no-second-chance launch into life in the ether. It simply dropped into space from the nest, and was then on its own – but hesitation was often considerable on the part of a chick whose 'only direct knowledge of the outside world has been what it can see by looking out of the entrance hole'. The humming and hawing could last for hours, till at last it plucked up courage and fell out into its future. 'There is', wrote Lack, 'perhaps no more striking instance in birds of the efficiency of inborn behaviour, than this of the young swift, which after its cramped life in the nest enters on its aerial life in a very wide world, feeds itself, finds some way of spending the night and migrates, all without help or guidance from its parents.'

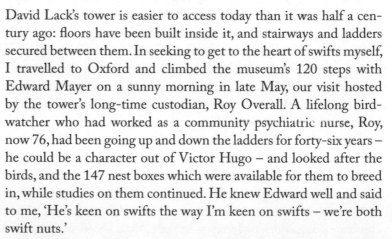

David Lack's tower is easier to access today than it was half a century ago: floors have been built inside it, and stairways and ladders secured between them. In seeking to get to the heart of swifts myself, I travelled to Oxford and climbed the museum's 120 steps with Edward Mayer on a sunny morning in late May, our visit hosted by the tower's long-time custodian, Roy Overall. A lifelong bird-watcher who had worked as a community psychiatric nurse, Roy, now 76, had been going up and down the ladders for forty-six years – he could be a character out of Victor Hugo – and looked after the birds, and the 147 nest boxes which were available for them to breed in, while studies on them continued. He knew Edward well and said to me, 'He's keen on swifts the way I'm keen on swifts – we're both swift nuts.'

And certainly visiting the tower is memorable and gets you close

to swifts in a way that is probably impossible anywhere else, at least in Britain. The nest boxes, haloed in the blackness with a thin thread of daylight, were not all occupied, so every time Roy lifted one of the screening cloth curtains there was a tingle of expectancy: sometimes there was just emptiness behind the glass plate, sometimes there was a single white, thumbnail-sized egg on the makeshift heap of aerial detritus that passes for a swift nest (and occasionally two), and sometimes there was a bird, a brooding bird, its dark elegance torchlit and present before you in startling intimacy.

But somehow the closeness didn't contain what I was looking for. I was seeking what it was that made swifts special to people now, and I was vaguely aware that this was . . . modern, in some way. Alone among the spring-bringers, swifts seemed to have an appeal which was relatively recent. It was partly that *Swifts in a Tower* changed things. It brought them into the public mind, giving them a fresh identity to replace the rusty folklore of devil birds; it let writers as well as scientists look at them anew, and allowed them to become the focus of growing interest, as the understanding of their mysterious life on the wing only invested them with more mystery. Edward with his conservation campaigns (and there were other swift enthusiasts like him) was a part of this process, it seemed to me; but what was at the heart of their appeal? What was it that struck a chord with people today, which yesterday failed to resonate? I began to understand only after receiving the invitation to a screaming party.

Being only a couple of miles north of the centre of London, Upper Holloway, N19, can properly be termed inner city, but, although not that far from parts of the capital which might justifiably be called deprived, its own situation is more fortunate. The solid Victorian houses of its quiet streets are much sought-after by middle-class families happy to raise their children in distinctly urban surroundings – families who, though affluent, would often be left-wing or at **155** least decisively liberal, in the manner of those from its better-known neighbour suburb of Islington, whose most famous resident (until moving on to grander things) was Tony Blair.

Upper Holloway's most famous resident is a character from a Victorian comic novel: Mr Pooter, the hero, or rather anti-hero, of George and Weedon Grossmith's *The Diary of a Nobody*. Charles Pooter, lower-middle-class clerk in the City of the late 1880s, is a figure slight and inconsequential in every way but one: his own estimation of himself. His innocent inflation of his own significance, his melodramatic recording of his trifling conflicts with tradesmen, neighbours and friends – virtually all of which he loses – have given him immortality and provided a word to the language: Pooterish (occasionally applied to Tony Blair's predecessor, John Major).

Naively pompous though he is, we are drawn to Mr Pooter because he is also good-hearted, honest and, above all, respectable. Admiration for Victorian respectability might have vanished many years ago, but there remains, as John Betjeman pointed out, something touching about the unthinking upright decency of Charles and his dear wife, Carrie, as they live out their uneventful lives (sometimes with their disreputable son, Lupin, in tow) in The Laurels, Brickfield Terrace, a street which has been plausibly identified with the real Tavistock Terrace, running off the Holloway Road. Even today some Pooterish respectability seems to cling to Upper Holloway – racy suburb it is not – and the thought occurred to me, What would the Pooters think, were they to see us now, sitting in the garden of a house barely three streets away from Tavistock Terrace, waiting for a screaming party to start? Not entirely decent, would they think? Perhaps even unseemly?

But, Charles and Carrie, we were not devotees of Arthur Janov and his primal therapy, the four of us sipping our wine in the balmy dusk: we were not about to join together in a primal scream. We were not even about to just let it all go vocally, as Dory Previn was doing in her seventies song, 'Twenty-Mile Zone', provoking her arrest by the police, who accused her of screaming in her car, alone, in a speed-restricted area. It was not us who would be doing the screaming. Swifts would be doing the screaming.

It was sometime after the visit to the Oxford tower; it was high summer, and here close to the heart of London we were waiting to witness what of all the extraordinary behaviour of *Apus apus* was the most extraordinary example of all. For on warm evenings like this one the birds gather in parties of perhaps a dozen – a typical number in Britain, though often many more in continental Europe, where populations are larger – to perform what amounts to a ritualistic tribal dance in the air.

It consists of a wild and seemingly ecstatic chase which brings them low down, almost to the ground, as they tear around the boundaries of their territory screeching frantically as they fly. The coming-together of these screaming parties, as they are known, is clearly a form of joint display and may be a behavioural mechanism for strengthening the social bonds of the colonies in which swifts habitually nest, with the birds seeming to be exhilarated by the ritual. What is certain is that it is just as exhilarating for the human observer caught up in the middle of it, surrounded by creatures possessed by a riotous, almost lunatic, flying frenzy which is doubled in its effect by their wild cries.

We were waiting for one such, the four of us in the garden, because for the previous few days it had been happening nightly around where we were sitting, around the Upper Holloway house belonging to my work colleague Jeremy Laurance and his wife, Angela. Jeremy had become so taken with the performance that he had been coming in to work in the morning full of it, as if he had been to a moving concert or a gripping play, reporting, 'The swifts were amazing last night!' And, knowing of my interest, Jeremy and Angela had invited me to the party, and I had brought Edward Mayer with me.

When we arrived just after eight and they installed us under the apple tree with a bottle of Pinot Grigio and a bowl of olives, there **157** were no swifts to be seen, but Jeremy laughed. 'Don't worry,' he said. 'It takes place between 8.45 and 9.15.' And, at ease in the large, green, bourgeois oasis which the garden formed with the gardens of neighbouring Victorian houses, we fell to talking about birds in cities, and swifts in particular.

'As we've shifted from country to town, we've become more aware of swifts,' said Edward. 'It started with the Romans. When the Romans put up their first buildings in Britain, they created ideal swift nesting places. And the Romans today are still using the same Roman roof tiles that they used then.'

'Really?'

'The swifts can get under these and nest on the beams below, so if you go to Rome now and go the Spanish Steps at dusk, you get a couple of thousand swifts screaming around you. We stayed in this Landmark Trust flat above the Keats Museum on the Spanish Steps, and we were in the top floor, and there were swifts nesting above us in our roof. So places like Rome and Madrid and Nice and Barcelona have huge numbers of swifts, and that's part of their atmosphere, part of their charm.'

I remarked that central London is not over-furnished with wild birds compared to many cities of continental Europe.

'The other night,' said Edward, 'we went to an open air play in Westminster Abbey. *She Stoops to Conquer*. It was in Dean's Yard. I made a note of the birds. There was a blackbird, a woodpigeon, and two blue tits. Oh yes, and a gull flying over. But recently we were in Salamanca, and there were things hopping all over the place – black redstarts, blackcaps, serins, white storks on the church buildings, all sorts of things right in the centre. We saw a peregrine attack a black kite and force it to drop its prey, and then dive after it – right in the centre of Salamanca. So yes, London's pretty poor, and the swifts are one of the best things we have.'

The birds had first made an impact on him, he said, when he was a small boy in Southampton. 'We had a house near the common, and I used to lie on the kitchen table with my head up, watching and listening to them screaming around. I would have been about 5. Even then I thought they were like no other birds. Most birds fly from A to B in a straight line, or hop around on the ground feeding. But swifts were instant drama.'

While he was talking, something had caught my eye: a flock of birds moving steadily towards us, and I pointed, and everyone looked, and we realized what they were in the same moment as they flew past. 'Starlings,' said Edward. 'Really boring flyers. Just travelling from A to B. It's as dull as watching commuters.'

I finally caught sight of what we were waiting for at 8.20: they were high up, tiny arrowheads swirling in a spiral like a cloud of gnats, black against the evening sky's fading duck-egg blue. 'There they are!' we shouted, and from then on we looked only upward. They seemed to disappear and reappear in different places, tumbling and wheeling, as if the gnat cloud were being blown about the heavens, and they seemed to be getting lower, then they seemed to be getting higher again, and the first pass – in the sense of the pass of a bomber over a target – came suddenly, at 8.30. Two birds appeared out of nowhere and dived screaming past the tops of the poplar trees at the end of the garden before pulling up steeply and parting, and I found myself shouting, 'Yes!' with Jeremy exclaiming, 'Fabulous!'

We were on our feet then, and on tenterhooks, and for several minutes nothing happened, as if the first two birds had been on reconnaissance – although we noticed that the full flock, which seemed to be about twenty strong, was much lower, circling us at a distance then coming in closer, and we could hear their screams. And then at 8.45, just as Jeremy had said, with the shadows lengthening and the yellowing sky in the west hung with small high clouds washed pink by the setting sun, it began. It was like an air raid. The military metaphors seemed unavoidable. It was like being on an airfield which was being bombed and strafed by enemy planes, as parties of birds peeled off from their circling and rocketed down towards us, through the gardens, around the trees, dispensing screams instead of **159** ordnance, dropping their vocal bombs, firing their vocal cannon, and the boyhood plane-spotter in me soared to the surface and the word that came with it was '*Weeeeeeowww!*'

We were cheering. The air show. Schoolboys watching jet fighters.

Weeeeeeowww!

'See the turns!' cried Edward. 'See the turns! You could never do the turns they're doing as a plane without falling out of the sky! They use leading-edge vortex technology' – I swear he shouted that – 'which is used by F-16s, look at that one!'

Weeeaarreeeowww!

'They turn on a penny! Look, it's just reversed its direction, forward now, now going back again. The main thing is the turns. They can turn much more quickly and sharply than any aircraft can. Look at them!'

Jeremy, though, saw something else as they chased each other around the house and came shrieking through the garden almost at head height. 'I just love them screaming round the place,' he murmured, watching admiringly, 'just going hell for leather. It's about them being together and chasing each other and yelling. You know what it is? It's kids.'

'Kids?'

'It's the exuberance of kids. When kids are happy they just tear round the house, their delight just bursts out of them, their delight at life. They're just like kids that are so happy to be alive.'

Edward saw F-16s. Jeremy saw children. And, as the screeching reached its climax, I saw something different again: I saw the wildness within.

We like to think of ourselves as rational creatures, but it is only half the truth. We have the faculty of self-control, but we also have the capacity to abandon it quite utterly; and to be reminded of that, to be jolted into the realization that we sometimes cannot rule our very selves, is not only unnerving, it holds a thrill, a forbidden thrill. **160** For, even though the wildness within us must be kept in check, for us to be able to live together, it has a claim on us that ultimately will not be denied.

The most disturbing of all the Greek tragedies gets to grips with this: *The Bacchae* of Euripides. It was Euripides' last play, written about 407 BC, when he had left Athens to retreat to the mountains of Macedon, a couple of years before the Athenians were finally crushed by the Spartans in the Peloponnesian War, and it cannot be read without disquiet: who knows what personal circumstances informed its frightening feel? It tells the story of the young god Dionysus, deity of wine and also of self-abandonment, arriving in the city of Thebes, where his cousin Pentheus is the ruler. Dionysus seeks to have his cult accepted in Thebes, and has driven the women of the city (who includes Pentheus' mother) into an ecstatic frenzy on the mountains; Pentheus, a believer in order and reason, forcefully seeks to put a stop to it all. But Dionysus tricks Pentheus into witnessing the wild behaviour of the women, by playing on his own hidden but powerful curiosity to see it; and the women discover him, and tear him to pieces.

In the bleakest way possible Euripides is underlining that the non-rational side of human beings cannot be completely suppressed, dangerous though it may be: any attempt at outright subdual will meet with disaster. Sooner or later it will out, because it is part of who we are: it was Pentheus's own desires which led him to his death. It is part of our animal nature, the wildness; and to me, in the screaming party in Pooterland, the swifts were making it manifest.

This, I thought, is what has drawn people to these birds in recent times: this seemingly ecstatic abandonment, found nowhere else in the natural world, which crowns all their mystery, and which echoes something deep in ourselves. For if past ages knew only imperfectly how to look beneath the surface of humankind, we have concentrated our gaze there, and have become comfortable with whatever may burst out.

Certainly, recent writers have been very taken by swifts in manic mode, a prime example being Ted Hughes in his much-praised and much-quoted poem 'Swifts', published in *Season Songs* (1976):

Fifteenth of May. Cherry blossom. The swifts
Materialize at the tip of a long scream
Of needle. 'Look! They're back! Look!' And they're gone
On a steep

Controlled scream of skid . . .

while Richard Mabey wrote longer but just as vivid prose descriptions of screaming parties in his 2005 book about his recovery from illness, *Nature Cure*. For Hughes and Mabey, and other recent writers, the frantic airborne chase puts the seal on the swift's special nature, and thus the bird is even more welcome as a spring-bringer, when it is suddenly appears overhead. Hughes writes:

They've made it again,
Which means the globe's still working, the Creation's
Still waking refreshed, our summer's
Still all to come –

But that evening in Upper Holloway, in Jeremy and Angela's garden, the summer was well advanced; the day's end was drawing on; and, as suddenly as it had begun, the show put on by the visiting troupe from Africa was coming to an end. We watched a bird hurtle towards the bottom of a neighbouring roof and disappear: there was the nesting site. We watched through binoculars and saw another one follow, appearing to shoot in like an arrow, without pausing, and then two more – they were the breeding birds of the flock – and then, when we turned and looked up, the others, the young non-breeders, had gone.

All of them.

Silence now.

The sky was empty – empty of the life which minutes earlier had so animated it; filled only with the blazing glow of the dying light.

TEN

The Wandering Voice

Cuckoo

I sought them all the spring and half the summer, the migrant birds; across the countryside and even in the cities I sought to find their essence and their worth to us, and when the essence became clear, so did the worth, it seemed to me, so did what they meant to us, why they moved us, and what they added to our lives – in every case but one.

The cuckoo was different. The essence of the cuckoo was not what touched our hearts. It was a paradox, bizarre: what moved us about the bird was simply an add-on, an accident of nature that could have taken a myriad different forms, and yet it moved us – certainly it moved many people – more than anything else among the spring-bringers.

But the essence, no. In sharp contrast to the others, like the swallow and the turtle dove, in contrast to them all, really, the cuckoo's essence, when eventually I came to understand it, had nothing about it of the beautiful. That's not to say that it wasn't absolutely riveting, but 'beauty' was not a word it prompted in your mind, any more than did the cuckoo's appearance, although you wouldn't call it **163** unsightly. It was curious, more than anything else: a bluish-grey bird of model-aircraft size with long wings and a long tail, and the general appearance (with its rapid flight) of trying to be a hawk, but not quite succeeding. This had been noticed for thousands of years, and the first thing Aristotle reported about it in *The History of Animals* was the rumour that it actually was a hawk which was transformed into a cuckoo state at certain seasons of the year.

Very few people in modern urbanized Britain seemed to know any more what a cuckoo looked like, although most knew the key facts about it: its two-note call was a signal of spring, and it laid its eggs and had its chicks raised in the nests of other bird species (it was a brood parasite, to use the technical term). These two entirely different aspects of its ecology had generated two entirely separate streams of folklore and literature which were implicitly contradictory – how can the bird celebrated as the herald of spring at one moment be reviled as a byword for deception the next? – but such are our abilities to compartmentalize our brains that we seem to have lived cheerfully with both.

Both aspects had been known and commented upon for thousands of years. If we are surprised that the ancients knew so much about birds, without the benefit of binoculars, guidebooks or TV documentaries, we should simply remember how close to the natural world they lived, 'even inside the city states', as John Pollard wrote in his *Birds in Greek Life and Myth*. 'Kites and ravens robbed the sacrifices, nightingales sang in the woods of Colonus, a mile from the centre of Athens, dazzlingly-hued bee-caters flitted up and down the banks of the Cephisus [a river outside Athens] while hoopoes fanned their crests in the local parks and gardens.' Cuckoos were mentioned as harbingers of spring by Hesiod, the earliest Greek poet apart from Homer, in about 700 BC, and by the time we reach Aristotle, nearly 400 years later, their egg-laying in the nests of other species is extensively documented.

The bird in question is the European or common cuckoo, *Cuculus* **164** *canorus*, one of the most widespread birds in all of Eurasia, breeding right across the connected continents from Ireland to China and Japan. It is one of two cuckoos in western Europe, the other being the great spotted cuckoo of the Mediterranean basin, which breeds irregularly from Spain through France and Italy to Turkey, and is also a brood parasite (this one specializing in laying its eggs in magpies' nests; boy, do the magpies hate it). But parasitism is by no means the rule: there are 140 cuckoo species in the world, and only 57 farm out their child care, as it were. For example, American cuckoos – the black-billed and the yellow-billed cuckoos – are not parasitic, the role of nest intruder being taken in America by another group, the cowbirds.

With *Cuculus canorus*, however, it would be fair to say that parasitism is at the centre of things, and in Europe this has exercised a morbid fascination down the centuries, both in the detail of its operation and in the moral lessons which could be drawn therefrom. In *The Parliament of Fowls* Chaucer refers to 'the cukkow ever unkynde' ('unkynde' here meaning 'unnatural') while 400 years later Gilbert White was livid: 'This proceeding of the cuckoo, of dropping its eggs as it were by chance, is such a monstrous outrage on maternal affection, one of the first great dictates of nature, and such a violence on instinct, that, had it only been related of a bird in the *Brazils* or *Peru*, it would never have merited our belief.' And of course the bird gave its name to a man whose own domestic nest has been violated – a cuckold.

The evidence for its deviant behaviour was all too obvious in the countryside in which most people then lived – the gripping sight of a small songbird sweating to feed a fat cuckoo chick many times its size, with its own young nowhere to be seen. Shakespeare, supreme observer of the natural world, makes telling use of this as an image in *King Lear*, when the Fool says to Lear, warning him of the predatory nature of his daughters:

> *For you know, nuncle,*
> *The hedge-sparrow fed the cuckoo so long*
> *That it had it head bit off by it young*

165

Hedge-sparrows (which we now call by their older name, dunnocks, as they are not true sparrows) are a frequent host species for the cuckoo in Britain, and have often been seen reaching so far down a giant cuckoo chick's gaping throat to feed it that their heads do indeed disappear (although they are not actually bitten off) – something Shakespeare may well have observed for himself.

The mechanism of how the cuckoo chick ended up as the sole beneficiary of its foster-parents' feeding was much longer in being unravelled. Aristotle gave several theories, including the cuckoo parents killing the hosts' young or eggs, the host parents themselves killing their own young or eggs, or the growing young cuckoo outcompeting its foster siblings. The astonishing truth – that the tiny cuckoo chick, soon after hatching, naked and blind, forcibly ejects the rival eggs or chicks or both from the nest, by manoeuvring them on to a hollow in its back and heaving them over the side – was finally discovered in 1787 by Edward Jenner, the country doctor from Gloucestershire now remembered as the pioneer of vaccination. Jenner, professional medical man and amateur ornithologist, discovered in 1796 that inoculation with cowpox gives immunity to the much more virulent smallpox, and won lasting fame; but his earlier discovery about the cuckoo, based on careful observation, was just as remarkable a finding, if one of less practical use to mankind – so remarkable, in fact, that the Royal Society at first refused to publish the paper in which he put it forward. (It was published the following year, and created a sensation.)

It was another century and more before the next astonishing aspects of the cuckoo's lifestyle were elucidated: how the bird got its egg into the nest of a host species, and how it fooled the host into thinking the egg was one of its own so it would brood it and hatch it out. More than 120 different songbirds have been identified as common cuckoo hosts, although a very much smaller number – from 15 to 20 – tend to be used regularly, and in Britain 5 species account for 90 per cent of all nests parasitized: the dunnock, meadow pipit, reed warbler, robin and pied wagtail.

The strangest fact which needed to be accounted for was that the egg of the cuckoo closely resembled the eggs of the host, whatever it was. This had first been reported in the eighteenth century, but was not generally believed. You have to admit it's pretty unlikely: for a cuckoo's egg to be just like the host's, from the greenish blotched egg of the reed warbler, to the brownish blotched egg of the meadow pipit, or even the brilliant blue in the case of a bird like the redstart – how on earth would a female cuckoo manage that? Could she switch egg types, egg patterns, egg colours at will? However, in the late nineteenth century two egg-collecting German ornithologists, Eduard Baldamus and Eugene Rey, showed that it was true, and offered an explanation – female cuckoos each specialized in parasitizing one particular host species, for which their eggs were a good match, and would normally lay only in those species' nests. It was almost as if they were subspecies themselves – reed warbler cuckoos, meadow-pipit cuckoos, and so on. (We now know that this is indeed the case, and there are different races of cuckoos – the technical term is gentes, singular gens – which parasitize one host species exclusively, and this trait is passed on down the female line.)

This was first confirmed decisively, with much more besides, in the 1920s by a wealthy British businessman with a passion for birds (but even more for collecting their eggs), Edgar Chance. Chance is one of the more extravagant characters in the history of British ornithology. The parallels with Eliot Howard at first sight seem uncanny – both were millionaire Birmingham industrialists (Chance was director of a glass firm) who made major contributions to ornithology as amateurs, working in the Worcestershire countryside, at the same time. Yet Chance was a far brasher type than the discoverer of territory in bird life, who was reticent and withdrawn. Chance had something of the adventurer about him, almost the buccaneer: for his fieldwork at Pound Green Common in the Wyre Forest, where from 1918 to 1925, with a group of helpers, he closely studied a small population of cuckoos, he would turn up in his Rolls-Royce.

He had found the site on egging expeditions. Luckily for natural history, his original and greedy project, of collecting cuckoo's eggs on a world-beating scale, metamorphosed into something of real scientific significance. Chance found that although locally there were several other potential host species, such as tree pipits and yellowhammers, the cuckoos of Pound Green Common laid virtually exclusively in meadow pipits' nests; and so keen, detailed and continuous was his observation that over three summers he worked out when they would lay (just after the pipits had started a clutch) and at what time of day (in the middle of the afternoon). This was all new to science. By 1921 he thought he could predict the time and place of a cuckoo laying; he set up hides on the common, hired a cameraman from the Commercial and Educational Film Co., and was rewarded with some of the most remarkable and dramatic wildlife pictures ever taken – the first views of a cuckoo depositing its egg in the nest of its host.

Chance at once turned this into a commercial documentary called *The Cuckoo's Secret* (which makes for terrific viewing, even now) and it was accompanied by a book of the same name, in which he noisily blew his own trumpet. My own copy, a first edition from 1922, has a printed appeal for further information about good cuckoo sites pasted on to the flyleaf; it begins, 'The phenomenal success of my film of *The Cuckoo's Secret* . . .' The preface is panting just behind, and opens thus:

> The claim made by the title of this book is based upon the fact that never before in the history of ornithology has any observer been able to foretell the time, place and circumstance of the laying of a Cuckoo's egg, and thus designedly to witness the act itself. It will be evident to readers of this book that without the necessary preparation which foreknowledge alone can make possible, all purely casual observations of the deposition of Cuckoos' eggs must lack the precision of detail which is essential to accurate knowledge, and which my system has secured.

Braggadocio, certainly; yet it was no more than the truth. Like Eliot Howard, Chance the amateur had secured a wonderful natural-history scoop, which offered substantial advances in scientific knowledge, not least of which was the discovery of the true manner of the cuckoo's egg-depositing. This had previously been the subject of a peculiarly persistent myth: that the bird laid its egg on the ground and took it to the host's nest in its bill. Cuckoos had been seen in flight carrying eggs in their bills, and the supposition had taken hold. It can even be found in the fount of Edwardian wisdom, the celebrated and revered eleventh edition of *Encyclopædia Britannica*, published in 1910–11, where the 3,300-word article on the cuckoo, authoritative in tone and written a few years earlier by the greatest of the Victorian ornithologists, Alfred Newton of the University of Cambridge, not only repeats the myth, but offers witnesses in support of it.

Chance's film exploded it for ever. The footage captures the actual event in irrefutable and dramatic detail. Hidden in a nearby tree, the female cuckoo watches for hours until the host's nest is briefly empty; it then glides directly to it, lands on top of it, picks up one of the host's eggs in its bill, lays it own egg in its place, and flies off. The whole procedure is over in virtually the wink of an eye: it takes less than ten seconds. Birds which had previously been observed flying with an egg in their bill were thus flying *away* from the laying site, not towards it; and the host's egg is swallowed shortly thereafter.

Nobody had ever seen all that, let alone captured it on film. To call it the cuckoo's secret was no exaggeration. Chance later got his comeuppance for his egg-gluttony when he was prosecuted for overstepping the mark and forced to resign from the British Ornithologists' Union – this was the period when egg-collecting was ceasing to be acceptable – but there is no denying his achievement. And so by 1922, after thousands of years of myth, the greater part of the cryptic conduct of the most secretive of all our bird species had been witnessed and properly described.

Described, but not understood. Understanding had to wait. It had to wait until the great neo-Darwinian revolution in biological **169** studies that began in the 1960s and '70s with the perception that different types of behaviour could be produced by evolution – that is, they had a genetic basis and could be inherited, passed on down the generations – just as much as physical traits such as gaudy plumage or a very long beak. Two books above all introduced this startling idea to the public: in America, *Sociobiology*, by Ed Wilson, in 1975; in Britain, *The Selfish Gene*, by Richard Dawkins, in 1976. *Sociobiology* gave its name to a discipline which at once became highly controversial, because in the final chapter of his long exposition Wilson, one of the world's leading experts on the social insects such as ants, moved on to apply the concept to human beings, as just another species, as it were. But the idea that human behaviour is inherited – that it is predetermined for us by our biology, rather than the social and economic environment in which we grow up – is anathema to many people, and bitter argument ensued.

In Britain, although Richard Dawkins himself became a contentious figure, not least for his attacks on religion, the new insights which evolutionary biology was starting to offer into animal behaviour were taken forward in a less controversial way, partly by leaving human beings out of the picture, and the discipline was given a less provocative, if slightly obscure, name: behavioural ecology. Two young and brilliant biologists from the ancient universities were its joint founding fathers: John Krebs from Oxford and Nick Davies from Cambridge. John Krebs went on to be Research Professor of Zoology at Oxford, then Sir John, and then Lord Krebs – one of the dominant figures in the British scientific establishment. Nick Davies went on to become the first Professor of Behavioural Ecology at Cambridge, and in the process he also became one of the world experts on the cuckoo.

Cuckoos clearly offer fertile ground for anyone interested in exploring and explaining animal behaviour, especially from an evolutionary point of view, and when he turned his attention to them Nick Davies had already done outstanding work on the dunnock, **170** Shakespeare's hedge sparrow (and Britain's commonest cuckoo host).

Studying the dunnocks of Cambridge University Botanic Garden, he discovered that a small bird which had always seemed so modest in its appearance as to be a model of unobtrusive sobriety, homely and uninteresting, actually led the wildest sex life imaginable: it had a complex mating system which involved not only one male with one female, but also two males with one female, two females with one male, and multiple males with multiple females. Both sexes sought copulation unceasingly and competed for it frantically, one of the most eye-catching aspects of this being that, before mating, a male would peck continuously at a female's bottom (oh, all right, its cloaca) until the sperm deposited by the last male suitor was dislodged. *Dunnock Behaviour and Social Evolution* teased it all out and showed how it all made sense in evolutionary terms – each individual was merely trying to maximize its rate of reproductive success under varyingly difficult circumstances – and the book became a wildlife classic as well as a masterly scientific text.

When he moved on to cuckoos, Nick Davies exchanged the Botanic Garden for a remoter study site: Wicken Fen. Ten miles outside Cambridge, this was one of the few surviving fragments of the great waterland which once covered nearly 3,000 square miles of the low-lying ground between Cambridge and The Wash, roughly bounded by Peterborough to the west and the Brecklands of Norfolk to the east. Far wilder as a wetland than the Norfolk Broads would ever be, the Fens had been England's equivalent of the Florida Everglades, an alien and impenetrable swampscape which the local inhabitants, who lived by wildfowling, peat-digging and cutting reeds for thatch, learned to walk through on stilts. It was a land of legends: from the Isle of Ely, deep in the Fens, the half-mythical figure of Hereward the Wake was supposed to have led his Anglo-Saxon resistance to William the Conqueror after 1066. But the primal wetland began to disappear in the seventeenth century, when local landowners brought over Dutch engineers skilled at draining large areas of marsh by cutting channels and dykes, and the drainage continued steadily for two centuries until reaching a peak **171** with the emptying of Whittlesey Mere near Peterborough, the largest stretch of open water in lowland England, in 1851. Now more than 99 per cent of the Fens had gone; only a handful of surviving fragments clung on as soggy islands in a sea of intensively farmed carrot fields.

Wicken Fen was the most celebrated of these, with an astonishing wildlife richness hardly equalled anywhere else in the British Isles for a single site: it held nearly 8,000 species of plants, fungi and animals. More than 1,000 types of moth, more than 1,500 types of beetle, and nearly 2,000 species of flies had been recorded there – I didn't know there *were* 2,000 species of flies – with over 400 higher plant species, and nearly 100 species of breeding birds. All this had long been appreciated, however; by some happy chance the fen had not been drained, and in 1899 the National Trust began to buy it up to turn it into Britain's first nature reserve, and now protected it in perpetuity. The association with Cambridge was just as old, and Wicken had traditionally been seen as the university's outdoor laboratory, especially for botanists and entomologists, much in the way that Wytham Woods outside Oxford had long performed a similar service for Cambridge's rival. Nick Davies had been working on cuckoos at Wicken Fen since the mid-1980s, and, given his reputation and his eminence, it was with some trepidation that I asked him if he would let me come and see him there, to try to get to the heart of the bird. But I need not have worried: he said he'd be happy to.

So it was that on 23 May, on a morning that was intermittently cloudy but warm and still – midgy weather – I walked out on to a flat landscape of sedge meadows and reed beds and beheld a character sporting a floppy hat and a long wooden staff, giving a welcoming wave: it was the neatly bearded figure of Nick, a man whose formidable intelligence, I quickly found, was blessedly equalled by his geniality. The hat was to keep the sun off: there was little shade on the fen. I discovered what the staff was for a few minutes later, when Nick was showing me the reason why Wicken was such a good place

for cuckoo studies: it held a substantial population of reed warblers,

perhaps the favourite cuckoo host species in Britain after the dunnock. The small brown birds with the stuttering song which Mark
Cocker had taught me to remember – *I-I can't-can't-quite-quite-
get-get-my-my-words-words-out-out-out* – nested in numbers in the
phragmites, or common reed, along both banks of Wicken Lode,
the ancient canal which divided the fen in two (a lode is a fenland
watercourse); they were singing everywhere as we walked beside it.
Set back from our bank of the lode, for the whole of its length, was
a row of trees which provided the essential cover for female cuckoos
to hide in and stealthily observe as the reed warblers patiently put
their nests together, every 20 yards or so. The nests were not difficult
to find, said Nick, and to illustrate the point he stepped to the edge
of the bank and with a sweep of his staff he parted the reeds like a
wizard; and there, fastened halfway up the stems, was a reed warbler
Mon Repos.

It was a deep cup. Very deep, said Nick, 'so that if it sways in the
wind the eggs stay snug and don't slip out'. The thrill of discovering a bird's nest is clearly a primeval one, deep in the genes; I felt
it strongly, and I felt it even more when I peered in and saw two
green eggs with dark splotches, virtually identical except that one
was slightly but quite distinctly larger than the other. I asked and
Nick confirmed it: there it was, the larger one, the living myth. The
cuckoo's egg. A tiny time bomb for the reed-warbler family at this
address, ticking away.

Edgar Chance and others might have documented it, but *how*
the cuckoo had evolved its astonishing egg mimicry, and indeed its
other tricks, Nick said, was the sort of question he and his fellow
researchers had been seeking to answer, and modern evolutionary
biology had given them a conceptual framework for understanding
it: the evolutionary arms race. This was the idea, first conceived by
Richard Dawkins and John Krebs, that if victims of parasites (or
predators, say) evolved defences, then eventually the parasites or the
predators would evolve new ways round them, which in time would
lead to new defences, and so on.

Nick explained it to me after we had climbed up into the tower hide which gives views across the whole fen. He had set out to test experimentally whether the bird had indeed been involved in an arms race – had it evolved mimetic eggs (ones which match those of the host species) in response to earlier rejection by the host? He did this by parasitizing nests of cuckoo hosts himself, with variously coloured model eggs – once facing arrest as an egg collector, until he persuaded the apprehending policeman that he and his colleague were putting eggs *into* nests, rather than taking them out, something the officer was disinclined to believe until he saw their licence.

The results showed that in the cases where a cuckoo gens, or race, had evolved mimetic eggs – reed-warbler cuckoos, meadow-pipit cuckoos – the host species was very fussy, and would reject any eggs which were not a good match. But in the case of a host species which was not fussy, the dunnock, which the experiments showed would accept 'any old eggs' in its nest, the cuckoos which parasitize it had not evolved an egg which matched.

Clearly, the matching eggs had been produced by natural selection as a way of getting round a discriminating host's defences. So had other cuckoo ploys and dodges, such as laying just after the host species had started – reed warblers, it was found, would always reject an egg placed in the nest *before* they began their own clutch, even if the match was perfect. Similarly, they would reject significantly larger eggs, which explained why the cuckoo's egg was extremely small for its body size, even if sometimes slightly bigger than the host's. The research even showed why it was the cuckoo chick, not the cuckoo itself, which ejected the eggs and young of the host from the nest – because host species will always desert a single egg if the other eggs have been removed (as would be the case if just the cuckoo's egg were left), but they will never desert a single chick.

I was riveted by all this. Talking to Nick, I began to have just the glimmer of a sense of seeing the world from a cuckoo's point of view, which he clearly possessed to a high degree, as proved by

what happened next. He spotted a cuckoo fly into a distant tree on the far side of the lode, about 250 yards away, and pointed it out to me, and we began to watch it, silhouetted on a branch, through our binoculars. And then Nick put his bins down, cupped his hands together, and blew through his thumbs, making a perfect, and very loud, cuckoo call.

I say perfect; don't take it from me, take it from the cuckoo. As I watched, and Nick cuckcooed, it straightened up on the branch and looked left and right in alarm – I was reminded of John Cleese's taunting French knight in *Monty Python and the Holy Grail* when he hears the sounds of the English knights building their Trojan rabbit – and suddenly it launched itself from the branch and came belting over the fen towards us, buzzed our tower, and landed in the trees just behind, cuckcooing loudly in what was clearly indignation.

I was astounded. This was the Professor of Behavioural Ecology at the University of Cambridge. Fellow of Pembroke College. Fellow of the Royal Society. And he had just done a faultless impersonation of Old Jethro the poacher from Four Mile Bottom. *Ole Jethro, he'm a man what can call a cuckoo over! Cuckoo thinks it be a cuckoo! But it be he!*

What did he do for an encore, I wondered? Tickle trout?

The cuckoo was cuckcooing incessantly somewhere near the hide, trying to flush out the rival male who had dared to invade his territory. Nick shot me a grin. He said, 'He's going to be worried about his paternity all morning.' We scanned the branches and eventually caught sight of him (or so I thought) to the side, and had marvellous views of a very handsome bird, its eye-ring shining yellow against the soft grey of its head and breast, but after a couple of seconds Nick said, 'Actually, I think that's the female.' She was perched in her tree watching the length of the lode for the reed warblers starting to lay: probably the bird which two days before had laid the egg we had seen earlier, now she was waiting for her next opportunity. We carried on scanning. After a minute or so Nick said, 'Hey, look, there's a turtle dove on that branch over there,' and as I strained to pick it up, he did his encore.

175

He cupped his hands and blew into his thumbs, and this time a perfect turtle-dove purr came out, loud and filling the hide, *purr-purrrrrrrrrr*, and once again it had its effect: the bird, which was about 100 yards away, took off and flew to us, circled the hide, and landed on a nearby tree, giving a call which reminded me not so much of a lazy summer afternoon as of a very irritated animal: *grr-grrrrrrrrrr* . . .

I had run out of terms of astonishment.

Nick said, 'Maybe we should move on.' He grinned again. 'I think we've caused enough trouble here for one morning.'

Over twenty years, the research which Nick and his colleagues had carried out had laid bare much of the cuckoo's armoury of tricks, yet the evolutionary arms race, he explained to me as we walked along the lode, was truly double-sided: just as the cuckoo's stratagems had evolved in relation to the host species, so host defences had evolved in relation to cuckoos. For example, some songbirds were unsuitable for cuckoos to parasitize, such as those which nest in holes (which cuckoos couldn't get into) or those which fed on seeds (as cuckoo chicks need insect food). Neither of these groups was ever likely to have been affected by cuckoos; and neither showed a tendency to reject eggs which were unlike their own, meaning that egg rejection had probably evolved specifically as a cuckoo-defence. The pied flycatcher, which nested in a hole, did not reject strange eggs in its nest; the spotted flycatcher, which built an open nest and was sometimes the victim of cuckoos, rejected them strongly.

That was remarkable. But that was all about the egg. What, I wondered, about the chick, the great fat cuckoo chick which ended up so many times its foster parents' size? Surely a reed warbler or a meadow pipit or a dunnock could see that this monster was not its own? Why did it keep on feeding it, working its claws to the bone?

Nick said, 'The cuckoo's egg is a visual trick, right?' I nodded. 'The chick uses a vocal trick.'

'How d'you mean?'

'Although it looks nothing like a reed-warbler chick, it's got this amazing begging call for food. When a reed-warbler chick is hungry, it goes *cheep cheep*. When a cuckoo chick is hungry it goes *cheepcheep-cheepcheepcheep* at a fantastic rate, so it doesn't sound like just a single chick, it sounds like a whole brood of hungry reed-warbler chicks. The fact that it sounds like a whole brood of chicks is sufficient to speed the reed warblers on to feed it at a very fast rate. Both parents feed it.'

And he and his colleagues had tested it, Nick said.

'We put a blackbird chick in the reed-warbler nest, which is much the same size as a cuckoo chick. If it was just a question of the black-bird's size, they should feed it like the cuckoo chick, but they didn't bring it much food at all. So we put in loudspeakers. Every time the reed warblers came back with food, and the blackbird chick begged, we played cuckoo begging calls through the little loudspeaker, to give the blackbird a helping hand.'

'Did it work?'

'Almost instantly the reed warblers jerked up their feeding rate, as if you were giving them the signal that they needed, and they would bring the blackbird chick as much food as it called for.'

Loudspeakers . . . I smiled at the ingenuity of it all. I said, 'Why are the reed warblers being so stupid?'

'They see the world in a different way from us. For them, sound is a key stimulus. When the chicks beg more rapidly, that's how the parents can tell they are hungry. It's a rule they follow. On average, a reed warbler does very well in raising its chicks if it follows these rules; it's just that they are not foolproof. We do the same, don't we? Anybody that spent time checking for any possible cause of a disaster before they did anything would never get round to doing anything. You've got to get on with it, and don't worry if you actually make a mistake. It's only a couple of per cent of the time it's going to misfire.'

177

I thought about it all. I said to Nick, 'Do you like cuckoos?'

'I love cuckoos,' he said. 'I admire their secrecy and their cunning. And the fact that they can get away with it – that amazes me. It's why I find them so interesting. I'll put it this way. Almost always birds know more about what's going on than you do. So when you start studying something, at first it doesn't make any sense. Then you realize it all makes perfect sense, and the birds are one step ahead of you.'

One step ahead: that seemed to be the essence of things. This was a very different creature, if you looked at it in human terms, from the rest of the spring-bringers I had been seeking. If you delved into the essence of the swallow or the nightingale or the swift, you could come back with beauty or wonder or wildness, but if you got to the heart of this one you found something of another order entirely, something exceptional, admittedly, but not at all likely to move you in the same way. At the heart of the cuckoo was trickery.

But that was only half the story.

When you thought about it, it could have been anything, the male cuckoo's vocalization: a squawk like a jay, a laughing yelp like a green woodpecker, a mewing like a buzzard, a chattering like a magpie, even the weird but fascinating bubbling which the female cuckoo makes (I heard it with Nick on Wicken Fen). Some sort of harsh laughing call would have suited well with the image of the deceiver. Instead, by a remarkable accident of nature – and you wonder what the odds against this happening were – it was the most perfectly musical sound in all creation.

Cuck-coo: two notes, that's all. But look at it this way: one note is a noise; two notes make a tune. The key thing was the interval, surely memorable to humans from the first time it was heard, but instantly placeable in western minds accustomed to music based on the twelve-tone scale: it is a descending minor third. At its simplest, in the key of C Major, it is G to E. (As to which key the cuckoo actually calls in, Gilbert White wrote that one of his neighbours 'who is said to have a nice ear' found the key varied in different individuals: 'for about Selborne wood, he found they were mostly in D; he heard two sing together, the one in D, the other in D sharp, who made a disagreeable concert; he afterwards heard one in D sharp, and about Woolmer Forest, some in C'.) The repeated call not only had pitch, it even had rhythm; you could represent it easily in a bar of 4/4 time as two quavers repeated with a crotchet rest in between – | cuck-coo! (rest) cuck-coo! (rest) | – although to capture the slight stress which the bird sometimes seems to be giving to the second note, it would probably be better written in 2/4, with the first note the final quaver of a preceding bar, the second note the first crotchet of the next bar (the stressed, down beat) and then a quaver rest, before the call begins again – cuck | Coo (rest) cuck | Coo (rest) – and so on.

Hardly any other birdsong was precisely transcribable in musical notation like this, accurately and simply. That was its uniqueness. There was just nothing else like it. It was famously set down on the stave in the seventeenth century by a German Jesuit, Athanasius Kircher (he wrote it as F to D). Father Kircher was a Rome-based linguist and polymath whose knowledge ranged over a vast area from Egyptology to astronomy (a recent biography of him was entitled *The Last Man Who Knew Everything*), and in 1650 he produced a hefty musical encyclopaedia, the *Musurgia Universalis*, which contains an often-reproduced and charming page showing pictures of six birds – nightingale, cock, hen, quail, parrot and cuckoo – with their calls transcribed alongside. The cuckoo's ('Vox cuculi') is by far the most distinctive, and in fact its distinctiveness had already begun to make it a motif in baroque keyboard and orchestral music. The first example was probably the *Capriccio on the Cuckoo* written for organ by Girolamo Frescobaldi, a now largely forgotten contemporary of Monteverdi, in 1624. From then on it can be found in composer after composer, from several little-known early Italian and German baroque names through Frenchmen like Couperin and Daquin to J. S. Bach, and then on to Haydn in the 'Toy' Symphony (although modern scholarship **179** now thinks that may have been written by Mozart's father, Leopold). The best-known cuckoo in the classical era is probably the one that calls in the lovely slow movement of Beethoven's 'Pastoral' Symphony (he also put one into a piano sonata), and later in the nineteenth century and into the twentieth the bird was calling, in Saint-Saëns' *Carnival of The Animals*, Humperdinck's *Hansel and Gretel*, Mahler's First Symphony, Delius's *On Hearing the First Cuckoo in Spring*, and numerous other works.

I discussed these with a friend who is a fine musician, Tom Lees (a master of the sackbut, among other instruments) and after listening to them carefully Tom pointed out to me that in some cases the composers had added a semitone to the interval of the natural cuckoo's call, and made it a major instead of a minor third. This is the case, for example, with Beethoven's 'Pastoral' Symphony cuckoo, and with Saint-Saëns' cuckoo in the depths of the woods, and with Delius's cuckoo – although at first hearing Delius's bird sings a minor third, then calls as a major third later on. (All of these, incidentally, are played on the clarinet, whose mellow tone best approximates to that of the real bird's call.) Why was this? Did they feel the slightly mournful edge of the minor third made the motif too weak? Making it a major third subtly changed it and turned it into a more positive, forceful, almost bouncy sound – which is perhaps why cuckoo clocks, which invariably use the major third, drive people nuts.

At all events, there is no gainsaying the call's intensely musical nature. Yet there is something more, even beyond the musicality, which makes it so exceptional. As *Cuculus canorus* was a secretive, shy and never very common bird, you hardly ever saw it: you only heard it. You couldn't *see* where the call was coming from; but it also had a sort of ventriloquial quality, which meant you couldn't *hear* where it was coming from either. It was a sound which didn't seem to come from anywhere: it was simply existing, disembodied, in the landscape. When I catch it, I am reminded of the music Ariel makes when invisible in *The Tempest*, which has such an effect on everyone who hears it, even the monster Caliban:

180

Be not afeard; the isle is full of noises,
Sounds and sweet airs that give delight and hurt not.

While Ferdinand, the young prince of Naples, exclaims:

Where should this music be? I' th' air or th' earth?

It was its ethereal, disembodied nature which made the ringing disyllabic call so magical. A corny word, but the only word for it, really, and Wordsworth eventually captured the phenomenon in his 'To the Cuckoo':

O blithe New-comer! I have heard,
I hear thee and rejoice.
O Cuckoo! shall I call thee Bird,
Or but a wandering Voice?

While I am lying on the grass
Thy twofold shout I hear;
From hill to hill it seems to pass,
At once far off, and near . . .

There was nothing in nature like the wandering voice. When it was paired, as an aural signal, with the most eagerly awaited change of the turning year, the coming of spring, it is not an exaggeration to say that in Europe it became one of the most significant and resonant sounds in human life. It produced a stream of folklore right across the continent which was quite colossal and which dwarfed the other strain emanating from the idea of the cuckoo as deceiver and cheat. 'The folklore of the cuckoo', wrote Charles Swainson in the late nineteenth century, 'is almost inexhaustible.' The nightingale may have prompted more poetry; the cuckoo has prompted more proverbs. Every European country has its big fat bundle of cuckoo sayings and stories and legends: where or when or how you **181** hear the call tells you what the weather will be like, what your luck will be, how good will be the harvest, how much money you will have, when you may be married, or how long you will live.

Britain has its own plentiful share of cuckoo lore and literature, and two examples of it in particular – one ancient, one recent – illustrate how the bird and its spring salute have taken a peculiar hold on the English mind.

The first is to be found in a manuscript in the British Library:

> *Sumer is icumen in,*
> *Lhude sing cuccu!*
> *Groweþ sed and bloweþ med*
> *And springþ þe wde nu.*
> *Sing cuccu!*
>
> (*Summer is a-coming in*
> *Loudly sing cuckoo!*
> *Groweth seed and bloweth mead*
> *And springs the wood anew*
> *Sing cuckoo!*)

Originating from Reading Abbey in Berkshire, 'Summer is icumen in' is a round, a song where four voices follow each other in turn through the tune; it was probably written about 1250. It is the oldest extant song in English: so people were singing about cuckoos even as the language was being formed.

The other striking example of the bird's grip on the English imagination is a modern myth, whose potency is with us still: the 'first cuckoo' letters to *The Times*.

It is widely believed that the newspaper once considered the official bulletin board of the British establishment still publishes an annual correspondence from readers claiming to have heard the first cuckoo of the spring. In fact it has not published a plain and simple 'first cuckoo' letter since 1940 (although witty variations on the theme occasionally make it into print). Yet for more than a century it did indeed feature such communications from readers, based around the fact that cuckoos tend to arrive in Britain from Africa (along with nightingales) about the end of the second week of April – 15 April being a good average date for the Home Counties. Any encounter substantially earlier than this would prompt a missive, an archetypal one being the note dashed off by Mr W. J. Courthope, and published on 3 April 1907:

> Sir, – I wonder whether many of your readers have heard the cuckoo at this unusually early date? I heard him two or three times this afternoon and I find that others in these parts heard him this morning. The Sussex legend that the cuckoo is let out of a basket by an old woman at Heathfield Fair – about the middle of April – marks the season when his arrival is commonly observed.
> Yours faithfully,
> W. J. Courthope
> The Lodge, Wadhurst, Sussex, April 1

Mr Courthope's letter brought forth an instant response from Mr David A. Horner (published the following day):

> Sir, – Referring to Mr W. J. Courthope's letter in your today's issue, I can claim to have heard an earlier cuckoo.
> On Sunday afternoon, outside the little village of Friday Street in Surrey, I was delighted and surprised to hear the bird's 'wandering voice' quite close at hand. That was on March 31.
> Yours, &c.
> David A. Horner
> Lidsdale, Epsom, April 3

Year in, year out, the paper gave space to letters like these. Why? Partly because they were written by gentlemen, for other gentlemen **183** to read, and in that more leisurely age many gentlemen took a keen interest in natural history – think of the solicitor John Masefield with his South African swallow – and the paper sympathized. For example, on 24 January 1933 it published a letter from Neville Chamberlain, the then Chancellor of the Exchequer, recording the fact that for the first time he had seen a grey wagtail – he specified it was a grey wagtail, Sir, not a pied wagtail – in London's St James's Park. (This was six days before Adolf Hitler became Chancellor of Germany and embarked on a career that would give Chamberlain something more than wagtails to think about.) But also the *Times* cuckoo letters took on a force of their own and became a tradition, which eventually became A Great British Tradition, nay, a very talisman of Englishness – up there with the Changing of the Guard and cricket at Lord's and tea at five o'clock – and the paper played up to the idea. It did not only publish 'first cuckoo' claims by readers, it published news stories about cuckoo arrivals (usually 'From A Correspondent'), letters from nature-minded vicars in rural rectories detailing years of first-cuckoo observations, and even cuckoo leaders. At least three times in the twentieth century it ran long articles in praise of the cuckoo and its heralding of spring, as the fourth or fifth leader, intended to be lighter in tone than the others– on 22 April 1924 (640 words), 18 April 1940 (766 words) and 29 March 1946 (558 words). And so hardy did this association between leaders-and-letters page and bird become that when in 1976 *The Times* published a best-selling anthology of its twentieth-century correspondence, it entitled the book *The First Cuckoo* – and went on to entitle subsequent selections *The Second Cuckoo* and *The Third Cuckoo*.

The modern, Rupert Murdoch-owned, tabloid *Times* is no longer interested in cuckoos. This was made quite explicit in a piece by Sally Baker, letters editor from 2003 to 2005, published in the paper on 11 February 2006, entitled 'Time to evict a legendary cuckoo from our nest', with the sub-heading: 'Contrary to myth, *The Times* long ago lost interest in this deceptive herald of spring.' Ms Baker, who had moved on to became the paper's feedback editor, wrote that, although 'first cuckoo' letters were still received each year, none was published. 'That we still publish "first cuckoo" letters is perhaps the greatest myth in *Times* lore and I am almost reluctant to explode it,' she wrote. But explode it she did, concluding her piece, 'So I extend a warm welcome, wherever he or she presently is, to the first cuckoo of this spring. But please, don't tell us about it.'

All written off then? For now, perhaps. Yet something of genuine substance can still be found in those earlier letters, available in the published volumes of correspondence, or in the *Times* online archive, and that is the pressure of real feeling. People cared about their cuckoos. The sentiment was naturally at its sharpest when they claimed to have heard a very early bird and were openly challenged, as in the case of Mr J. R. Aitken of Siriol House, Olney, Bucks, who in a letter published on 22 February 1896, claimed to have heard a cuckoo on 20 February, two days previously. Not impossible: the earliest generally accepted record in recent decades is a bird heard on 20 February 1953, at Farnham in Surrey. However, a subsequent letter signed with the nom de plume 'Ornithologist' poured scorn on his claim, suggesting he had met with a sparrowhawk or, worse, a small boy doing a cuckoo imitation. On 2 March Mr Aitken hit back indignantly and at length, protesting loftily, 'Under extraordinary circumstances, the wonderful happens.'

Yet even the birds with an ordinary date were special for people, as the century or so of *Times* correspondence illustrates beyond doubt. The feelings the cuckoo inspired were intense. Never mind the bird's true nature, crafty and deceiving: it was the add-on, the physiological accident of its call, that mattered – the voice, the unique voice, the wandering voice which suddenly was heard in the air. That touched something deeper in many people than anything the other spring-bringers did, wonderful though they were, perhaps because it was so exceptional in its mysterious musicality as to do full justice to the magnitude of the change in the world it was marking. 'For human nature, the spring comes round in sufficient intervals that it's a surprise each time,' Nick Davies said to me. 'If spring happened every couple of months you would still remember the last one, but a year seems just enough time to forget how wonderful spring days are. So every time it seems to comes as a fresh surprise. And the cuckoo is the symbol of that.'

Two notes, that's all; but nothing else is quite like them in nature. In my spring, seeking out the migrant birds and seeking to get to the heart of them, I was lucky and heard the two notes echo across the countryside in a number of places, and my heart lifted every time. But I didn't go only where cuckoos were: I also went where cuckoos were no longer, and that let me see it even more strongly – just how much the two notes mean to us, now that they are going.

ELEVEN

Vanishings

Yellow Wagtail

Julia Jeffries lives in the Ashdown Forest in Sussex, one of the last wild areas of southern England, a far-ranging mosaic of lowland heath and woodland which has never been put to the plough. A designer and writer, she is a handsome woman of 57 with ash-blonde hair and grey eyes, just divorced. She wears a single string of pearls, silver leaf earrings with a pearl stud, white slacks, and sandals.

Her house consists of two sandstone woodman's cottages knocked together, with a conservatory built on the end; there is forest all around. It is 28 April, and the forest is in its spring glory: the gorse in bright yellow bloom, the birches and beeches just coming into misty green leaf, and the wild flowers startling in their loveliness – clumps of primroses, swathes of bluebells, sheets of wood anemones.

In her garden Julia has gathered together and intensified everything that is happening with the flowers of the forest: she has bluebells and primroses too, and also ramsons, the white stars of wild garlic, while beneath the blossom of her apple trees cowslips glisten in the grass. She has been passionate about flowers since girlhood. **187**

('I do a lot of rushing off during the orchid season.') While she makes me a coffee to go with a piece of fruitcake from the farm shop, I glance at the books scattered on a side table and I see *The Oxford Book of Wild Flowers*; *The Collins Pocket Guide to Wild Flowers*; *Sussex Wild Flowers*; *Britain's Rare Flowers*, by Peter Marren; *Wild Orchids of Britain*, by V. S. Summerhayes; *Wild Flowers of Chalk and Limestone* by J. E. Lousley. I also see *The Buildings of England: Sussex* by Ian Nairn and Nikolaus Pevsner, and *England's 1,000 Best Churches* by Simon Jenkins.

There are walking sticks in the umbrella-holder, and green Hunter wellies by the door. Julia is a county lady. I don't think she would take issue with that description.

She sweeps the cat off the sofa, sits down, and says, 'It was April 1992. I remember the Easter weekend was very hot, and I was very pregnant. I went into hospital on the Tuesday, 21 April, the Princess Royal in Haywards Heath, and on the 22nd I had her, I had Harriet, and I came back here with this tiny baby on the 23rd and there were cuckoos calling everywhere. There had been none when I went in, but when I came out they were all calling.

'Every single year there have been cuckoos on her birthday or the day before, and not just one. I put it in my internal calendar. They were part of my life and her life. The cuckoo came on her birthday, or the day before. The little boy next door has a birthday on the 21st, and we have a competition for whose is the cuckoo that comes up first.'

She said, 'Sometimes there were so many of them that you would wake up in the early hours of the morning and think, "Oh God, the cuckoo", and you would have to get up and close the window. Getting up to feed the children, you would just get back to sleep and the cuckoo would start calling. When the children were small, I would wear them out trailing them round the garden in the push-chair, and the cuckoos would be calling, calling all the time, down in the valley there.'

It was in 2007 that they stopped coming, she said. 'It was last year that I didn't hear the cuckoo, for the first time. There were none, for the first time ever. I was . . . I was absolutely traumatized. I just felt like . . . like the life blood was being taken away. I minded absolutely.

'Every year the same things happen in this garden and I look for them, like the starlings nesting in my eaves. There's huge relief when the cuckoo comes back and the starling starts nesting – it's a sign that everything is still . . . that God's in his heaven and all's right with the world. Harriet has her birthday on 22 April, and every year since she's been born we always hear the cuckoo. The sign of the cuckoo is the sign of good happening in life. But if it's gone . . .'

She said, 'Last year I thought, "The conservators of the Ashdown Forest have been cutting a lot of trees down to restore heathland," and I thought maybe it was that, it was linked in to the forest clearances: no trees, no cuckoos. Whereas this year . . . I don't know.'

We walked out into the garden, resplendent with its spring flora. She said that foxes and badgers, squirrels and rabbits all came into the garden, as well as tawny owls and woodpeckers, goldfinches and greenfinches. 'In this garden I've seen adders, grass snakes, smooth snakes. It's fantastic for moths. It's the complete garden for wildlife. There's always a cuckoo here at this time of year.'

'I mean there was.'

We listened.

'At this time of year I would absolutely be able to bring you out here and you would hear a cuckoo.'

There was nothing.

We drove then to one of the high points of the forest, where a local resident had said in a letter to the local newspaper that cuckoos could still infallibly be heard.

We listened for twenty minutes maybe. The line of the South Downs was on the horizon.

There was only the wind.

Julia said, 'I was born halfway through the century and I've seen all these things go in my lifetime, but I never thought the cuckoo would be one. The bird of spring. That's the worst of all.

189

'It's just not right without the cuckoo, it just isn't. Something really is wrong if the cuckoos are not here. There's something wrong. There's something rotten in the state of Denmark.'

Julian Langford lives in a brick semi-detached house in the small town of Wellington in Shropshire, now part of Telford New Town, the sprawling conurbation at the foot of the Wrekin, the wooded hill which A. E. Housman also celebrated and which can be seen for miles around. A retired civil servant, he is 70, and he has been ringing birds – his passion – for more than half a century, keeping a meticulous note of every one of the 208,000 avian legs upon which he has placed a metal band. Most of his ringing has been done around a series of small lakes belonging to a sugar factory at nearby Allscott, which hold a substantial population of reed warblers and, as a result, have always attracted cuckoos, eager to parasitize them.

Julian and his fellow ringers were often able to ring cuckoo chicks in the nests of the deceived and hard-working hosts; it was such a superb cuckoo site that one year, 1987, they ringed five, and Julian remembers from about the same time the spectacular sight of six male cuckoos chasing each other around a tree. He pointed out the tree to me as we walked around his lakes on the morning of 2 May. He said, 'We've still got just as many reed warblers. Nothing's changed in the habitat here.'

But in 2006 he heard only one cuckoo at Allscott; and in 2007, for the first time, none at all. 'No, I didn't hear a single cuckoo in Shropshire last year,' he said. 'And I used to hear them everywhere. Everywhere. They've become very scarce. My wife and I have lived in our house for forty-seven years, and for the first thirty-five we would be woken up by cuckoos calling while we were in bed. We used to lie in bed and listen to them cuckooing. But not any more. They've just gone.'

He said, 'It would be a miracle if we heard a cuckoo today.'
We did not.

John Taylor is the head of the Tring Ringing Group in Hertfordshire, which was started by Chris Mead before the BTO moved from Tring to Norfolk in 1990; John has run it ever since, and I talked to him on the edge of Tring's Wilstone Reservoir in the early morning of 4 May. His group were busy about him, catching and ringing the small songbirds which cluster in the scrub at the reservoir's edge, in particular the reed warblers which breed in the reed beds – prime cuckoo hosts.

'There have always been cuckoos here in my time,' said John. 'Normally we would be hearing them now, at this time of the year. About three years ago there were fewer and I started thinking, "What's happening to the cuckoos?" Then in 2006 we had just the one, but last year, for the first time ever, none at all.'

And there were none at Wilstone that day.

'We should be hearing them now,' said John. 'We should be shouting at them, shouting, "Bugger off, you're getting on my nerves!" It feels strange.'

It feels strange for many people. Say goodbye to the cuckoo. The bird is rapidly disappearing from Britain, at a scarcely conceivable rate, along with a cluster of the other summer visitors which bring us the spring from sub-Saharan Africa, some of them vanishing even faster. Say goodbye to the spotted flycatcher, the wood warbler and the turtle dove; make your farewells to the tree pipit, the yellow wagtail and the pied flycatcher; look out when you can for the willow warbler and the garden warbler, the whinchat and the swift. Oh, and cherish your memories of the nightingale.

These migrant birds which, despite all the travails of their journeys, have reached us so unfailingly for so many thousands of years, and have meant so much to us, have now begun to decline on slopes **191** which in many cases point in short order towards extinction. They are dropping in numbers every year – not in Britain alone, but across Europe, failing to arrive in the fields and forests and hedges and heathlands where they have been known since the memory of man, leaving great gaps in the landscape and in the soundscape, leaving the people who love them perplexed and distressed in a way they hardly know how to articulate. There is no conventional response to the situation of not hearing a cuckoo where a cuckoo has always been heard; it is new, and on the face of it trivial, but the people who are experiencing it sense profoundly that it is important, even if they are unable to say why. A man or woman who laments that they have lost their spotted flycatchers will as like as not be treated by society with amused condescension, society not appreciating that the loss is symptomatic of something much greater going awry in the working of the world.

It is a phenomenon which has crept upon us, the disappearance of the spring-bringers, and it is only now being recognized, but it is increasingly clear that it is real. The losses which bird-lovers have been registering in private disquiet for a decade or more have at last begun to show up in the statistics: their personal losses have become national losses, even European losses, and a great pattern of vanishing is in evidence now which cannot be gainsaid.

It is perhaps worth explaining in some detail just how we know this, how we can be sure there is a pattern and not just a random assemblage of piecemeal events – a nightingale absent here, a cuckoo missing there. For birds are the most mobile of all living things. Even when they come to a stop and nest, one year they nest in this place, one year they nest in that. It's hard enough to count them accurately in your garden: how on earth can we possibly count the numbers of birds in a *country*? And then see if they're going up or down year by year? And *then* see if those fluctuations are really significant, not just merely the annual variations in numbers which are common to all animal populations? And never mind doing it in a country – how can **192** we do it for a *continent*? How can we do it for Europe as a whole?

The answer is that we can make a shot at this seeming labour of Hercules by intensive sampling, which reflects fairly well the underlying situation. One of the consequences of the great pesticide massacre of birds in the late 1950s and early 1960s, documented so angrily and unforgettably by Rachel Carson in *Silent Spring*, the 1962 book which lit the flame of the modern environmental movement, was the creation of the modern bird census. If birds were disappearing in huge numbers, poisoned by DDT and other agricultural chemicals, scientists needed to be able to measure that properly; and in 1966 national bird censuses began to operate and produce annual data on population levels both in Britain and the United States: the Common Bird Census (CBC) in Britain, the Breeding Bird Survey (BBS) in the US.

Britain's CBC involved volunteers, who needed to be fairly expert birdwatchers, choosing a site – a wood, say, or a farm – and making about ten extensive visits to it a year, with the object of recording all the territories of the resident avifauna, and thus getting a very good idea of local numbers. Once a baseline figure was established, year-on-year fluctuations could be measured against it by repeating the surveys annually, and natural variation and other statistical 'noise' would tend to be smoothed out by the long-term trend which would gradually take shape.

Run by the British Trust for Ornithology, the CBC came along just in time to provide damning statistical evidence of a disaster. After Britain in 1973 joined what was then the European Economic Community and began to participate in its Common Agricultural Policy – the crazy CAP, with its fat production subsidies tempting farmers to turn their fields into factories – the consequent intensification of agricultural processes had a mortal effect on farmland birds. The vastly increased use of pesticides, the ripping-out of hedges, the ploughing-up of stubbles in the autumn to sow crops in winter as well as in spring, the replacement of old wildflower-rich hay meadows with highly fertilized monoculture grassland, the specialization of farms into units which raised livestock or grew crops but **193** did not do both, as before – all these combined to shrink severely the amount of seed and insect food which was available to birds in the countryside, and their populations began to plunge. The CBC documented the process in graphic detail. By the 1990s its figures were showing incontestably that a whole series of well-loved farmland birds, from the skylark to the corn bunting, from the tree sparrow to the grey partridge, had crashed appallingly in numbers – in some cases by 90 per cent. It was the biggest collapse in avian populations ever seen. Breeding farmland bird numbers in England are now 52 per cent lower than in 1966, the CBC base year. Imagine: just in the time since the Beatles gave their last concert, half the birds of the fields of England have disappeared.

Vital though the figures it provided were, however, the CBC was far from perfect. It was very labour-intensive, so only about 350 people took part in it – 350 samples for the country as a whole. The volunteers could choose their own site, which in the nature of things was likely to be a pleasant and easily accessible one, so some areas – the uplands, the cities – were barely covered at all. To rectify the weaknesses of the CBC, in 1994 a new British scheme was set up with the same name as its long-standing US counterpart, the Breeding Bird Survey (BBS).

This was much simpler to operate, involving only two visits a year to a 1-kilometre grid square, through which volunteers would merely walk two parallel transects, noting down what birds they encountered. The advantages were that the grid squares were not chosen by the volunteers, they were randomly generated by computer, so all habitats and areas of Britain were covered; and, because it was so much less labour-intensive, many more observers took part. Jointly run by the BTO and the RSPB, the Breeding Bird Survey now involves more than 3,500 volunteers, a tenfold increase in the coverage of its predecessor.

One of the troubles with discussing these schemes is that you descend into abbreviation hell. But, for the record, the CBC carried on running alongside the BBS (see what I mean?) for some years, until the BBS incorporated it and continued alone, so it is now Britain's principal bird censusing instrument. It generates annually two population trends for each of the species it covers: a long-term trend, dating from 1967 (when the CBC data were first published) to the present moment, and a short-term trend, using just the BBS data from 1994 onward. Only the short-term trend is now published in the annual survey, but the long-term trend is available from the BTO.

So what do the latest figures, from the Breeding Bird Survey 2007, tell us about the fortunes of the spring-bringers? They tell us a lot – and very little of it is of comfort.

Let's start with the cuckoo. *Cuculus canorus* has declined by 59 per cent over the long-term period 1967–2007. In forty years, the number of cuckoos in Britain has gone down by nearly three-fifths, and the slope is getting steeper: just since the BBS was introduced, in 1994, the number has declined by 37 per cent. Well over a third of the population that was left in 1994, gone in thirteen years. However you look at it, this is a slide towards silence for the wandering voice.

But that's nothing. The spotted flycatcher – inconspicuous and understated, yet so dearly loved by its English admirers – has declined by 84 per cent over the long term, since 1967, and by 59 per cent over the short term, since 1994. This is the high road to extinction. Yet there is more: a quite staggering decline recorded just between 2006 and 2007 of 41 per cent. Such year-on-year changes are often statistical 'noise' – maybe it was a bad summer with fewer observers, so the figures were skewed – but this one is marked with an asterisk by the BBS as 'statistically significant', meaning it is regarded as evidence of a real phenomenon. The plunging numbers of *Muscicapa striata* plunged even more steeply over the most recently recorded twelve-month period. What conclusion can we draw, other than that the bird is on its way out?

195

It is far from alone. The turtle dove, the bird with the purring sound of summer in its voice, is right alongside it, having declined by 82 per cent over the long term and an astounding 66 per cent over the short term. The tree pipit – the meadow-pipit relative with the bubblegum-pink legs we watched performing its song flight over the hillside at Dinas – has declined by even more over the long term, 83 per cent, with an 11 per cent decline over the short term; while the yellow wagtail, the prettiest of all the small farmland birds, is down by 70 per cent since 1967 and by 47 per cent since 1994.

These species are just vanishing. So are others for which there is only a short-term trend, as the limitations of the Common Bird Census mean that before 1994 they were not picked up in the surveys. Heading the list is the wood warbler, the living spirit of the western oakwoods: since the BBS began (and started to pick it up), it has declined by 67 per cent. Try to get your head around that: to use another recent historical comparison, just in the time since Tony Blair became leader of the Labour Party, more than two-thirds of the wood-warbler population has gone. Say goodbye to *Phylloscopus sibilatrix*.

The other warblers also show some spectacular declines: the marsh warbler, the bird with all the African imitations in its song repertoire, is down 76 per cent in the long term and 53 per cent in the short term, but it should be said that this is from a tiny population, a very small base, and a similar situation applies to Savi's warbler, a recent colonizer of southern England, down 53 per cent and 58 per cent short and long term respectively.

Other declines are more significant. The willow warbler, the bird with the silvery descending song, perhaps the most numerous of all the spring-bringers – it was once thought that 4 million willow warblers came to Britain every spring – is descending sharply in numbers: it is down 60 per cent over the long term. The short-term figure, 1994–2007, shows it holding steady over the UK as a whole, but this does not reflect the situation in England, where there has been a short-term decline of 27 per cent. (This is balanced by a rise in Scotland over the period of 31 per cent.)

The whitethroat shows an even bigger decline, of 62 per cent over the last forty years, but this is partly due to a population crash in the late 1960s, and numbers have since recovered. The lesser whitethroat, however, is on a shallow but continuous downward gradient, with declines of 15 per cent and 12 per cent, long and short term respectively, while the garden warbler, the bird with the ultra-sober dress sense, is on a steeper downward slope and shows a decline of 21 per cent over the long term and 5 per cent since 1994.

Other warbler species are holding their own: the figures show sedge warblers coming back over the last decade or so from a long-term decline of nearly 30 per cent, while the reed warbler appears to have doubled its population over the last forty years, and the grass-hopper warbler has also shown a marked rise. The two short-distance migrant warblers, the chiffchaff and the blackcap, which generally winter in the Mediterranean basin or in North Africa – or even, now, as far north as Britain – are doing well, both being up hugely since 1994, and the fact that they do not go south of the Sahara may well be significant, as we shall see.

What of the swallow and its hirundine relatives, and the swift? The picture is mixed. In his comprehensive millennium review, *The State of The Nation's Birds*, Chris Mead suggested that swallow numbers were much lower than they once were, especially in the Home Counties, perhaps because of the disappearance of livestock farms. 'Many younger birdwatchers have no memory of just how common swallows used to be in rural areas,' he wrote, adding that there were 'serious concerns' about the bird. However, the BBS shows a 20 per cent long-term rise in swallow numbers, and a 25 per cent rise since 1994. The house martin is down 53 per cent since 1967 (although there is a 9 per cent recent rise). The sand martin is down by 9 per cent long term and up by 25 per cent short term; but the one-year figure 2006–7 shows a colossal drop of 40 per cent, and this too is marked as 'statistically significant', meaning all with the sand martin is not well. The picture is much less ambiguous with the swift, for which there is only a short-term trend, since 1994: it is down 41 per **197** cent. The creature which commands the sky, the supreme exponent of flight, in numbers is only falling.

And so we come to the bird with which we began. Wondrous in song but scarce, and skulking in behaviour, the nightingale has long been one of the more difficult birds to census in Britain (or rather in England, as it is extinct in Wales and has not bred in Scotland in recorded times). It was too rare for the mere 350 plots of the Common Bird Census to pick it up in any meaningful way before 1994. But what at least had become evident over recent decades was that its range was rapidly shrinking back towards the south-east corner of England, and in particular the four coastal counties of Sussex, Kent, Essex and Suffolk.

This was revealed by the comparison of the two versions of *The Atlas of Breeding Birds in Britain and Ireland*, the first, published in 1976, covering the period 1968–72, and the second, published in 1993, covering 1988–91. The distribution of the nightingale in the latter shows a conspicuous retrenchment from the earlier map, with the bird vanishing from the counties at the north and west of its range, such as Lincolnshire and Dorset, and the population becoming concentrated more and more in England's bottom right-hand corner.

However, when the BBS took over in 1994, with its tenfold increase in sampling plots, *Luscinia megarhynchos*, like the wood warbler, began to be picked up more regularly. For a long time the organizers declined to publish a population trend, as it was a rule that this would be done only if a species was being recorded from at least thirty grid squares, the minimum sample size for which a trend could reliably be calculated, and the nightingale wasn't. But as the BBS continued to expand, the thirty-site qualification was eventually met, and a population trend for the bird, from 1994 onward, was published in the 2007 Breeding Bird Survey for the first time. Released on 17 July 2008, just twelve weeks after Seb and I had had our nightingale encounter on Great Bookham Common, this showed how it had fared in the previous thirteen years: it had **198** dropped in numbers by 60 per cent.

These declines are desperate. That they have not yet been the cause for national alarm is remarkable. In many cases the descending lines on the graph hit zero not very far in the future at all. If it be thought that to raise the prospect of extinction is to overdramatize, let us remember that the two species which have become extinct as breeding birds in Britain since the Second World War were also long-distance, trans-Saharan migrants: the wryneck and the red-backed shrike. The former, the small brown woodpecker said to be capable of turning its head right round (whose spring arrival in Selborne was always keenly anticipated by Gilbert White), became extinct in England in 1974, and, although a tiny population clung on in Scotland, by 2003 there were no breeding records in Britain at all. The latter, a captivating chestnut-and-grey 6-inch-long predator with the habit of impaling its insect and small bird prey on the spikes of thorn 'larders' for future consumption, ceased regular breeding in 1989 (although occasional pairs have bred since).

Are they to follow them over the edge, then, the nightingale and the turtle dove, the spotted flycatcher and the wood warbler, the tree pipit and the cuckoo? What prompts fears that they very well might is that their British declines are being closely paralleled across Europe: this is more than just a national problem. We know this because other European countries now run censuses like the BBS, and the results of them are brought together and amalgamated in the Pan-European Common Bird Monitoring Scheme (whose appalling abbreviation, PECBMS, is at least pronounced 'Peckhams').

Peckhams – let's call it that – now takes in censuses from 21 European countries and can currently give annual trend data for 135 species of European common birds, 44 of them being trans-Saharan migrants (out of a total European avifauna of more than 500 species). At the top of the list of those declining is the ortolan bunting, the fat-packed morsel which provided François Mitterrand with his farewell dinner. It has declined over the long term (in Peckhams terms, 1980–2005) by no less than 79 per cent, and in the short term (1990–2005) by 28 per cent, and whether the pressure of illegal **199** hunting is contributing to its fall is a very relevant question. (The ortolan is completely protected, throughout the European Union, under the EU Wild Birds Directive.)

Emberiza hortulana does not occur in Britain, but following it closely in the European slide downward are most of our own declining spring-bringers. The bird with the second biggest fall in population across the continent is the turtle dove (66 per cent long term); the third, the wryneck (63 per cent); the fourth, the nightingale (63 per cent); and the fifth, the yellow wagtail (61 per cent). The sixth is another bird not found in Britain, the river warbler, but the next four are the whinchat (55 per cent long-term decline), the wheatear (52 per cent), the spotted flycatcher (50 per cent) and the tree pipit (47 per cent). The wood warbler, the willow warbler and the pied flycatcher are showing long-term declines of 27, 26 and 22 per cent, respectively, with the cuckoo's long-term decline at 12 per cent. It is also interesting to note that in the Peckhams data both the swallow and the house martin are shown as dropping in numbers over the short and the long term (the sand martin is not covered in the survey).

So there seems to be no doubt that many of the spring-bringers are in severe decline across Europe. But an important point needs to be made now: *so are many other birds.* The Common Agricultural Policy decimated bird populations right across the continent, and, even though its worst excesses have been curbed, farmland-bird numbers are continuing to drop, while many more increasing pressures, from development to hunting, are being felt by bird communities in Europe – and also beyond. In September 2008 BirdLife International, the Cambridge-based global alliance of bird-protection groups, held an international conference in Buenos Aires to discuss the future of bird conservation, and released a report entitled *The State of The World's Birds*, which offered a startling and depressing message: never mind the rarities, on which so much conservation effort has been expended, common birds are now in decline all over the globe. On every continent, in every country, species which have always been familiar and taken for granted are steadily dropping in numbers, providing, said BirdLife, compelling evidence of a rapid deterioration in the world environment as a whole.

Are the declines of the spring-bringers simply part of this, or do the migrants have special problems of their own which go with their special lifestyle? Is it possible that conditions on their migratory journeys, or conditions on their African wintering grounds, might be behind their falling numbers, in whole or in part? Or – a new and intriguing possibility – might the fact that they start breeding in Britain later than resident birds be to blame?

To get an indication we need to look at the figures again, and go into number-crunching mode. Take the BBS 2007 data for the short term. The report gives 1994–2007 population trends for 104 British bird species, including many familiar favourites such as the robin, the wren and the blackbird. The first thing we notice is that four of out of the five most rapid declines in the whole list are long-distance migrants (wood warbler, turtle dove, spotted flycatcher and pied flycatcher) and so are seven out of the leading ten (add yellow wagtail, swift and cuckoo). But let us slice the data another way.

Out of the 104 species trends recorded, there were 41 declines, which is 39 per cent. Now let us look at the long-distance migrants, 24 species out of the 104: the number of declines amongst them was 13, which is 54 per cent. And now let us look at the remaining residents and short-distance migrants, 80 species in total: the number shown declining is 28, which is 35 per cent. So long-distance migrants are declining as a group in Britain (as far as the BBS is concerned) by 54 per cent, compared with declines in all birds of 39 per cent, and declines in residents and short-distance migrants of 35 per cent.

Pretty suggestive? Well, we find this correlation to be exactly paralleled when we do it for all of Europe with the short-term data from the pan-European monitoring scheme. Leaving out three species which are migrants to Asia, there are 132 species in total, and 82 of them are declining, which is 62 per cent. The long-distance migrants **201** number 44 out of the 132, and, of these, 31 are declining, which is 70 per cent. The remaining resident and short-distance migrant birds number 88, and, of these, 51 are declining, which is 58 per cent. So long-distance migrants are declining as a group in Europe by 70 per cent, compared with declines in all birds of 62 per cent, and in residents and short-distance migrants of 58 per cent.

There are caveats, of course: the UK Breeding Bird Survey covers only about half of Britain's breeding species, and the Peckhams data only about a quarter of Europe's. But the figures are strongly suggestive of the fact that many Afro-Palaearctic migrant birds are not only rapidly decreasing in numbers but are doing so because of their migrant identity, meaning they have problems of their own; and this conclusion has been backed by the first piece of thoroughgoing scientific analysis of the issue.

It was based on another way of counting the birds of the continent: a massive assessment by BirdLife International of the conservation status – that is, are their populations going up or down? – of *all* of the 515 breeding species in *all* 52 countries and territories of Europe, from Gibraltar to the Faroes. This gargantuan number-crunching exercise, entitled *Birds in Europe – Population Estimates, Trends and Conservation Status*, has been produced by BirdLife twice, in 1994 and 2004. As precise information from national monitoring schemes is available (via Peckhams) only for a score or so of countries, the gaps for the rest have to be filled by lesser-quality data, such as local surveys and informed estimates from experts, so specific figures for increases and declines in each case cannot be given, only more generalized 'trend classes'; but the enormous value of the report is that all species and all countries are covered.

The introduction to the *Birds in Europe* 2004 edition signalled for the first time that the migrants appeared to be having special problems, and after publication its data were analysed to explore this possibility by a group of five researchers who were expert in statistics – Fiona Sanderson, Paul Donald, and Deborah Pain from the RSPB, and Ian Burfield and Frans van Bommel from BirdLife. Their study, now generally referred to as *Sanderson et al.*, was published in 2006 in the journal *Biological Conservation* with the title 'Long-Term Population Declines in Afro-Palaearctic Migrant Birds'. Their conclusion was not only that the trans-Saharan migrants had indeed shown 'a pattern of sustained, often severe decline' as a group, but also that species which were migratory had declined more than closely related species which were not, irrespective of breeding habitat. (The researchers examined thirty separate pairs of migrants and closely-related non-migrants, and the conclusion held true for every pair.)

Sanderson et al. sounded the alarm bell for the spring-bringers. This was science, not anecdote, not I-can't-remember-when-I-last-saw-a-turtle-dove. For the first time, their analysis suggested in clinical detail that something enormous was happening: that the flow of the vast aerial river out of Africa was starting to weaken; that Europe was starting to lose its heralds of the changing seasons which had come to it so unfailingly down the ages. But why? Why was it happening?

Migrant birds, wrote Ian Newton, Britain's leading migration expert, 'live in multiple jeopardy'. They can be caught up in problems on their breeding grounds, but they can also face problems on their journeys, and then problems on their wintering grounds (their 'non-breeding grounds' is more strictly accurate) which are not encountered by the resident birds, which remain behind.

Any of these can affect their numbers on a large scale. So let us look first at the problems the spring-bringers may have been encountering once they have finished their spring odysseys and arrived at their nesting sites. There is no doubt that the population declines of some of the migrants to Britain and Europe have been largely caused by breeding-ground difficulties. The corncrake was the earliest example, the chicken-like bird of the hayfields: its **203** populations were decimated as haymaking became mechanized from the beginning of the twentieth century, and in Britain it is now virtually confined to the Western Isles of Scotland (although English reintroduction schemes are taking place). But a much more widespread and severe problem was the intensification of farming which followed the introduction of the CAP, to which Britain adhered in the early 1970s, and it is depressing to a degree to realize that the declines caused by intensive agriculture are still going on. In the 1990s conservationists vigorously took up the issue, and eventually governments did so too, bringing in farmland wildlife schemes to restore the lost lapwings and skylarks to the fields, and by the turn of the millennium these schemes seemed to be working: the declines were being slowed, and between 1999 and 2004 farmland bird numbers in Britain stabilized. But in 2005 they started falling again, and between then and 2007 they fell to their lowest recorded level. The calamity continues.

Two migrants in particular, specifically classed as farmland birds, have been very hard hit by agricultural change: the yellow wagtail and the turtle dove. The yellow wagtail (47 per cent decline since 1994) has been hammered by big reductions in some of its nesting habitat, such as wet grassland, and also by the switch from spring-sown to autumn-sown crops, which means that the crops are too tall and thick when the birds try to nest in them. The turtle dove (66 per cent decline since 1994) has faced a different problem, Stephen Browne found in his four-year study of the bird: it experienced a significant drop in its reproductive rate, probably because its could no longer find enough of the weed seeds (especially fumitory) which were its principal food.

It is possible also that the cuckoo has been hit by a significant side effect of intensive farming: insect decline. Not being 'charismatic megafauna', insects and other invertebrates are largely neglected by the public, if not viewed with downright distaste, so there is little general perception of the enormous shrinkages in their populations over the last fifty years, caused principally by the great

204

tide of pesticides which has washed over the land. Yet the reduction in insect numbers may be behind the extinctions in Britain of the wryneck (eater of ants) and the red-backed shrike (eater of big beetles), and the mysterious disappearance from towns and cities of the house sparrow (eater of aphids, at the young-chick stage).

With cuckoos – and with bats, many of which are also declining – the issue is moths. But whereas bats take the adult moths in their night-time flight, cuckoos take the caterpillars during the day, especially the big, very hairy and toxic caterpillars which all other birds find entirely unpalatable. It's one more cuckoo peculiarity, up there with the trickery and the minor third: the niche in the food web they've carved out for themselves. However, some of the moths whose caterpillars cuckoos take have dropped in numbers precipitously in Britain in recent decades. We know this from one of the biggest data sets on insect populations anywhere in the world, the records of the countrywide network of moth traps run since 1968 by the Rothamsted agricultural research station in Hertfordshire. When this data was analysed in 2003, it was found that 226 out of the 337 moth species examined had decreased over the thirty-five years, many by alarming amounts: 75 species had decreased by more than 70 per cent, another 57 by more than 50 per cent, and a further 60 by over 25 per cent. Among the big losers were several moths of the Arctiidae family, whose 'woolly bear' caterpillars cuckoos so much enjoy: the garden tiger moth (and what a fantastic insect that is) had declined by 89 per cent, the white ermine by 77 per cent, the buff ermine by 73 per cent.

The jury is out for now on cuckoos and moths. But the effects of intensive farming are not the only problems the spring-bringers may be meeting on their breeding grounds, for over the last decade it has become apparent that not only farmland birds, but also woodland birds have been experiencing difficulties. A whole suite of woodland species has been found to be in trouble, led by the willow tit, Britain's most rapidly declining bird – down 77 per cent since 1994 in the Breeding Bird Survey, and now extinct in many parts of southern

England – while another species giving great concern is the stunningly attractive lesser spotted woodpecker: black, white and scarlet and the size of a mobile phone, too rare to be picked up by the BBS, but estimated in a joint RSPB–BTO study of woodlands published in 2006 to have gone down in numbers by nearly 60 per cent.

Several of the most rapidly declining migrants can also be classified as woodland birds: the wood warbler, the two flycatchers, the tree pipit and the nightingale. Is it possible that some cause or set of causes is specifically triggering woodland-bird declines, which would catch the wood warbler and its migrant fellows in its ambit as well as the willow tit? Maybe. The issue has been examined in several scientific papers, and several drivers of decline have been suggested. One is increased predation, the principal candidate being the grey squirrel, introduced to Britain from the US in the late nineteenth century: having displaced the native red squirrel from most of England, its population continues to soar, and in its American homeland it is a major predator of birds' nests. Grey squirrels may well be affecting nesting success in some species, not least the spotted flycatcher, but this is not yet certain.

Another potential driver of woodland bird decline is the increase in the deer population in British woodlands. Virtually all British deer species are increasing, led by the muntjac, a pint-sized Bambi introduced from China, whose speciality is breeding all the year round, and in many of Britain's woods its browsing is now so extensive that it is causing large-scale structural changes to the vegetation. In effect, Bambi and his pals are eating the undergrowth to bits. This may be having consequences for nightingales and willow and garden warblers, birds for which woodland undergrowth is a prime habitat; it may be the reason why nightingales seem to be moving out of woodland, where they survive in England, and into scrub. The over-browsing by deer is paralleled by a change in woodland management by humans, which is the widespread disappearance of coppicing – cutting trees down to ground level and letting new **206** shoots grow back up from the resultant stumps. These eventually provide a supply of poles, but in their early stages they produce a dense shrubby layer which is perfect for nightingales in particular. And coppicing is being increasingly abandoned.

Yet the best candidate of all looks like climate change. Research from the UK Met Office, released in 2006, showed that England has become a full degree Celsius warmer on average since 1960, and this rise may be hitting a species like the willow tit directly, in making damp woodlands drier, as *Parus montanus* is the only tit which excavates a nest hole, and to do that it needs damp, soft wood. But there is a subtler and more widespread effect in play, which is more likely to hit the spring-bringers, to do with timing.

In the past twenty years there has been a big revival in the study of phenology, or the timing of natural events, as it was gradually realized that the natural world was responding to rising temperatures with fundamental shifts in its long-established routines, ranging from the leafing of trees and the emergence of insects to the laying of frogspawn and the nesting of birds. One academic in particular spotted the importance of this and made the field his own, Tim Sparks from the Centre for Ecology and Hydrology at Monks Wood in Huntingdonshire, and over the course of fifteen years and in more than 100 publications, Dr Sparks has demonstrated the extent of the change in what is sometimes referred to as 'Nature's calendar'. His key discovery was that budburst on oak trees was getting earlier and earlier. This could, of course, be ascertained only by comparing present leafing dates with previous ones, but, strange though it may seem now, half a century ago nobody was bothering to note down when an oak tree put forth its leaves. (The Victorians had done so, but the practice had fallen out of favour.) However, after publishing an article on earlier phenological records, in 1995, Dr Sparks was contacted by Mrs Jean Combes of Ashtead in Surrey, who had – to his amazement and delight – a full list of the leafing dates of oak, ash, horse chestnut and lime in her area, compiled by herself and dating back to 1947. It enabled him to show at once that oaks in southern England were now putting out their leaves an average of 26 days, on **207** average, before they did half a century earlier; and many other trees and plants were following suit.

If tender young leaves are appearing earlier, the billions of caterpillars which feed on them need to hatch earlier too, before the leaves toughen and become unpalatable, and so the insect world in its turn is affected. And if the 'caterpillar flush' is earlier, the woodland birds which eat the caterpillars, and which take advantage of this peak of prey availability to feed their young in the nest, will correspondingly have to adjust the dates of their egg-laying. Just such a phenomenon was demonstrated by Humphrey Crick and other researchers from the BTO in a paper published in *Nature* in 1997, showing that twenty species of birds had significantly shifted their egg-laying to earlier dates between 1971 and 1995, the shift averaging 8.8 days over the period.

The birds are doing this in reaction to the situation around them, either by responding to changed stimuli or through natural selection. This is fine if you're a resident bird, in the woodlands all year long. But what if, when the caterpillar flush starts appearing earlier, you're still in Africa? What if you have no way of leaving Africa earlier to catch it, because you are not aware of what is happening in Europe, and anyway the cues that prompt you to depart for Europe are all African cues, such as the change in day length? Then, if you are a migrant bird, you may arrive back on your breeding grounds and find you have missed the peak of prey availability, and food for your nestlings is now much scarcer than it should be; and this asynchrony, this mistiming between breeding bird and food supply, threatens the spring-bringers very seriously indeed. And it works the other way round: the two shorter-distance migrants, the blackcap and the chiffchaff, which generally do not cross the Sahara (or which even, in the case of the blackcap, sometimes now winter in Britain), can get back to the breeding grounds and begin nesting very much earlier than the long-distance travellers, and, far from declining, the figures show them shooting rapidly up in numbers – the chiffchaff by 46 per cent and the blackcap by 62 per cent since 1994.

208

That the threat from mistiming is real has been graphically illustrated by two Dutch biologists, Christian Both and Marcel Visser, studying pied flycatchers in the Hoge Veluwe National Park near Arnhem in the Netherlands. In an initial piece of research in 2001 they showed that these birds had indeed brought their egg-laying dates forward when they arrived in Europe, to try to catch up with the earlier breeders all around them, but not by enough, because they could not alter their arrival dates. The timing of their spring migration from Africa relied on internal rhythms which were unaffected by climate change and so constrained their ability to adapt to new European conditions. The implication was that the flycatchers would suffer, and this was demonstrated in a subsequent study by Both and Visser and other Dutch colleagues published in 2006, which showed that in areas where food peaks had become earlier, pied flycatcher populations had indeed declined, by 90 per cent.

Could mistiming be the cause, or a constituent cause, of the 59 per cent decline in British spotted-flycatcher populations recorded between 1994 and 2007 by the Breeding Bird Survey? Or, for that matter, for the startling declines in the rest of the woodland migrants over the same period – the wood warbler down by 67 per cent, the nightingale by 60 per cent? We do not yet know; but the possibility must be a real one. There is potential trouble in plenty for the spring-bringers, then, on their breeding grounds in Britain and the rest of Europe. What about elsewhere?

The power of conditions in Africa to affect severely British and European migratory-bird populations suddenly burst upon the world of ornithology in 1969, when the whitethroats failed to return. Previously one of the commonest spring migrants, *Sylvia communis*, with its scratchy chattering song, its white throat, grey head and chestnut wings, and its generally perky appearance, would usually bounce out of every other thorn bush in April and May; but not **209** that year. The birds didn't arrive. Most places went whitethroatless. People shrugged at first, or shook their heads; but soon the infant Common Bird Census showed that this was a real, serious and national phenomenon: the whitethroat population of Britain had crashed by a quite incredible 77 per cent in one year; and furthermore, over succeeding years it showed no sign of bouncing back. The birds had enjoyed an excellent breeding season in Britain in 1968, so what on earth had caused the crash? Pesticides, perhaps, the cause of notorious earlier bird crashes? No. It was gradually realized that this was something in evidence right across Europe, and eventually the reason was tracked down (in a paper published in 1974): the failure of the rainfall in the Sahel, the belt of semi-arid grasslands, shrublands and savannahs which runs west–east across Africa from Mauritania to Eritrea, just to the south of the Sahara Desert.

The Sahel is one of the key wintering grounds for Afro-Palaearctic migrants. When, at the end of the summer, birds from Britain land there exhausted, having slogged their way over the Sahara, the zone is at the end of its rainy season and at its richest in terms of food supplies, and the migrants can quickly recover their energy levels. It then slowly deteriorates until the rains return the following year, so some migratory species drift south towards the humid forest zone or even further; but others, including the whitethroat, tend to stay in the semi-arid Sahel all year round. They find a living, for even outside the rainy season the zone has much more life and nourishment than may appear from photographs, containing groups of shrubs such as *Salvadora persica*, the toothbrush tree, whose berries allow birds to fatten themselves effectively; and the Sahelian ecosystem usually still contains enough resources for the crucial refuelling period just before the birds slog back across the Sahara in the following spring.

But not in 1969. Over the preceding twelve months the rains had dropped 25 per cent below their normal levels, and a whole series of Sahel-wintering species were very hard hit, including sedge warblers and redstarts as well as whitethroats; and in later years subsequent Sahel droughts affected returning numbers of other species, such as sand martins in the mid-1980s, though never quite with the astonishing severity of the original whitethroat crash. Drought remains, however, a latent threat.

Yet drought is not the only difficulty the spring-bringers have to cope with in Africa. A major and increasing problem is the general degradation of the environment. In June 2008 the Nairobi-based United Nations Environment Programme, UNEP, published *Africa: Atlas of Our Changing Environment*, which sent out shock waves. Launched by Thabo Mbeki, then president of South Africa, it offered a picture of destruction of the natural world on a scarcely imaginable scale. Using 'before and after' satellite photos taken in all 53 countries of the continent, some of them spanning a 35-year period, the UN geographers had put together a deeply disturbing portfolio. Its purpose was to inspire African governments to improve their records as environmental custodians, and so its language and tone were studiously neutral, generally referring to environmental 'change' rather than destruction. However, although there were some examples of change for the better, the vast majority of the case studies were of large-scale environmental degradation, and the atlas compilers accepted that this represented the true picture. They wrote of 'the swell of grey-coloured cities over a once-green countryside; protected areas shrinking as farms encroach upon their boundaries; the tracks of road networks through forests; pollutants that drift over borders of neighbouring countries; the erosion of deltas; refugee settlements scattered across the continent causing further pressure on the environment; and shrinking mountain glaciers'.

The atlas found deforestation to be a major concern in no fewer than 35 African countries, including the Democratic Republic of the Congo, Rwanda, Nigeria and Malawi: Africa is losing more than four million hectares of forest every year – twice the world's average deforestation rate. Closely following in significance is major loss of wildlife, occurring in 34 countries, such as Angola, Ethiopia, Gabon and Mali. Land degradation is similarly a major worry for 32 countries, including Cameroon, Eritrea and Ghana, with some **211** areas across the continent said to be losing more than 50 tonnes of soil per hectare per year. The atlas showed that erosion, as well as chemical and physical damage, had degraded about 65 per cent of the continent's farmlands.

Some points need to be made at once. We cannot contemplate this without recognizing that it is overwhelmingly a human problem, a terrible load to bear for Africa's people. Some might say it is *only* a human problem, rather than an environmental problem, but there is a growing recognition, in Africa as much as elsewhere, that it is both: if you trash your natural-resource base because of need, you are trashing your future. That recognition was the impetus behind the atlas. Secondly, we can hardly feel superior in Europe: we have trashed our own part of the natural world just as effectively, and it is doubtful if any African wildlife collapse could equal the halving in numbers of Britain's farmland birds in just thirty years. So the spring-bringers have an increasingly degraded environment at both ends of the migratory journey.

We have looked at their difficulties in Britain; how the migrants are coping, and will cope, with degraded landscapes and habitats in Africa is a great unknown. It is possible their mobility will help them, for the African continent is enormous and of course much pristine landscape still remains. No one can say as yet. Much of the migrants' lives in Africa, much of their ecology and their distribution, remains shrouded in mystery.

It was fortunate, nevertheless, that in 2008 scientists in Britain and Europe at last began to address seriously the question of the vanishings: the vanishing cuckoo, the vanishing nightingale, the vanishing turtle dove, the vanishing warblers, the vanishing flycatchers, and all the other disappearing heralds of spring. It was the year of the recognition of the problem, when the ornithological science establishment creaked into gear and began to work. The initial results were encouraging: the RSPB produced a lengthy review of the declining population trends and potential factors contributing to them, while the BTO produced a piece of analysis which suggested new lines of inquiry (both are unpublished at the time of writing). The RSPB review, by a young Scottish research biologist, Steven Ewing, is a model of lucidity, convincingly setting out the evidence for the migrant declines being a real and serious phenomenon which should be given a high priority in conservation policy. It notes that drought in the Sahel does not appear to be a driver of the current population losses, and this is echoed in the BTO research paper, by Nancy Ockendon and Phil Atkinson, which reports that birds which spend all their non-breeding time in the Sahel latitudes, such as the whitethroat, the reed warbler and the sedge warbler, seem to be able to adjust the date of their migration back to Britain, and are doing fairly well, while birds which winter further south, in the 'Guinea forest' humid zone, including both flycatchers, the nightingale, the cuckoo, the turtle dove and the wood, willow and garden warblers, seem much less able to do so, and are doing badly.

Does this imply mistimed arrival on the breeding grounds in Britain? Or does it perhaps imply habitat degradation in the humid Guinea forest? No one yet knows, but people are trying to find out. On 6 May 2008 the small group of European scientists who are experts on Afro-Palearctic migrant birds – nineteen researchers, from eleven countries – met at the Vogelwarte Radolfzell, the bird observatory at Radolfzell on the banks of Lake Constance in southern Germany, which is the spiritual successor to Johannes Thienemann's Rossiten from a century ago. They agreed to set up a network to promote research within Africa itself to identify how changing conditions are affecting bird populations, and, co-ordinated by Volker Salewski from Radolfzell and Will Cresswell from the University of St Andrews, this has now begun work.

BirdLife International, the global partnership of bird protection groups, was the third body which woke up to the issue of migration and migrant declines, realizing that it now had to be treated as a major international concern, at a strategic level. BirdLife published a substantial review of the subject in its conservation journal, and **213** began to plan a Flyways Campaign to raise awareness of migratory birds and their problems all around the world.

Thus at the end of 2008 an effort was at last under way to come to grips with the vanishings; scientists recognized there was a problem, and a truly serious one, and had began to reorientate their research efforts to take it on board, sketching out new programmes which prompted the hope that the declines of the birds which brought us our spring out of Africa might now be properly addressed, and might, sooner rather than later, be understood.

Whether or not they can be halted, of course, is another matter entirely.

TWELVE

A Loss of a Different Order

Red-Backed Shrike

The riches of the natural world in its pristine state are difficult for us to conceive of now. When the cod fishery of the Grand Banks off Newfoundland was discovered by the Basques, and then at the end of the fifteenth century by the English and the French, the cod were said to be so plentiful that a basket merely dipped into the water would be brought up brimming with fish. You could walk on the backs of the cod, it was said. (The fishery collapsed in 1989, was formally closed in 1992, and has not reopened.) When Europeans arrived in the American continent and came across the passenger pigeon, a bird which nested in large colonies, the magnitude of its migrating flocks left them staggered: some were estimated to be a mile wide and perhaps 300 miles long, took several days to pass a given point, and may have contained a billion birds. (The last passenger pigeon died in Cincinnati Zoo in 1914.) Yet even the seemingly untouched riches of the Americas, such as the bison herds which stretched from horizon to horizon, were in reality only a remnant of the life which had flourished there 10,000 years earlier: a whole megafauna of giant mammals, from mammoths, mastodons and sabre-toothed cats to giant sloths, giant beavers and giant bears, had roamed the plains and forests for millions of years until they were abruptly driven to extinction in what may have been as little as a millennium. The culprits are thought to have been the humans who came into the American continent from Asia, via the prehistoric land bridge between Russia and Alaska, which since the end of the last Ice Age has been swallowed up by the sea. These first Americans gradually made their way southward down through the whole of North, Central and South America, hunting the giant mammals as they went, and in the process wiping them out.

Until the advent of humanity, life on earth, in its natural state, seems to have been characterized by abundance; that animal celebrity of our times, the rare creature, was unknown. Human contact with this abundance has in essence been a long, continuous and savage process of whittling it down until it is a tiny fraction of what it was, or might be again in our absence; yet few people have noticed. The reason is a curious one: each generation tends to take what it finds around it to be the norm. American marine biologists have recently focused on this and have coined an evocative term for it: the shifting-baseline syndrome. It was first applied to the management of fish stocks – you may think the baseline, or natural state, of a stock is what it was at the start of your career, yet actually it may once have been very much greater – but of course it applies to all forms of life, and Nick Davies and I discussed it in the tower hide overlooking Wicken Fen as he told me there were now only half the number of cuckoos that there were on the fen when he began his research, twenty-five years earlier. 'People don't listen to their parents who used to see thousands of skylarks,' said Nick. 'They see twenty. Their children will see one. And each generation grows up to see the natural world and thinks that's how it normally is.'

That has surely been true down the ages, and has masked from a general understanding the relentless war of attrition which humanity has pursued against nature. Succeeding generations are unaware of what has gone, and the endless erosion of the natural world which humans have carried on has not been seen as the primal human characteristic which it is. In the second half of the twentieth century, however, with the world population doubling from 3 billion to 6 billion roughly between 1960 and 2000, the human impact upon the earth became so egregious as to be unmistakable, and society at last woke up to loss: loss of species, loss of habitats, loss of ecosystems, loss of natural resources.

Half a century of losses, gathering speed: by the time the new century was under way, loss was happening everywhere. According to the 2008 Red List of the International Union for the Conservation of Nature, 12 per cent of the world's birds, 21 per cent of the world's mammals, 30 per cent of the amphibians, 31 per cent of the reptiles, 37 per cent of the fishes and 70 per cent of the world's plant species were threatened with extinction. The great majority of marine fish stocks were fully exploited or over-exploited; some, such as the Mediterranean bluefin tuna, were on the verge of collapse. All seven species of sea turtle were threatened, as were 19 of the 21 albatross species. The population of the African elephant had dropped from 1.3 million to 625,000 in a decade, before the international ban on the ivory trade was introduced in 1989; the plunge had been halted, but population was dropping still. The Asian elephant was dropping faster. Very few of the world's five rhinoceros species survived outside protected areas: Javan rhinos, Sumatran rhinos and three subspecies of the African black rhino were listed as Critically Endangered on the Red List, while Africa's northern white rhino was probably extinct. The great apes were everywhere under pressure: the habitat of the orang-utans of Borneo and Sumatra was fast disappearing under the chainsaw, while hunting was remorselessly reducing the numbers of Africa's chimpanzees and gorillas. As for the majestic tiger, its numbers were down to probably fewer than 4,000, in scattered pockets across Asia, and falling fast because of poaching and habitat loss. Even in Britain, with our wildlife on a much more modest scale, loss is ubiquitous: the wildflowers of our cornfields virtually extinguished; 70 per cent of our butterfly species **217** dropping in numbers, farmland birds of course in freefall – lapwings, corn buntings, grey partridges, skylarks, down, down, down.

When I began to look at the declines of the migrant birds which annually came out of Africa and brought the spring to Britain and the rest of Europe, I first saw them very much in this context: yet another set of losses to document alongside the larks and lapwings, the poppies and cornflowers, the butterflies and moths. Yet I also had a niggling feeling that there was something peculiar about the potential loss of the spring-bringers, which set it apart from other wildlife declines; and my seeking them out, seeking to get to the heart of them, spending a spring on that quest, was an attempt not only to define and reaffirm their worth, but to understand what their disappearance might really mean.

Certainly, I found what it meant to many, for I not only spent time with people who were showing me the migrant birds, I also spent time with people who had lost them. For example, just as I had seen how a village could be graced and enlivened by spotted flycatchers, by little brown jobs of such character – and that did seem to be the only word for it – I also saw how a village which had lost its flycatchers could seem to have something vital missing.

Wingrave in Buckinghamshire is a picture-postcard corner of the Vale of Aylesbury: it has a fifteenth-century church, a duck pond with fat white ducks, a village green with a war memorial, a pub called the Rose and Crown, and the Chilterns on its southern horizon. It also has many walled gardens, and creeper-covered cottages and grander houses, in which several pairs of spotted flycatchers bred when David Snow arrived in the village in 1965. David had been one of Britain's leading academic ornithologists: until he retired in 1984 he was head of the British Museum Bird Collection (now the bird section of the Natural History Museum) at Tring in Hertfordshire, a few miles away, and after retirement he and his wife paid special attention to the birds of the village, of which *Muscicapa striata* was one of the highlights. 'When we first came here, we knew of half a dozen or more nesting pairs, and we probably didn't know all of them,' he said. 'I was very fond of them. I was always fascinated watching them flying on sallies. One year, one nested in one of the church windows, although most nested in creepers on houses.' I looked around: it was exactly the same sort of place as John Clarke's villages at the foot of Bredon Hill, full of quiet, hidden overgrown corners, and David nodded. 'It's an absolutely archetypal place for spotted flycatchers,' he said.

But not any more. Over the last decade, the number of pairs steadily diminished, until in 2003 they bred no more. 'They went down and down, to two, and one, and then, in recent years, nothing.'

'They've gone?'

'They've absolutely gone.'

I could see the loss through David's eyes. The small but self-possessed hunters on their fence posts, come from Africa – one of them in a corner here, one in a corner there – must have made the village so much more than it was without them.

'I do miss them,' David said. 'I'd love to have them back. Maybe they will come back some time – we have dozens of good places for them in the walled gardens.' He looked at the gardens. 'But I don't feel very hopeful about it.'

I spoke to several people about the loss of their flycatchers. I say 'their', for without exception they felt a strong personal attachment to the birds, and without exception they were dismayed by their disappearance. I spoke to several people about the loss of turtle doves; they felt the same. Mark Avery, in addition, was incredulous. Over dinner in Llandovery, the night before we sought out the wood warbler, he said to me, 'I've just spent three full days birding in East Anglia and I didn't see a turtle dove. It was amazing.'

'Why amazing?' I asked him.

Because, he said, when he was 12 he had persuaded his parents to take him on a trip from their home in Bristol to East Anglia, to see birds he had never seen before, and the turtle dove was high on his list. 'And it felt like the type of experience you get when you go abroad now, and there's some bird you've never seen before, and **219** because you've gone to a foreign country it's really common and you see it everywhere. That was what going though East Anglia was like as far as turtle doves were concerned in 1970, when I was 12. You drove through the fens and you would see them sitting on the telegraph wires. They would fly up from the road. You would see them in the fields. When you stopped in a village, you would hear them purring. The fens were just full of them, they were all over the place, they were a really common bird and you felt slightly foolish for never having seen them. They were so common there, you felt, "Oh! Why used I to be bothered about seeing them?"'

He shook his head.

'Three days birding in East Anglia and I didn't see a single one.'

But the next day we did see the wood warbler: we saw and heard the jewel of the western woods. And when I got home I emailed Mark Cocker, who had urged me to find it, and he emailed me back at once. He wrote, 'It's very much a bird of my childhood, and I remember vividly watching males singing in beech trees by my house in '73–75. I was 13. It was always a key moment each spring. You have to remember the iron-hard deadness of winter woods in Derbyshire. You cannot believe these places will ever awaken. To have a bird like a wood warbler return to it and make it home had something of the miraculous about it. It filled me with an intensity. I used to get up before school – about five in the morning – and go to the woods above the house and see ring ouzel and wood warbler, and hear cuckoos, and watch twite. It seems, now, not just like another century: it feels like a lost era. All of those birds have gone from my area in Derbyshire.'

The wood warbler had gone too from Norfolk, Mark's present home, as had many of the spring-bringers – or at least their numbers had tumbled precipitously – and I came across a man who had watched it all happening with dismay: he was David North, the education manager of the Norfolk Wildlife Trust. He remembered flocks of yellow wagtails on Cley Marshes, spotted flycatchers in his garden, turtle doves at Fakenham, cuckoos everywhere across the county, lots of pieces of roadside scrub that were special because they held a nightingale – all gone now, or very rare. 'The changes are very drastic,' he said. 'There's a real sense of loss.'

All these people, and many others, could certainly have told you what the disappearance of the summer migrants meant to them. Without putting words into their mouths, I feel sure they would have said that in every case it was a significant absence in their own lives, a hurt, a bereavement even, and more: a major diminishing of the beauty and the value of the natural world – one more defeat, one more loss to go with all the other losses which have been piling up for half a century as the human impact on the planet has become ever more extensive and extreme. And they were right.

But that wasn't it.

One of the aspects of the declines of the spring-bringers which struck me as distinctive was that they seemed very difficult to bring to a halt, and might well lead to extinctions, at least locally. This was largely because of the 'multiple jeopardy', as Ian Newton put it, in which the migrants lived out their lives. Take the cuckoo: nobody knew why it was declining so fast, but it was possible it was being hit by a double, or even a triple, whammy, as it were. The colossal declines in the moths whose caterpillars it fed on in Britain might be a problem; and if those caterpillars were hatching earlier because of rising temperatures, the bird might be coming back too late to take advantage of the peak of what was left. Then there might well be quite separate problems on its migratory journeys – it is estimated that a *billion* birds of passage are shot by hunters in the Mediterranean every year – or on its African wintering grounds. It would be virtually impossible to take conservation action to cope with all of these.

A further threat hanging over the future of all the migrants was climate change in Africa. The fourth report of the UN's climate-change panel, published in 2007, was gloomy in the extreme about what global warming would probably bring to the African continent **221** in the course of the twenty-first century: agricultural production is likely to be 'severely compromised' by climate variability and change. The focus and emphasis were of course, and rightly, on what the future held for Africa's people, and one might think a subject such as the future of European migratory birds in the continent too obscure for consideration; yet it is being researched, and the initial results are not encouraging.

In January 2008 a major piece of research by the universities of Durham and Cambridge, in association with the RSPB, introduced a new idea to the study of birds: their 'climate space', meaning the climatic range in which different species can comfortably exist. The *Climatic Atlas of European Breeding Birds* showed how these 'bioclimatic envelopes' could be calculated, using variables such as summer heat, winter cold, and moisture, and showed that they correspond very well with the birds' actual observed range. The point was that, with global warming, these climate spaces are likely to change: they may shrink severely in extent, or shift, and if they shift, it may well be to areas where the birds cannot follow (for lack of suitable breeding habitat, for example). The atlas suggested that three-quarters of the breeding birds in Britain and Europe are likely to decline during the twenty-first century as their climate space decreases with rising temperatures.

After the atlas was published, two of the principal researchers, Professor Brian Huntley and Dr Steve Willis of Durham University, joined with their colleague Natalie Doswald in turning their attention to Africa and began to calculate the future climate spaces of all the continent's avifauna. I asked them about the principal Afro-Palaearctic migrants, and in November 2008, just as this book was being completed, they released to me stunning maps of the future climate spaces in Africa of nine British species: cuckoo, turtle dove, swallow, swift, spotted flycatcher, wood warbler, willow warbler, nightingale and lesser whitethroat. They showed that for most of them the available wintering, or non-breeding, range was likely to shrink significantly or shift as global warming took hold, with the explicit implication that this would lead to further significant reductions in population.

It was clear that the declines of the migrants were different from the declines of farmland birds, say: they appear to be unusually intractable and difficult to restrain. But that was not what set them apart; and by the end of my quest for them I knew that the real meaning of their disappearance lay elsewhere.

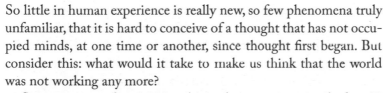

So little in human experience is really new, so few phenomena truly unfamiliar, that it is hard to conceive of a thought that has not occupied minds, at one time or another, since thought first began. But consider this: what would it take to make us think that the world was not working any more?

Spinning around at 1,000 miles an hour, on its axis tilted at 23 degrees to the plane of its orbit around the sun, the earth in its motions seems dependable to the last degree. In human history it has always worked entirely reliably, giving us day and then night, spring and then summer, autumn and then winter, with a regularity so unshakeable that these are the only real certainties, apart from death itself, in our uncertain lives. That any of this should alter, other than on the Day of Judgement, has never been part of our intellectual currency. But what if one of the world's profoundest motions, a living announcement of spring, were to come to an end?

Since before human memory the miraculous aerial river has flowed out of Africa into Europe, the river of intrepid small creatures which flew from one continent to become part of the soul of the other, signalling that winter was past and the rain was over and gone. We may only have understood this phenomenon as a whole and grasped its extraordinary scale for less than fifty years, and even today appreciation of it is not widespread; but the beings which were borne on its tide, the summer migrant birds, we have in Europe for millennia taken to our hearts. For in making their marathon journeys **223** here from south of the Sahara, their barely believable desert-crossing, strength-exhausting, hunter-dodging migrations, these trivial packets of feathers have given people something deeper than delight: they have given them the proof of renewal. The cuckoo's minor third, the nightingale's cantata, the swallow's loopings round the farmyard: all have been instant assurance, on being heard or seen again, that the greatest of all changes is under way – not just the seasonal shift from winter to spring, exhilarating though that is, but the profoundest movement of all, from death to rebirth. No wonder that our responses to them have been animated, and universal. Over thousands of years they have inspired us to poetry and prompted us to proverbs, they have been the source of a vast treasury of European folklore, legends and literature, and they have been so woven into the fabric of our culture as to become part of the continent's idea of itself. A Europe without its spring-bringers is almost as unthinkable as a Europe without its cathedrals.

And now the great river is shrinking back, its current is slacking, and the spring-bringers are failing to return to the woods and forests and fields, the hedges and heathlands, the groves and copses and orchards, in Britain and all over Europe, where people have smiled to see them, time out of mind. We have grown accustomed to loss in the natural world. The litany grows ever longer: whales and turtles and albatrosses, elephants, rhinoceroses and tigers, fishes and amphibians and reptiles, plants all across the planet, our own skylarks and our butterflies vanishing from our chemically drenched farmland. But the loss of the birds that brought the spring is a loss of a different order entirely. This is more than a loss of species: this is a loss of meaning, on an enormous scale. It is a sign that something is going awry at the heart of things.

The person who understood this was Julia Jeffries in the Ashdown Forest, and I came to understand it myself through thinking about her reaction. I was trying to work out why it was quite so intense and I went back to my notes and read them again, and there were the words 'I was absolutely traumatized by losing my cuckoos'. Coming to them cold, on the page they seemed wildly hyperbolic, comical even; but I remembered Julia uttering them, and they had not seemed out of place then. They had seemed of a piece with her body language and her demeanour. For her feelings were very strong, and different from those of others who were seeing the migrants fail to return. You might say that with the others the emotion aroused was dismay, even deep dismay; but with Julia it was distress. She had strong personal reasons to be upset, of course: the cuckoo had come on her daughter's birthday every year for the first fifteen years of Harriet's life, and then stopped. Wouldn't you be troubled by that? But there was something more which troubled her. Julia had understood at once, instinctively and profoundly, the implications.

For living in the forest with her passion for wild flowers, waiting for them to bloom every year, rushing off in the orchid season, she was attuned to the rhythms of the natural world in a way which is now very unusual, *and she had witnessed a disruption of them which was completely new*. For the cuckoo not to arrive – there had never been anything like that. The cuckoo had always come back. It wasn't only part of the spring: it was part of the eternal cycle of death and rebirth. If the cuckoo did not return – well, there was something seriously wrong, she said, shaking her head: 'something rotten in the state of Denmark'.

She wasn't exaggerating. She was right. She merely had more sensitive antennae than most people. She understood in her bones that something very large was happening – something to do ultimately with complex global processes which was made manifest by the absence of a bird in the Sussex countryside one April morning. With his dazzling insight into the natural world, Ted Hughes also understood the scale and complexity of those processes, and their fragility as well, how much was involved in the spring-bringers' return, and how we should give thanks for it. 'They've made it again,' he wrote, 'Which means the globe's still working . . .' He was focusing on swifts, but he was speaking for them all.

But what if they don't make it? By 2007, forty-one per cent of Britain's swifts had failed to return since 1994. Thirty-seven per cent of the cuckoos. Forty-seven per cent of the yellow wagtails. Fifty-four per cent of the pied flycatchers. Fifty-nine per cent of the spotted flycatchers. Sixty per cent of the nightingales. Sixty-six per cent of the turtle doves. Sixty-seven per cent of the wood warblers. All gone already in thirteen years, with the remainder on slopes of decline which stretch sharply down towards the zero at the bottom of the graph. Is the globe still working when this is happening?

Humanity's long war of attrition against nature, its unending erosion of the abundance of nature's pristine state, has taken species after species, flower after flower, forest after forest; and yet through indifference, or through ignorance, or through shifting the baseline, still we are able to comport ourselves as if the world were carrying on as it always has. But sooner or later the war of attrition had to come up against something fundamental. Forests perhaps we can regrow; tigers perhaps we can save in captivity; but how will we mend the loss of the spring-bringers? How could we restore their coming, once they go? And they are going, now.

I was blessed, in seeking to get to the heart of them when I did, in seeking to celebrate them and restore them to their rightful place in a world turned urban and electronic, for I was able to find them. I listened to the nightingale and felt the sense of wonder; I listened to the warblers and stepped inside the soundscape; I gazed on the jewel of the western woods; I heard the promise of high summer in the turtle dove's springtime purr; I grasped what was special about the swallows and their beauty; I saw what was special about the spotted flycatchers in their plainness; I sensed the wildness of the swifts; and I caught the bell-like wandering voice of the cuckoo ringing out across the countryside and I rejoiced in it. For during my quest for them they were not all gone, the summer migrant birds: some of them had made it back from Africa, and for that unforgettable springtime, the world was still working.

But for how much longer?

Acknowledgements

In writing about Britain's summer migrant birds and their dismaying decline I have been deeply indebted to two groups of people. First I should like to thank those who helped me get close to, and understand, the migrants themselves, and indeed their losses. For the birds on Gibraltar: Ian Thompson, Yvonne Benting and John Cortes. For cuckoos: Nick Davies, Julia Jeffries, Julian and Angela Langford, John Taylor, David North and Tom Lees. For swifts: Edward Mayer, Roy Overall, Jeremy Laurance and Angela Coles. For spotted flycatchers: John and Pamela Clarke, Mary Doney, Ros Long, David Snow and Elliot Morley. For swallows: Angela Turner and Angela Plowright. For turtle doves: Stephen Browne, Harriet Mead and Mrs Vee Mead. For wood warblers: Mark Avery and David Anning. For warblers: Mark Cocker and Mary Muir. For nightingales: Ian Swinney, Sebastian McCarthy, Polly Munro and Richard Mabey. I should particularly like to thank Richard Mabey, whose incomparable account of the nightingale, *Whistling in the Dark*, is a model study of a legendary bird in both its natural and its cultural habitats. Richard gave me freely of his time and expertise but, as may be evident from the text, I ultimately felt unable to see nightingales through his eyes, for the simple reason that, as they used to say in Chicago, he knew too much.

Secondly I owe special thanks to the group of ornithological scientists and researchers who are expert in the Afro-Palearctic migrants, in particular Ian Newton, Tim Birkhead, Peter Jones, Will Cresswell, Volker Salewski, Bob Dowsett, Steven Ewing, Phil Atkinson, Ian Burfield, Richard Gregory, David Noble, Brian Huntley, Steve Willis, Natalie Doswald and Tim Sparks. Any errors in the text are of course mine rather than theirs. I have also been greatly assisted by other members of the staffs of the three main ornithological organizations based in Britain. From the British Trust for Ornithology: Andy Clements, Graham Appleton, Rob Fuller, Juliet Vickery, Dawn Balmer, Mark Grantham, Dave Leech, Rob Robinson, Kate Risely and Jacquie Clark. From the Royal Society for the Protection of Birds: Euan Dunn, David Gibbons, Alistair Gammell, Fiona Sanderson, Paul Donald and Deborah Pain (now with the Wildfowl and Wetlands Trust). From BirdLife International: Richard Grimmett, Ania Sharwood-Smith, Adrian Long and Nick Askew.

Beyond this, for help in solving thorny individual problems I would especially like to thank Susanne Blankemeyer, Maureen Dodd, Graham Madge and Barnaby Wright; for further assistance I would like to thank Dalya Alberge, Sally Baker, Sir John Boardman, Mike Collins, Anna Guthrie, Angus Murray, Dominic Mitchell, Catherine Pepinster, Ben Sheldon, Kate Simon, Dyfri Williams, Stuart Winter and Dom Henry Wansbrough, OSB; and for consistent encouragement and moral support I would like to thank Robert Verkaik, Heather Schiller, Brian Clarke and Diane Revill. I am grateful to two successive editors of the *Independent*, Simon Kelner and Roger Alton, for allowing me leave of absence to write this book, and to my two successive editors at John Murray, Rowan Yapp and Helen Hawksfield, for their patience and sympathetic understanding, as well as to Joe Mclaren, who illustrated the superlative cover, and to Sara Marafini, the art director.

Acknowledgements

Most of all, for insisting on me working hard while simultaneously preventing me from taking myself too seriously, I would like to thank my children, Flora and Sebastian, and my wife, Jo Revill; to her this book is dedicated.

Most of the sources of quotations are identified in the text, but the translations from Homer are by E. V. Rieu, those from Aristotle from the revised Oxford translation, ed. Jonathan Barnes, and those from Pliny are my own. Reg Moreau's autobiographical notes are held in the Edward Grey Institute, Oxford. Ian Newton's comment about migrant birds living 'in multiple jeopardy' is quoted from 'Population Limitation in Migrants', *Ibis* 146 (2004), pp. 97–226; the paper which identified the cause of the decline in whitethroat numbers was D. Winstanley, R. Spencer and K. Williamson, 'Where Have All the Whitethroats Gone?', *Bird Study* 21 (1974), pp. 1–14.

The author and publisher would like to thank the following for permission to reproduce copyright material: extract from 'Swifts' by Ted Hughes, from *Season Songs*, published by Faber & Faber Ltd, (1976); extract from 'The Thyrsus Retipped' by Ronald Bottrall, from *Collected Poems*, reproduced by arrangement with Anthony Bottrall; extract from 'These Foolish Things' by Jack Strachey and Eric Maschwitz, reproduced by permission of Boosey & Hawkes Music Publishers Ltd; extract from 'A Nightingale Sang in Berkeley Square', words and music by Eric Maschwitz and Manning Sherwin © 1971, reproduced by permission of Peter Maurice Music Co. Ltd, London W8 5SW.

Index

Index

Index

Ovid, 118
Owain Glyndwr, 86, 89
Oxford University Museum of
    Natural History, 146, 152, 154
oystercatcher, 98

Pain, Deborah, 202
Palearctic (region), 37
Pan-European Common
    Bird Monitoring Scheme
    (PECBMS; 'Peckhams'), 199,
    202
passenger pigeon, 113, 215
passerines (Passeriformes), 52
peacock, 129
pelicans, 23
Pennant, Thomas, 85
Pervigilium Veneris (*The Festival
    of Venus*), 7, 20
pesticides, 193–4, 205
pheasants, 98
phenology, 207
Philomel and Tereus (myth), 7,
    20
pied flycatcher, 11, 17, 19, 87, 90,
    94, 176, 191, 200–1, 206, 209,
    212–13, 226
pied wagtail, 166
pigeons (doves), 100, 113
Plato, 23
Pliny the Elder: *Natural History*,
    100
Pliny the Younger, 100
240 Plowright, Angela, 122–3, 125–6

Plowright, Paul, 123
Pollard, John: *Birds in Greek Life
    and Myth*, 164
Pompeii, 117
poorwill, 24
Pound, Ezra, 47
Pound Green Common, Wyre
    Forest, 167–8
Previn, Dory, 156

quail, 23, 106

Radolfzell, Germany, 213
Raphael Sanzio, 130
red-backed shrike, 45, 199,
    205
red kite, 87
red-legged partridge, 98
red-rumped swallow, 120
redshank, 51–2, 90, 94
red squirrel, 206
redstart, 87, 167, 210
reed warbler, 5, 65–6, 74,
    76–7, 166–7, 172–4, 176–7,
    190
Rey, Eugene, 167
Richard II, King, 86–7
Richard, Cliff, 104
ring ouzel, 5, 25
ring-necked dove, 106
ringing (of birds), 17, 30–4,
    108–9, 190–1
river warbler, 200
robin, 18, 166, 201

243